Experiencing Archaeology

Related title:

Experiencing Archaeology: A Manual of Classroom Activities, Demonstrations, and Minilabs for Introductory Archaeology Instructor edition

Lara Homsey-Messer, Tracy Michaud, Angela Lockard Reed, and Victoria Bobo
ISBN 978-1-78920-350-9 ebook

Experiencing Archaeology

A Manual of Classroom Activities, Demonstrations, and Minilabs for Introductory Archaeology

Lara Homsey-Messer, Tracy Michaud,
Angela Lockard Reed, and Victoria Bobo

berghahn
NEW YORK • OXFORD
www.berghahnbooks.com

First published in 2020 by

Berghahn Books

www.berghahnbooks.com

Library of Congress Cataloging-in-Publication Data

Names: Homsey-Messer, Lara, author. | Michaud, Tracy, author. | Lockard Reed, Angela,
author. | Bobo, Victoria, author.
Title: Experiencing archaeology : a laboratory manual of classroom activities, demonstrations,
and minilabs for introductory archaeology / Lara Homsey-Messer, Tracy Michaud, Angela
Lockard Reed, and Victoria Bobo.
Description: First edition. | New York : Berghahn Books, 2019.
Identifiers: LCCN 2019033046 | ISBN 9781789203493 (paperback)
Subjects: LCSH: Archaeology—Laboratory manuals.
Classification: LCC CC75.7 .H66 2019 | DDC 930.1078—dc23
LC record available at hcps://lccn.loc.gov/2019033046

British Library Cataloguing in Publication Data

A catalogue record for this book is available from the British Library.

ISBN 978-1-78920-349-3 paperback

CONTENTS

FIGURES AND TABLES

Figures

Tables

ACKNOWLEDGMENTS

Most of the activities in this volume have their origins in our teaching experiences with the Johns Hopkins University Center for Talented Youth (CTY), an academic summer program for gifted and accelerated high school students that several of us participated in from the early 1990s through the mid-2000s. Timothy Scarlett was the first of us to teach for CTY, and several of these activities are his brainchild. Some have proved so powerful that we still use them today in their original form. Many have evolved, to accommodate either additional age groups, or educational settings such as public education events and general science programs. In addition to acknowledging the CTY program and coordinators who supported the archaeology class, we would like to thank the university campuses that hosted the archaeology class and generously provided invaluable laboratory space and materials to conduct these activities, including Skidmore College, Saint Mary's College, Franklin & Marshall College, and the Universidad de las Américas (UDLA). Many of these activities would not have come fruition if it were not for the support and efforts of our CTY teaching assistants over the years, including Pascale Meehan, Axel Ramirez, and Jenny Remmel. Pascale Meehan developed chapter 19 ("What's for Dinner? Faunal Analysis") during the 2007 summer program in Puebla, Mexico. Axel Ramirez provided inspiration for chapter 15 ("Tree Ring Match-Up) and what eventually became chapter 26 ("Tree of Life: Human Ecology") by biking miles across the UDLA campus for a cut log with well-preserved tree rings going back nearly two centuries during the 2008 summer program in Puebla, Mexico. And, of course, we are deeply grateful to the hundreds of CTY students we have collectively taught over the years, who enthusiastically participated in these activities, provided inspiration for improvement over the years, and who now serve as stewards of the archaeological record and role models for the generation following them.

As we transitioned to teaching at the university level and participated in community outreach events, we began to adapt many of these exercises to work with college and middle school students. As a result, these "minilabs" have evolved in such a way as to be appropriate for a wide audience, ranging from middle and secondary school students to college undergraduates. As with the CTY program, several students and teaching assistants deserve special thanks for their efforts toward this laboratory manual. Genevieve Everett and Jessie Hoover, graduate students in the applied anthropology program at Indiana University of Pennsylvania, developed chapter 26 ("Tree of Life: Human Ecology") as part of a service learning project associated with the public archaeology graduate seminar taught by Lara Homsey-Messer. This activity was initially used in an Upward Bound Math and Science Saturday Academy workshop for high school juniors and seniors. Eleanor Schultz, an undergraduate anthropology student at IUP, developed the groundwork for the concluding chapter, "The Ethical Archaeologist." Assisted by fellow undergraduate Harley Burgis, Schultz's chapter is an important contribution to module 6, "Archaeological Ethics and Stewardship," for which there are unfortunately too few exercises available to teachers who want to address ethics but frequently feel constrained by time and class size. Finally, Joseph Bomberger, a master's student in applied archaeology at Indiana University of Pennsylvania, ably drafted original artwork for several of the chapters.

Our passion for experiential learning stems in large part from the teachers and mentors who shaped our own educational experiences, and to them we are grateful. Thanks to Marc Bermann, Kathleen Allen, and Rosemary Capo, who were inspiring examples of engaging learning activities with University of Pittsburgh undergraduate students that many of us modeled ourselves after as their teaching assistants. We have continued to grow as teachers from the collegiality and mentoring of many of our current and former colleagues at the Johns Hopkins University's Center for Talented Youth, Murray State University, Indiana University of Pennsylvania, University of Southern Maine, and Grand Valley State University. We especially thank those who provided constructive feedback and encouragement on earlier versions of these activities and Caryn Berg for having faith in this project. Finally, we would like to thank our families for their support as we worked long hours to convert these activities from informal classroom teaching strategies into a useable laboratory manual. We hope these exercises will be useful to secondary and collegiate instructors alike and that they may inspire additional experiential teaching strategies down the road.

INTRODUCTION

Welcome!

Welcome to the world of archaeology! Archaeology, the study of human culture through material remains, is an inherently hands-on discipline. We have designed this manual to capitalize on the unique experiential opportunity archaeology represents. We have created short, hands-on, inquiry-based exercises as a fun and creative supplement to traditional classroom lectures. Some activities will require you to work actively in teams (as real archaeological work is done), while others are more individually based. These activities will engage both majors and nonmajors using tactile experiences, problem-solving skills, and discussions and debates. Another unique aspect of archaeology is how it relies on so many different disciplines—there is literally something for everyone! Math, geology, art, religion, environment, chemistry, animals, and agriculture are only a few aspects regularly incorporated into archaeological studies of human populations. We hope you will find the activities in this manual engaging and that they will help you appreciate the breadth of archaeological research.

What's Inside?

This volume is divided into six modules focused on a different aspect of archaeology. Module 1 focuses on how archaeology fits into its parent discipline of anthropology. These chapters explore concepts such as the scientific method, cultural relativism, and the uniquely human trait of using symbolism and art. Module 2 examines how archaeologists attribute meaning to artifacts. Using everyday objects such as buttons or kitchen gadgets, these chapters will help you learn how to interpret artifacts from an emic (i.e., insider) perspective. These chapters are also designed to make you aware of the biases and difficulties archeologists face when interpreting artifacts, particularly when we are unaware of our own etic (i.e., outsider) tendencies. Module 3 uses everyday materials and ideas to explain how archaeologists date the past. Module 4 allows you to explore common archaeological specialties such as lithics and ceramics. It also explores the interdisciplinary nature and teamwork approach of today's archaeology. Module 5 tackles explanation in archaeology through various philosophical and theoretical lenses such as evolutionary theory and human agency. We've sought to relate these more difficult concepts to your daily lives to create analogies from which you can better interpret the past. Finally, Module 6 explores ethical topics that are often overlooked, such as the preservation ethic, stewardship, and accountability to descendent communities.

Many of these activities are designed as debates to get you thinking about all sides of these issues, as well as to challenge assumptions and stereotypes arising from our own cultural paradigm, such as assuming agriculture is inherently positive. These last chapters will introduce you to the Society for America Archaeology's Principles of Archaeological Ethics that govern contemporary archaeological practice, guide ethical behavior, and support all public stakeholders in the protection of cultural resources. The ultimate goal of this chapter, and the entire volume really, is to cultivate an appreciation for, and attitude of, stewardship for past and present cultures. Your instructor will provide you with copies of any reading materials that are not freely available online and will show you any videos that require a subscription or purchase to stream or download. If any of the provided links to free video-sharing websites are broken or no longer active, ask your instructor for updated ones, or try finding them by searching for the title in a search engine. *Enjoy!*

MODULE 1

Frameworks for Exploring Anthropological Archaeology

CHAPTER 1

The Scientific Method (TSM) Cube

Processual Archaeology

Processual archaeology, sometimes called "new archaeology," is a theoretical and methodological framework for archaeological inquiry that became popular in the 1960s and remains widely practiced today. Its earliest roots originate in the work of the archaeologists Gordon Willey and Philip Phillips (1958: 2), who famously said, "American archaeology is anthropology or it is nothing." This idea implied that the goals of archaeology are essentially the same as the goals of anthropology—that is, to answer questions about human behavior. From this emerging sense of identity, these "new" archaeologists began to strongly critique the former period, called the culture-historical phase, in which archaeologists focused largely on the artifacts themselves (e.g., cataloging, describing, and classifying them), rather than the underlying *behavior* of the people who produced them. By the 1960s, influential archaeologists such as Lewis Binford and Kent Flannery began to heed the call that "pots are not people," thereby ushering in a new era focused on understanding cultural *processes* (hence the name) that shape society. According to Binford (1978), archaeologists needed to develop a theory that would create a bridge between static artifacts in the ground and the dynamic behavior of people. This "middle-range theory," Binford argued, can be achieved only by adopting a scientific approach to the study of the past.

The Scientific Method

To this end, proponents of processual archaeology largely emphasized the rigorous use of statistical data analysis and the scientific method. Only in so doing is it possible to get past the limits of the archaeological record and learn something about how the people who used the artifacts lived and behaved (i.e., cultural processes). At the core of this process is hypothesis testing. A *hypothesis* is a specific and testable statement about something, generally tied to a broader concept about our understanding of the past.[1] For example, an archaeologist might hypothesize that people living in southwestern Turkey around 9,500 BCE shifted from hunting and gathering wild foods to farming domesticated foods and that population pressure to feed more people forced them to do so. To test this, the archaeologists would conduct excavations in the area to look for changes in the plant foods and population size present in lower (older) versus higher (younger) layers. Wild plant seeds tend to be smaller than domesticated seeds (see chapter 20); an increase in the proportion of domesticated seeds relative to wild seeds would support the first part of the hypothesis. Population increases often result in greater numbers of houses spaced more closely together; such a trend before the increase in domesticates would support the second part of the hypothesis. If, however, you saw an increase in houses after the increase in domesticated seeds, that would contradict the hypothesis and force you to reject, or perhaps revise, it.

The scientific method consists of five general steps: (1) making observations, (2) asking a question based on those observations, (3) proposing a hypothesis to answer the question, (4) testing a hypothesis through experimentation, data collection, and/or statistical analysis, and finally drawing a conclusion. Unfortunately, archaeologists—like all scientists—cannot "prove" their hypotheses to be correct. They can, however, accept, reject, or refine their hypotheses. When the data support a hypothesis, they have more confidence in their ideas and will accept it. If the data refute it, they have little confidence and reject it. Sometimes, the data indicate the hypothesis is mostly correct with a minor adjustment; in this case, we refine (i.e., "tweak") the hypothesis and test it again. Thus, the scientific method essentially constitutes a never-ending process of making and refining hypotheses, continually testing them with new data and reformulating them when new data are available.

The Activity

In this classroom demonstration, your teacher will review the steps of the scientific method (TSM) using a cube. Your job will be to make observations, ask a question, propose a testable hypothesis, test it, and finally accept, reject, or revise it. We think you'll have fun with it.

Suggestions for Further Exploration and Application

Your instructor may ask you to watch or read additional materials for classroom discussion or individual reflection. Write your answers in the space provided in Worksheet 1.1.

- **"Mystery of Easter Island" (PBS 2012)** (*53 minutes*). This episode of *NOVA* follows a team of archaeologists seeking to answer a long-enduring question about Easter Island: how and why did the ancient islanders build and move nearly 900 giant statues (*moai*), weighing up to 86 tons?
- **"Egyptian Pyramids" (PBS 2014)** (*52 minutes*). Using high-tech instrumentation, the *Time Scanners* research team travels to Egypt to find out how the pyramids evolved from simple mud-brick mounds to the most impressive buildings in the ancient world and to answer the controversial question of whether the Bent Pyramid at Dahshur was built that way intentionally or accidentally.
- **"Fort Raleigh, North Carolina" (PBS 2009)** (*53 minutes*). In 1587, the English sent a group of colonists to the New World, but when English ships returned with supplies three years later, they found the settlement empty and the colonists gone. This *Time Team America* episode seeks to discover what happened to the Lost Colony.
- **"The Development of Indigenous Archaeology" (Curtis 2010).** This is an excellent discussion of the extent to which we can rely on "science" and of the role indigenous knowledge plays in the reconstruction of the past—an excellent piece to use if you are in a class of archaeology majors.

Worksheet 1.1

1. Make observations.	*List relevant observations:*
2. Ask a question.	*State research question:*
3. Propose hypothesis.	*State your hypothesis:*
4. Test hypothesis.	*Check all that apply:* ☐ field or laboratory experiment ☐ results consistent with previous observations ☐ results fit the prediction(s) generated ☐ statistical analysis of data
5. ☐ **Accept hypothesis.** ☐ **Reject hypothesis.** ☐ **Refine hypothesis.**	*Explain your answer:*

1. What additional information would make you more confident in accepting your hypothesis?

_____

_____

_____

_____

_____

2. Watch the short video "The Pharaoh That Wouldn't Be Forgotten" (Green 2014). Can you think of another archaeological scenario (natural or cultural) that may be similar to our "missing 2" phenomenon?

_____

_____

_____

_____

_____

_____

For Further Exploration and Application

Your instructor may ask you to watch or read one of the suggested videos or readings for classroom discussion or individual reflection. Answer the appropriate questions(s) afterward.

☐ *NOVA*   ☐ *Time Team America*   ☐ *Time Scanners* (check one)

1. How did the research team use the scientific method? Be sure to address each of the five steps.

_____

_____

_____

_____

_____

_____

2. Read "The Development of an Indigenous Archaeology" by Wayne Curtis (2010). Is the scientific method inherently superior to Indigenous knowledge? Can the two go hand in hand?

_____

_____

_____

_____

_____

_____

Note

1. Contrast this with a theory, which is a systematic explanation that consistently explains large quantities of existing data and accurately make predictions about what to expect from new data. Examples include the theory of relativity and the theory of evolution.

References

Binford, Lewis R. 1978. *Nunamiut Ethnoarchaeology*. Cambridge, MA: Academic Press.

Curtis, Wayne. 2010. "The Development of Indigenous Archaeology." *American Archaeology* 14 (3): 37–43.

Green, Kate. 2014. "The Pharaoh That Wouldn't Be Forgotten." Video, 4:33. Animation by Steff Lee. Uploaded by TED-Ed, 15 December. https://www.youtube.com/watch?v=8bYRy_wZEJI. Accessed 4 June 2019.

PBS. 2009. "Fort Raleigh, North Carolina." *Time Team America*, season 1, episode 1. Aired 8 July. http://www.pbs.org/time-team/explore-the-sites/fort-raleigh. Accessed 4 June 2019.

———. 2012. "Mystery of Easter Island." *NOVA*, season 39, episode 14. Aired 7 November. https://www.pbs.org/video/nova-mystery-easter-island-pro. Accessed 4 June 2019.

———. 2014. "Egyptian Pyramids." *Time Scanners*, season 1, episode 1. Aired 1 July. https://www.pbs.org/video/time-scanners-preview-egyptian-pyramids. Accessed 4 June 2019.

CHAPTER 2

Cultural Bingo

Culture

Archaeologists are curious about the past—not just because artifacts are interesting but also because we want to learn how people lived back then. In other words, we seek to reconstruct the culture of past people. There are many definitions of culture, but the one we prefer, developed by our colleague Timothy Scarlett, is a "learned conceptual framework that allows us to (1) generate behavior, (2) communicate ideas, and (3) interpret experience." The first half of that definition refers to the fact that culture is learned—from our family, relatives, friends—rather than biological. A baby born in China but raised in France will *be* French culturally: they will speak French, grow up liking French food, and experience the world through a French lens, not Chinese. Culture is what generates the behavior we consider normal; if we behave differently, we often earn the derision of those around us. For example, in the United States, we have a "personal bubble" of about two to three feet around a stranger. But other cultures don't mind coming within a foot or so of someone. Imagine yourself in an elevator in, say, Germany and someone else gets on and stands elbow to elbow with you. Uncomfortable? For most Americans, yes; we would prefer the new person to stand on the other side, putting as much distance as possible between us.

Culture also determines how we communicate ideas. For example, in the United States, we often give a "thumbs-up" sign to indicate "good job." We even have an emoji for it. But the gesture simply communicates the number one in Germany and the number five in Japan. Malaysians use a thumb simply to point to something; the American meaning would be completely lost on them. In Saudi Arabia, it means "I'm winning!" yet it is an insult in Ghana. Imagine giving a thumbs-up to someone from Ghana—you would inadvertently offend someone you intended to compliment! Finally, culture determines how we interpret experience. For example, as we write this, the Black Lives Matter movement dominates the airwaves and social media. Many white Americans have had positive experiences with police; like me, "Officer Friendly" visited us in grade school, gave us cute stickers, and assured us they would always protect our families. But for Americans of color who live in school districts *not* visited by "Officer Friendly," who have been racially profiled and/or witness police violence in their neighborhoods, a police presence may be unsettling rather than comforting. It is a difference not merely of *opinion* between black and white Americans but rather of learned *cultural experience*.

Cultural Diversity

Because we are so used to behaving a certain way within our own culture, experiencing cultural diversity can be uncomfortable and even difficult at first. Anyone who has traveled outside the country has likely experienced "culture shock" as a result. In the United States, even the mention of "diversity" can lead to anxiety and conflict. Supreme Court justices disagree on the virtues of diversity and the means for achieving it. Corporations spend billions of dollars to attract and diversity, yet they still face discrimination lawsuits, and the leadership ranks of the business world remain predominantly white and male. It is therefore reasonable to ask what good diversity does us. Diversity of occupational *expertise* confers obvious benefits—you would not think of building a skyscraper without a diverse array of engineers, designers, and quality-control experts—but what about *cultural* diversity? If cultural differences can cause discomfort, awkward social interactions, and mistrust, then what good comes from diversity of race, ethnicity, gender, and sexual orientation?

While it may seem counterintuitive at first, decades of research by organizational scientists, psychologists, sociologists, and economists all show that culturally diverse groups are more innovative and productive than homogeneous groups. For example, research on large companies that prioritized innovation saw greater financial gains when women were part of the top leadership ranks. Similarly, a recent University of Texas study found that, for innovation-focused banks, increases in racial diversity were clearly related to enhanced financial performance (in Phillips 2014). According to the researcher Kathleen Phillips (2014), the key to understanding the positive influence of diversity is the concept of *informational diversity*. When people are brought together to solve problems in groups, they bring different information, opinions, and perspectives to bear on a problem. This makes obvious sense when we talk about diversity of disciplinary backgrounds—think again of the interdisciplinary team building a skyscraper. But the same logic applies to cultural diversity. People who are different from one another in race, gender, ethnicity, and other cultural dimensions (including sexual orientation, physical disability, and socioeconomic status) bring unique knowledge and experiences to bear on the task at hand. A male and a female engineer or architect might have perspectives as different and complimentary from one another as an engineer and a designer—and that is a good thing.

The Activity

Tear out the Cultural Bingo card as directed by your instructor (they will choose which one you'll use). Circulate the room to find people who characterize the various spaces. Students can then sign their name to a space. The center is a free space. Play as you would normally play Bingo: the first person to get five tiles horizontally, vertically, or diagonally wins. Your instructor may choose to play several rounds or play a "blackout" round in which the winner must complete the entire Bingo card.

Suggestions for Further Exploration and Application

Your instructor may ask you to read one of the following short articles or watch the short TED Talk for classroom discussion and/or individual reflection.

- **"Armor against Prejudice" (Yong 2013).** This short article explores the concept of *stereotype threat,* or the fear of failing in a way that reinforces derogatory stereotypes of one's cultural or social group.
- **"Diversity Makes You Smarter"** (*14 minutes*). Kathleen Nalty (2017) argues that the key to being the smartest person in the room is to surround yourself with people who are socially different and to look through different lenses.
- **"How Diversity Makes Us Smarter" (Phillips 2014).** Decades of research show that diverse groups are more innovative than homogeneous groups.
- **"Reaping the Benefits of Diversity for Modern Business Innovation" (Walter 2014).** This article looks at diversity from the point of view of business but is applicable to a broader discussion of how society as a whole benefits.

Worksheet 2.1

Cultural Bingo

Find someone who . . .

Is trilingual (fluently)	Has an *abuela/o* living at home	Celebrates Kwanzaa	Celebrated a bar/bat mitzvah	Fasts during Ramadan
Has traveled to two or more countries	Has eaten kimchi, bun, or biryani	Knows what Juneteenth is	Knows where potatoes originated	Can say "hello" in five languages
Is of Asian ancestry	Is a nontraditional student	**FREE**	Has relatives in another country	Attends mosque or temple
Can spell their name in sign language	Speaks English as a second language	Has studied abroad	Self-identifies as multiracial	Has participated in a Seder celebration
Has three or more generations living at home	Has eaten naan, lavash, or injera	Has attended a powwow or had fry bread	Has celebrated a quinceañera	Is vegan or vegetarian

1. Which blocks were the most difficult to fill? Why? What other diversity categories might we have included?

_____

_____

_____

_____

2. Did you hesitate to ask a fellow classmate about any of the spaces? If so, why?

_____

_____

_____

_____

3. Did you make any assumptions about *others* during the game? For example, did you assume someone who looked "foreign" spoke English as a second language? Conversely, did you overlook someone "American-looking" who was Muslim or trilingual? In other words, did you find yourself inadvertently "profiling" at any point in an effort to win?

_____

_____

_____

_____

4. Similarly, did anyone make assumptions about *you* that you found humorous, annoying, or even offensive? Similarly, did you feel uncomfortable being asked about any spaces, perhaps even to the point of lying to avoid being singled out? (You don't have to elaborate if it makes you uncomfortable.)

_____

_____

_____

_____

_____

Worksheet 2.2

Cultural Bingo

Find someone who . . .

Learned a second language	Knows ancestry on both sides	Knows the significance of Kwanzaa	Has celebrated a bar/bat mitzvah	Is Muslim, Jewish, or Hindi
Has traveled outside the United States	Knows what LGBTQ stands for	Knows what Juneteenth is	Has eaten Korean or Vietnamese food	Can say "hello" in five languages
Is of Asian ancestry	Has eaten baklava	**FREE**	Lives on a farm	Knows where the Aztec capital was
Can spell their name in sign language	Speaks English as a second language	Knows what year US women gained the right to vote	Knows where potatoes come from	Was born in a different state
Grew up in a military family	Is wearing something made overseas	Has attended a powwow	Knows what a quinceañera is	Is vegan or vegetarian

1. Which blocks were the most difficult to fill? Why? What other diversity categories might we have included?

_____

_____

_____

_____

2. Did you hesitate to ask a fellow classmate about any of the spaces? If so, why?

_____

_____

_____

_____

3. Did you make any assumptions about *others* during the game? For example, did you assume someone who looked "foreign" spoke English as a second language? Conversely, did you overlook someone "American-looking" who was Muslim or trilingual? In other words, did you find yourself inadvertently "profiling" at any point in an effort to win?

_____

_____

_____

_____

4. Similarly, did anyone make assumptions about *you* that you found humorous, annoying, or even offensive? Similarly, did you feel uncomfortable being asked about any spaces, perhaps even to the point of lying to avoid being singled out? (You don't have to elaborate if it makes you uncomfortable.)

_____

_____

_____

_____

_____

Worksheet 2.3

For Further Exploration and Application

Your instructor may have you do these questions as part of an in-class discussion or independent reflection.

1. Read Ed Yong's (2013) "Armor Against Prejudice." This short article explores the concept of "stereotype threat," or the fear of failing in a way that reinforces derogatory stereotypes. Have you ever experienced this phenomenon or known someone who has?

_____

_____

_____

_____

_____

_____

_____

_____

2. Read Ekaterina Walter's (2014) "Reaping the Benefits of Diversity for Modern Business Innovation." This article examines diversity from the point of view of business but is applicable to a broader discussion of how society as a whole benefits. Give an example, from either the article or personal experience.

_____

_____

_____

_____

_____

_____

_____

_____

3. Read Katherine Phillips's (2014) "How Diversity Makes Us Smarter." This article explores the science behind why culturally diverse workplaces are more innovative, profitable, and adept at solving problems. Have you ever experienced a situation in which you benefited from someone culturally different from you?

_____

_____

_____

_____

_____

_____

_____

_____

_____

4. Watch Kathleen Nalty's (2017) TEDx Talk "Diversity Makes You Smarter," in which she asks a quesiton to which most of us want to answer yes: Do you want to be the smartest person in the room? The key, Nalty argues, is to surround yourself with people who are socially different from you, avoiding our cultural "blind spots." Give an example of a cultural blind spot, from either personal experience or perhaps something you saw in a commercial, on TV, or on social media.

_____

_____

_____

_____

_____

_____

_____

_____

_____

References

Nalty, Kathleen. 2017. "Diversity Makes You Smarter." Video, 13:46. Uploaded by TEDx Talks, 11 September. https://www.youtube.com/watch?v=kJx7_JpxlxA. Accessed 4 June 2019.

Phillips, Katherine W. 2014. "How Diversity Makes Us Smarter." *Scientific American*, 1 October. https://www.scientificamerican.com/article/how-diversity-makes-us-smarter. Accessed 4 June 2019.

Walter, Ekaterina. 2014. "Reaping the Benefits of Diversity for Modern Business Innovation." *Forbes*, 14 January. https://www.forbes.com/sites/ekaterinawalter/2014/01/14/reaping-the-benefits-of-diversity-for-modern-business-innovation/#2f15c2cc2a8f. Accessed 4 June 2019.

Yong, Ed. 2013. "Armor against Prejudice." *Scientific American* 308 (6): 76–80.

CHAPTER 3

Eclectic Challenge

The Eclectic Nature of Archaeology

Archaeology sits at the unique intersection of the physical and social sciences. Archaeologists employ the methodologies and theories of science (such as the scientific method—discussed in chapter 1—and experimentation) to answer questions about human social behavior (such as why we began farming and why social inequality exists). As a result, modern archaeology has become very *eclectic*. Eclectic is defined as "composed of elements drawn from various sources" and "selecting what seems best from various styles, doctrines, ideas, methods, etc."[1] In other words, archaeology is multifaceted, heterogeneous, and varied in terms of both *what* it studies and *how* it studies. You will meet all kinds of specialists in archaeology: biologists, chemists, physicists, geologists, psychologists, forensic anthropologists, sociologists, historians, and philosophers. The eclectic nature of archaeology is what draws many people to the field in the first place, and many professional archaeologists have a secondary specialty in another discipline. For example, a zooarchaeologist may have degrees in both archaeology and biology; a linguistic archaeologist may have degrees in Classics and undergone intense language training in addition to holding a degree in archaeology or anthropology.

The Holistic Approach

Archaeology, like its parent discipline, anthropology, embraces a *holistic* approach when it comes to studying and understanding human social behavior. Holistic means archaeologists are concerned with all aspects of humankind and the relationships among these different aspects. Although different archaeologists often study different parts of human behavior, the *whole* can be understood only in relation to all the other parts, sort of how different doctors study different parts of the body, but they must understand how those parts relate to and affect one another. Like doctors, an archaeologist's job is put all the pieces together, stand back, and look at the complete, or whole, picture. For example, to understand the entirety of the Mayan "collapse" some two millennia ago, it was necessary to piece together data about climate change, farming practices, population growth, deforestation and construction of temples, political factions and competition, disparities and inequalities within the accepted social hierarchy, and religious practices and beliefs about the natural and spiritual world. It turned out to be very complex—indeed very eclectic!

The Activity

In this activity, the "Eclectic Challenge," your instructor will challenge you to think of three topics archaeologists do not (or cannot) study. Your instructor may run the challenge as a class activity or break you into teams; if the latter, they will tell you whether to use Worksheet 3.1 or 3.2, and may assign readings and questions under "For Further Exploration and Application." What do you think: can you win this challenge? Or is archaeology simply too eclectic . . . ?

Suggestions for Further Exploration and Application

Your instructor may ask you to do Worksheet 3.3 and/or read one of the following articles to illustrate a truly eclectic topic you would not initially think archaeologists would study. Write your answers in the space provided in Worksheet 3.3.

- **"Archaeology of the Homeless" (Albertson 2009).** Homelessness has long been a significant subculture of American society. Archaeologists are now examining the material culture of the homeless to understand its rules, realities, and patterns, with the goal of improving public programs that aid the poor.
- **"The Beer Archaeologist" (Tucker 2011).** This Smithsonian Magazine article shadows the "Beer archaeologist" Pat McGovern (and his partner in crime, Dogfish Head Brewery) as he uses everything from historical texts to chemical residues on beer pots to reconstruct (and recreate) ancient beer recipes.
- **"A Coprological View of Ancestral Pueblo Cannibalism" (Reinhard 2006).** This article studies enzymes and parasites trapped in human coprolites (i.e., fossilized feces) to investigate possible cannibalism among the ancestral Pueblo.
- **"How Will Future Archaeologists Study Us?" (Baraniuk 2018).** This article summarizes a new technology under development that will not store cultural material on hard drives but rather encode it into capsulated DNA: what seems like the stuff of science fiction of today may instead be the "material culture" of the future!
- **"A Tale of Garbage" (McTaggart 2015).** This article demonstrates how contemporary garbage is nothing more than modern-day material culture and that the study of garbage from an archaeological perspective, including its types and patterning, can shed light on the human societies both past and present.

Worksheet 3.1

Team A

List 4 topics that archaeologists don't or can't study.	In the boxes below, write W if the topic wins the challenge, or L if it loses the challenge. If L, explain.
1. _____ 2. _____ 3. _____ 4. _____	1. ☐ _____ _____ 2. ☐ _____ _____ 3. ☐ _____ _____ 4. ☐ _____ _____

tear here

Team B

List 4 topics that archaeologists don't or can't study.	In the boxes below, write W if the topic wins the challenge, or L if it loses the challenge. If L, explain.
1. _____ 2. _____ 3. _____ 4. _____	1. ☐ _____ _____ 2. ☐ _____ _____ 3. ☐ _____ _____ 4. ☐ _____ _____

A	**B**
Antarctica Quantum physics The Big Bang Medicine	Volcanoes Genetic engineering Oceans Dinosaurs
C	**D**
Brain surgery Quantum physics Plate Tectonics Astronomy	Mathematics Oceans Nutrition Plate tectonics
E	**F**
Antarctica Origins of the solar system Climate Art	Nutrition Origins of the universe Dinosaurs Mathematics

Worksheet 3.3

For Further Exploration and Application

Your instructor may have you do these questions as part of an in-class discussion or independent reflection. Use the back of this sheet if you need more space.

1. Archaeology is both eclectic, as you saw in this challenge, and holistic. As previously discussed, holistic means archaeologists are concerned with all aspects of humankind and the relationships among these different facets. Although different archaeologists often study different parts of human behavior, the *whole* can be understood only in relation to all the other parts, sort of how different doctors study different parts of the body, but they must understand how those parts relate to and affect one another. Like doctors, an archaeologist's job is put all the pieces together, stand back, and look at the complete, or whole, picture. Read the article assigned by your instructor. In what way is the research described both eclectic and holistic?

_____

_____

_____

_____

_____

_____

_____

2. Read the article "How Will Future Archaeologists Study Us?" and watch the associated video. It describes perhaps the most eclectic aspect of all: the study of how we will study ourselves in the future! Toward the end of the article, the researchers note this technology is expensive, and we will have to pick and choose what we record. How is this different from traditional archaeology, and is this a good or bad thing, considering preservation limitations?

_____

_____

_____

_____

_____

_____

_____

Note

1. *Merriam-Webster*, s.v. "eclectic (*adj.*)," https://www.merriam-webster.com/dictionary/eclectic, accessed 30 March 2019; Dictionary.com, s.v." eclectic" (*adj.*), https://www.dictionary.com/browse/eclectic, accessed 30 March 2019.

References

Albertson, Nicole. 2009. "Archaeology of the Homeless." *Archaeology* 62 (6). https://archive.archaeology.org/0911/abstracts/homeless.html. Accessed 4 June 2019. Reprinted in *Annual Editions: Archaeology*, 12th ed., chap. 22 (New York: McGraw-Hill, 2016).

Baraniuk, Chris. 2015. "How Will Future Archaeologists Study Us?" *BBC*, 30 November. http://www.bbc.com/future/story/20151127-how-will-future-archaeologists-study-us. Accessed 4 June 2019.

McTaggart, Ian. 2015. "A Tale of Garbage." *Earth Common Journal* 5 (1). http://www.inquiriesjournal.com/articles/1331/a-tale-of-garbage. Accessed 4 June 2019.

Reinhard, Karl J. 2006. "A Coprological View of Ancestral Pueblo Cannibalism." *American Scientist* 94 (3): 254–261. Reprinted in *Annual Editions: Archaeology*, 12th ed., chap. 11 (New York: McGraw-Hill, 2016).

Tucker, Abigail. 2011. "The Beer Archaeologist." *Smithsonian Magazine*, August. https://www.smithsonianmag.com/history/the-beer-archaeologist-17016372. Accessed 4 June 2019.

CHAPTER 4

A Symbol Worth a Thousand Words

Symbolism

A *symbol* is a mark, sign, or picture that represents an idea, object, or relationship. One of the hallmarks of human culture is our use of symbols to generate behavior, communicate ideas, and interpret cultural meaning with others in our social group (notice that this mirrors the definition of culture as introduced in chapter 1). Symbols carry meanings that depend upon one's cultural background. In other words, the meaning of a symbol is not inherent in the symbol itself but rather is culturally learned. Undoubtedly, you immediately recognize the cultural meaning behind each of the symbols shown in Figure 4.1. Symbols can be both arbitrary and subtle. Sometimes, symbols are so subtle we don't even recognize them consciously, but often pick up on them without realizing it. To illustrate this subtly, read the *Mental Floss* article (English 2013) and see how many "hidden symbols" you can find in familiar company logos. Were you surprised by any?

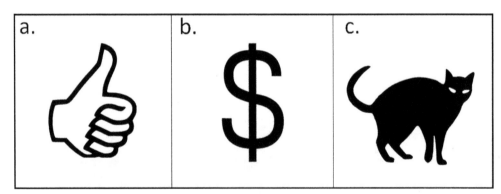

Figure 4.1. Thumbs-up (a), dollar sign (b), and black cat (c) symbols.

Symbols are also arbitrary. In other words, despite our familiarity with them, they are unrelated to the object is it supposed to represent. For example, $ is the American symbol for money (Figure 4.1b), and although this symbol in no way physically resembles our modern currency, Americans—and most Westerners, for that matter—recognize it immediately as the "universal" symbol for money. But if you are Yanomami or !Kung San, that symbol has no inherent meaning whatsoever. As another example, the "thumbs-up" symbol (Figure 4.1a) in American culture is a positive gesture symbolizing a job well done or indicating "way to go!" But elsewhere, this common symbol we take for granted may mean vastly different things. For example, in countries such as Australia and Ghana, it is an offensive, insulting gesture. In other countries, such as Japan and Germany, the gesture simply signifies a quantity, "five," in Japan, and "one" in Germany. Finally, in Saudi Arabia it means "I'm winning!" Colors are also arbitrary symbols that vary from one culture to another, and often with no apparent rhyme or reason. For example, Americans use the color black to represent death, mourning, grief, and bad luck. This is why we traditionally wear black to funerals and cringe when a black cat (Figure 4.1c) walks in front of us. Yet, for many other cultures, black carries no negative connotation at all. In modern China, and some other Asian countries, black is considered a neutral color and is worn as everyday attire, while white symbolizes death and is worn at funerals. And in some African cultures, black symbolizes age, maturity, and masculinity. Thus, color, like written symbols and hand gestures, are culturally specific rather than universal.

Emic and Etic Points of View

Because symbols are culturally specific, understanding them can come from only what anthropologists and archaeologists call an *emic* perspective (i.e., the insider's view of the world), or, to put it more colloquially, the "native's point of view." An outsider, who has what anthropologists call an *etic* point of view, is often unaware of these culturally specific nuances to human behavior. And, as a result, they may find themselves sinking in cultural quicksand, as former US President George H. W. Bush did when he inadvertently offended an Australian audience after innocently flashing a two-fingered "V" during a speech (with the palm facing inward, toward the himself)—a symbol that means "peace" to Americans but to Australians is the equivalent of the middle finger (Borcover 1992).

Former US President George W. Bush experienced a similar cultural misunderstanding as his father, when an Iraqi journalist threw a shoe at him during a press conference about the Iraqi War. Bush later said the incident was "one of the most weird moments" of his presidency—which it would be to an American with an etic perspective of Iraqi culture (Myers and Rubin 2008). But anyone familiar with Iraqi culture—that is, with an emic understanding—knows that hurling shoes at someone isn't just weird: in Iraq, the gesture is a symbolic sign of contempt. On a more humorous note, in 2003, then Democratic presidential nominee John Kerry stopped at a famous cheesesteak joint in Philadelphia and ordered a cheesesteak with Swiss cheese instead of the traditional, and culturally appropriate, Cheez Whiz. This shocked the restaurant owners (and most of Philadelphia!) to say the least. As Craig LaBan (2003) wrote in the *Philadelphia Inquirer*, "Swiss cheese, as any local knows, is not an option." The lesson? When in Rome, do as the Romans do (i.e., emic behavior), and don't do as the Romans absolutely don't (i.e., etic behavior)!

The Activity

In this activity, your instructor will ask you to make some drawings to illustrate the power of symbolism (use the blank sheets provided in your workbook). Keep an open mind for this one, and have fun with it, even if you initially feel awkward with what is asked of you. The logic will become clear at the end.

Suggestions for Further Exploration and Application

For homework or class reflection, your instructor may ask you to also complete Worksheet 4.3 and/or read one of the following articles:

- **"Body Ritual among the Nacirema" (Miner 1956).** This is the earliest anthropological description of the Nacirema, a little-known tribe living in the territory between the Canadian Cree, the Yaqui and Tarahumare of Mexico, and the Carib and Arawak of the Antilles.
- **"Weight of the World: The Battle of the Bulge Goes Global" (Niranjana 2006).** Without losing or gaining any weight, the author describes how she went from being "too thin" to "chubby" after moving from India to the United States.

Worksheet 4.1

Sketch below according to your teacher's instructions

Worksheet 4.2

Sketch below according to your teacher's instructions

Worksheet 4.3

For Further Exploration and Application

Your instructor may have you do Worksheet 4.3 as part of in-class discussion or independent reflection. Write your answers in the space provided.

1. INSTRUCTIONS.

Symbol	American (emic symbolism)	Etic symbolism (there can be multiple answers)
$		
✌		
#		
👍		
!		
✡		
∞		
the color white		
➤		
🍎		

2. Create your own "hidden message" and explain the symbolism behind it the space below.

_____

_____
_____
_____
_____

3. Read "Body Ritual among the Nacirema" (Miner 1956). Who are the Nacirema? At what point (if any) did you recognize them? Did this perspective make you think any differently about your own culture when you read if from an etic perspective, that is, an "outsider's" point of view?

_____
_____
_____
_____
_____
_____
_____
_____
_____
_____

References

Borcover, Alfred. 1992. "Hands Off." *Chicago Tribune*, 26 January.

English, Jason. 2013. "11 Hidden Messages in Company Logos." *Mental Floss*, 11 October. http://mentalfloss.com/article/53146/11-hidden-messages-company-logos. Accessed 4 June 2019.

LaBan, Craig. 2003. "Photo Oop: Kerry Eats a Cheesesteak Hoagie . . . with Swiss." *Philadelphia Inquirer*, 16 August.

Meyers, Steven Lee, and Alissa J. Rubin. 2008. "Iraqi Journalist Hurls Shoes at Bush and Denounces Him on TV as a 'Dog.'" *New York Times*, 14 December.

Miner, Horace. 1956. "Body Ritual among the Nacirema." *American Anthropologist* 53 (3): 503–507. http://www.sfu.ca/~palys/Miner-1956-BodyRitualAmongTheNacirema.pdf. Accessed 4 June 2019.

Niranjana, Iyer. 2006. "Weight of the World: The Battle of the Bulge Goes Global." *Smithsonian Magazine* 37 (5): 104. http://www.smithsonianmag.com/people-places/last-page-weight-of-the-world-125124175. Accessed 4 June 2019.

CHAPTER 5

Smokescreen
Hidden Symbols

Levels of Material Culture

In 1962, influential processual archaeologist Lewis Binford asserted that archaeologists must interpret material cultural on several levels, not necessarily just a functional level, if we are to correctly interpret the entirety of cultural behavior. For example, the function of a candle is to provide light (and perhaps warmth). But a candle can also symbolize more ethereal things such as age (i.e., a birthday candle) or forgiveness for sins (i.e., a baptismal candle). If we miss any one of these meanings, our overall knowledge of a culture is diminished. Thus, Binford argued that artifacts can, and should be, evaluated at three distinct levels: technomic, sociotechnic, and ideotechnic (Figure 5.1). An artifact's *technomic* meaning is strictly utilitarian and relates to the technology, or function, of the artifact. In our example, a candle's technomic meaning is to provide lighting or warmth. Similarly, a cup functions to hold liquid. An artifact's *sociotechnic* meaning involves its social, rather than technological, use. For example, a birthday candle represents one year of life, so a child turning 10 will often blow out 10 candles on their birthday cake, one for each year of their life. Similarly, an expensive antique cup displayed prominently may indicate wealth, or a Starbucks cup may show brand loyalty. An artifact's *ideotechnic* meaning relates to its use in a religious or ideological context. A baptismal candle represents the forgiveness of sins in the Christian Church, and the central black Kwanzaa candle represents African unity. In the cup analogy, a chalice may represent Christ's blood in the Christian church, or the essence of femininity in the Wicca and similar pagan traditions.

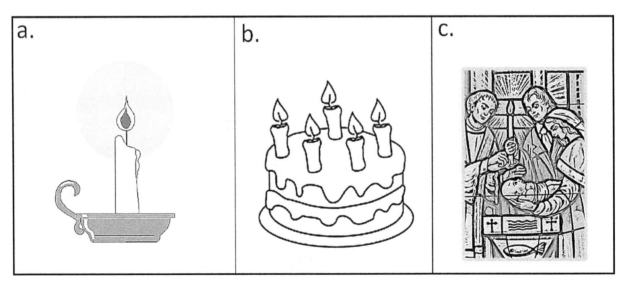

Figure 5.1. A candle in its technomic (a), sociotechnic (b), and ideotechnic (c) context.

The Old Copper Complex

With these three levels of meaning explained, Binford provides an archaeological example of the copper tools found at Native American sites associated
with the Late Archaic period "Old Copper Complex" in the western Great
Lakes region between 6000 and 3000 BCE. Binford raises several points that
call into question the use of these copper implements as just tools. First, copper is difficult to work, yet the result of so much effort is no more durable
than stone or bone (perhaps less even). Second, the "tools" do not appear
to be reworked (i.e., recycled) as is typical of bone and stone tools. This is
surprising, especially given how time consuming it is to manufacture copper;
it certainly doesn't seem efficient to waste the copper, at least not from a
technological or functional point of view. Finally, many of the tools appear
to have been intentionally buried in what archaeologists call "caches," a collection of items of the same type stored in a hidden or inaccessible place. This
phenomenon suggests some kind of social or ideological significance. Binford
suggests that as societies became more densely populated, the copper implements morphed into symbols of status and/or rank, no longer serving a technomic, technological purpose. Binford refutes the popular notion that falling
away from copper tools was odd, an inexplicable loss of technological skills.
Rather, while Great Lakes populations initially created copper tools during
the Middle Archaic, Late Archaic populations (toward 3000 BCE) returned
to stone and bone for everyday tools, with copper reserved for symbolic and
ornamental functions. Thus, over time, the implements' function changed
meaning, and archaeologists must recognize that what may look like a "tool"
may in fact be something quite different. Just like in our example, while the
baptismal candle may be capable of functioning to give light, most Chris-
tians would do so only in an extreme emergency because that kind of candle
carries a very different meaning, one imbued with a great deal of religious
symbolism.

The Activity

This short activity will ask you to brainstorm a contemporaneous "artifact"
and determine its three levels of meaning. You will then apply the concept to
the archaeological record and evaluate the benefits, as well as the difficulties
in unraveling, an artifact's potential multiple meanings.

Suggestions for Further Exploration and Application

For homework or class reflection, your instructor may ask you to complete
the back side of Worksheet 5.1, which entails watching and/or reading one
of the following:

- **"Contemporary Aboriginal Art" (Lubow 2010).** This is an excellent,
  short article on the resurgence in Australian Aboriginal artwork and its
  hidden symbolism of the "Dreamtime." While Westerners often note only
  the basic animal shapes and dots, Lubow shows just how complex the
  symbolism is.

- **"The Day Pictures Were Born" (BBC 2005)** *(54 minutes)*. Europe's famous Paleolithic cave paintings were originally interpreted from only a technomic point of view, but recent research suggests an ideotechnic interpretation instead, one in which the prehistoric artists were experiencing powerful hallucinations.
- **"What This Awl Means: Toward a Feminist Archaeology" (Spector 1991).** *(excerpt reprinted with permission in Worksheet 5.2)*. Janet Spector, an influential processual archaeologist, takes some artistic license—coupled with solid archaeology and interviews with living members of the Dakota Sioux—to tell the compelling story of a Sioux girl's prized awl, bringing the object to life in a compelling story everyone can relate to.

Worksheet 5.1

1. Read "11 Hidden Messages in Company Logos" (English 2013). Which company logo surprised you the most? Why? Did it make you see the company/brand differently than before?

_____

_____

_____

_____

_____

_____

_____

_____

_____

2. Pick two "artifacts" and distinguish among the three levels of meaning for each, following the example of the candle in the chapter introduction.

"Artifact" 1: _____

Technomic	Sociotechnic	Ideotechnic

"Artifact" 2: _____

Technomic	Sociotechnic	Ideotechnic

For Further Exploration and Application

Your instructor may have you do these questions as part of an in-class discussion or independent reflection.

1. Watch "The Day Pictures Were Born" (BBC 2005) (through minute 46). How did the archaeological setting/appearance of the cave paintings suggest that the original technomic interpretation was wrong? How did the researchers use the modern-day San to *emically* (re)interpret the Ice Age paintings' *ideotechnic* meaning? How did they use TSM (the scientific method)?

_____

_____

_____

_____

_____

_____

_____

_____

2. Read "Contemporary Aboriginal Art" (Lubow 2010) or "What This Awl Means" (Spector 1991) Based on these articles, and the BBC video, how can archaeologists infer the more nuanced sociotechnic and ideotechnic meanings of artifacts in the lack of written records? Are there any problems with these methods that might call our conclusions into question?

_____

_____

_____

_____

_____

_____

_____

_____

What This Awl Means

By Janet Spector

The women and children of Inyan Ceyaka Atonwan (Little Rapids) had been working at the maple sugar camps since Istawicayazan wi (the Moon of Sore Eyes, or March). At the same time, most of the men had been far from the village trapping muskrats. When Wozupi wi (the Moon for Planting, or May) came, fifteen households eagerly reunited in their bark lodges near the river . . .

One day some villagers brought their tanned furs and maple sugar to the lodge of jean Baptiste Faribault. He lived among them a few months each year with his Dakota wife, Pelagie. In exchange for furs and maple sugar, Faribault gave them glass beads, silver ornaments, tin kettles, and iron knives, awl tips, axes, hatchet, and hoes for their summer work . . .

Mazomani (Iron Walker) and Hazawin (Blueberry Woman) were proud of their daughter Mazaokiyewin (Woman Who Talks to Iron). The day after visiting Faribault, they had given her some glass beads and a new iron awl tip. The tip was the right size to fit into the smaller antler handle that Hazawin had given Mazaokiyewin when she went to dwell along at the time of her first menses. Mazaokiyewin used the sharp pointed awl for punching holes in pieces of leather before stitching them together with deer sinew. Though young, she had already established a reputation among the people at Inyan Ceyaka Atonwan for creativity and excellence in quillwork and beadwork.

Mazaokiyewin's mother and grandmothers had taught her to keep a careful record of her accomplishments, so whenever she finished quilling or beading moccasins, she remembered to impress a small dot on the fine awl handle that Hazawin had made for her. When Mazaokiyewin completed more complicated work, such as sewing and decorating a buckskin dress or pipe bag, she formed diamond-shaped clusters of four small dots which symbolized the powers of the four directions that influenced her life in many ways. She

liked to expose the handle of this small tool as she carried it in its beaded case so that others could see she was doing her best to ensure the well-being of their community.

When she engraved the dots into her awl handle, she carefully marked each one with red pigment, made by boiling sumac berries with a small root found in the ground near the village. Dakota people associated the color red with women and their life forces. Red also represented the east, where the sun rose to give knowledge, wisdom, and understanding. Red symbolized Mazaokiyewin's aspirations to these qualities.

When the designated day in Wasuton wi arrived, Mazomani led the people in the medicine dance near the burial place of their ancestors. Members of the medicine lodge danced within an enclosed oval area, separated from the audience by a low, hide-covered fence . . .

One hot day following the dance, Mazaokiyewin gathered together all of the leatherwork she had finished since returning to Inyan Ceyaka Atonwan after the spring hunting and sugaring seasons. . . . Now, Mazaokiyewin eagerly anticipated the quilling contest and feast called by a woman of a neighboring household to honor a family member. Mazaokiyewin knew she had produced more beaded and quilled articles than most of the community's young women, and she looked forward to bringing recognition to her parents and grandparents . . .

She started uphill carrying the mniapahatapi (skin water bags) carefully, but near the quilling contest lodge she slipped on the muddy path where water had pooled in the driving rain. As she struggled to regain her footing without dropping the bags, the leather strap holding her awl in its case broke, and the small awl dropped on the ground. It fell close to one of the cooking fires outside the lodge entrance.

Mazaokiyewin did not miss her awl that day, because as soon as she entered the lodge with the water, the host of the contest took her hand and escorted her to the center of the crowd. The host had already counted each woman's pieces and distributed a stick for each. Mazaokiyewin had accumulated more sticks than all but three older women. The host then led the four to the place of honor in the lodge and gave them their food first to honor their accomplishments. Later, the results of this contest would be recorded for all to see on the hides lining the walls of the lodge. This pleased Hazawin and Mazomani.

The heavy rain that day had scattered debris over the village and on the day after the quilling contest and medicine dance, people joined together to clean up the encampment. Using old hides, and baskets, they carried off loads of fallen branches, wet fire ash, and charcoal, and the remains of the feast to the community dump above the slough. Somehow, Mazaokiyewin's small awl was swept up and carried off with other garbage from the quilling contest. It disappeared in the dump as the villagers emptied one basket load after another on top of it.

Later, the loss of the awl saddened Mazaokiyewin and Hazawin, but they knew the handle was nearly worn out, and both realized it was more of a girl's tool than a woman's. Mazaokiyewin was almost a woman ready to establish her own household, no longer a child of her mother's lodge. It was time to put aside her girl-tools, she knew, but she had intended to keep this awl. Its finely incised dots and engraved lines showed how well she had learned adult tasks, and she took as much pleasure in displaying it as her mother did in watching others admire it . . .

The following day, they packed the equipment that the family would need over the next several months. As they assembled their hide-working tools, they spoke again of Mazaokiyewin's missing awl. They realized that their feeling of loss was not simply about that one small tool. Instead, as fall approached, and they prepared to leave Inyan Ceyaka Atonwan, they had troubling premonitions about the future.

Extract from Janet D. Spector. 1993. *What This Awl Means: Feminist Archaeology at a Wahpeton Dakota Village*. St. Paul, MN: St. Paul Minnesota Historical Society Press.

References

BBC. 2005. "The Day Pictures Were Born." *How Art Made the World*, season 1, episode 2. http://www.pbs.org/howartmadetheworld/series/buy. Accessed 4 June 2019.

Binford, Lewis. ¹962. "Archaeology as Anthropology." *American Antiquity* 28 (2): 217–225.

English, Jason. 2013. "11 Hidden Messages in Company Logos." *Mental Floss*, 11 October. http://mentalfloss.com/article/53146/11-hidden-messages-company-logos. Accessed 4 June 2019.

Lubow, Arthur. 2010. "Contemporary Aboriginal Art." *Smithsonian Magazine*, January. http://www.smithsonianmag.com/arts-culture/contemporary-aboriginal-art-10885394. Accessed 4 June 2019.

Spector, Janet D. 1991. "What This Awl Means: Toward a Feminist Archaeology." In *Engendering Archaeology: Women and Prehistory*, edited by Margaret W. Conkey and Joan M. Gero, 388–406. New York: Wiley-Blackwell.

MODULE 2

Attributing Meaning to Artifacts and Formation of the Archaeological Record

CHAPTER 6

Archaeological Chaos

Antiquity of the Archaeological Record

Envision an archaeological site in your mind . . . perhaps it's an ancient Roman city overlooking the Colosseum, or perhaps it is much older, such as a pueblo village in the Southwestern United States. Or even older yet: a Neanderthal camp in a cave in southwestern Germany. What objects do you see? What are the houses constructed of? What are the people eating? What kinds of tools are they using? What kinds of games are the children playing? If you are imaging a historic period scenario like Rome or Greece, you may know the answer to some of these questions based on the many written records their cultures left behind. For Rome, togas and mosaics might immediately come to mind, or perhaps the famous Colosseum with its heaps of spectators watching gladiator fights and mock naval battles. Or perhaps you think of Hadrian's Wall and the Romans' efforts to protect their empire from the people they called "barbarians." We know these details in part through archaeological excavation but also from the ruins that stand today and the copious writings the Romans left behind. But consider this: humans did not begin to invent writing until very recently in our human journey: only about 5,000 years ago. Modern humans have been around for nearly 150,000 years. That means we have been recording how we lived for less than 1 percent of our time on Earth! If we convert that to a 24-hour day that began at midnight, that means we did not begin writing until 11:45 p.m. the *next* day!

Material Culture

Thus, for the 99 percent of time that has no written records, we must rely on the physical remains people left behind in order to reconstruct what their houses looked like, what they ate, and the tools they used—things such as pottery, bricks, and stone tools. The physical materials left behind by people's activities is referred to as *material culture*. Think of it as individual pieces in a 1,000-piece jigsaw puzzle, one that has to be put together without the aid of the picture on the front of the box. Much of the puzzle pieces come from garbage, from litter, from stuff that has been used and discarded. Archaeologists often find themselves digging the remains of ancient garbage dumps, which we call *middens*. Sounds gross, but trash is a treasure trove of material culture that is our window into the past.

Even for the historical period, we cannot always trust what we read in books. For example, one of America's oldest religious sects, the Ephrata Cloister, who lived in central Pennsylvania in the 1740s, wrote down many things about their lifestyle—what they considered to be God's work. One interesting fact they wrote about themselves is that they ate only one small vegetarian meal a day (their leader, Conrad Beissel, considered meat spiritually undesirable). Yet, when archaeologists from the Pennsylvania Historical and Museum Commission excavated at the Cloister in the 1990s, they recovered butchered deer bones, calling their strict vegetarianism into question (Warfel 1993). Although the Cloister valued singing (they printed many self-composed hymns), they believed musical instruments were to be avoided as part of their focus on self-denial and separation from the outside world. Yet, excavations revealed a mysterious glass trumpet buried intentionally in a clay refuse pit behind one of the buildings; because the mouthpiece was missing, it is unknown if it was ever played, nor where it came from (see State Museum of Pennsylvania 2016 for a picture of the trumpet). Thus, the material culture at Ephrata Cloister not only tells us much about how people lived but may also be more truthful than our historical records. As Steve Warfel (1993), director of the Ephrata Cloister archaeology project, once said, "trash is a sort of democratic record. Documents are written for a purpose [but] what we find in the ground is what they actually did."

The Activity

In this activity, you will explore the various kinds of material culture that makes up the archaeological record and consider how preservation affects how much of the record gets preserved. The archaeological record is a collection of puzzle pieces in which some have decomposed, blown away, or been eaten by other animals, making the work extra challenging. This is the topic of the chapter 9. For now, we'll simply explore these three classes of material culture.

Suggestions for Further Exploration and Application

Your instructor may ask you to complete Worksheet 6.2 as part of additional classroom discussion or personal reflection. They may also ask you to watch a video to supplement Worksheet 6.2. Write your answers in the space provided.

- **"The Day Pictures Were Born" (BBC 2005)** *(54 minutes)*: Europe's famous Paleolithic cave paintings were originally interpreted only from a technomic point of view based on the features alone, but recent research suggests an ideotechnic interpretation instead, one in which the prehistoric artists were experiencing powerful hallucinations. This new understanding comes from some cool science, but also closer inspection of the features' appearance and location, as well as other classes of material culture found at the site.

Worksheet 6.1

1. As objects found at archaeological sites are called out, place them in the same column as your instructor does. Your instructor will give each category a name at the end.

Material Culture Category			
Examples			
Characteristics			

2. Which of these categories of material culture would preserve the best? The worst? How might that affect how archaeologists interpret past human behavior?

_____

_____

_____

_____

_____

_____

_____

_____

_____

_____

_____

3. Consider the size of these different classes of material culture. How might size affect how archaeologists interpret past human behavior?

_____

_____

_____

_____

_____

_____

_____

_____

_____

_____

_____

Worksheet 6.2

For Further Exploration and Application

Your instructor may have you do these questions as part of an in-class discussion or independent reflection.

1. The artifact, ecofact, and feature below were found by itself at an archaeological site from a society you know nothing about. Based *solely* on observation, what might you conclude/ assume about that society—not what you know or what is American, but what might you infer based on the object? In other works, this is an *etic* interpretation.

Artifact	Ecofact	Feature

2. List at least two reasons why using *multiple* lines of evidence (i.e., artifacts, ecofacts, *and* features) is so important to making sound, emic interpretations of culture. What other information might you want to interpret these?

_____

_____

_____

_____

_____

_____

_____

_____

_____

_____

3. If you haven't already watched it, your teacher may have you watch "The Day Pictures Were Born" (BBC) 2005), about the famous Paleolithic cave paintings in Europe. What about the archaeological setting/appearance of the cave paintings suggested that the original technomic interpretation was wrong? What other lines of evidence, or classes of material culture, did the scientists look at to interpret the paintings differently than the original researchers?

_____

_____

_____

_____

_____

_____

_____

_____

_____

_____

References

BBC. 2005. "The Day Pictures Were Born." *How Art Made the World*, season 1, episode 2. http://www.pbs.org/howartmadetheworld/series/buy. Accessed 4 June 2019.

Isakk, Leonora. 1994. Artifact Interpretation. *Archaeology and Public Education* 5 (2): 6.

State Museum of Pennsylvania. 2016. "Ephrata Cloister's Glass Trumpet Is Likely 'One of a Kind.'" 3 May. [Picture of trumpet available,] http://statemuseumpa.org/ephrata-cloister-glass-trumpet-one-kind. Accessed 11 June 2019.

Warfel, Steve. 1993. "The Ephrata Cloister." *The Reading Eagle*. 25 July.

CHAPTER 7

Name That Thingamajig

Archaeological Context

One of the most important concepts in archaeology is *context*. Context refers to the relationship artifacts have to one other, as well as the situation in which they are found. Without this information, we are forced to interpret artifacts' functions and/or purpose through our own subjective perspective, which is clouded by our own biases and beliefs, sort of like putting together a puzzle without having the picture to guide you. Context consists of three parts: matrix, association, and provenience—or MAP for short. This acronym will help you remember these three aspects since an artifact's context is very much related to mapping. Let's review provenience first, since this concept is most obviously related to mapping.

Provenience

Every artifact found on an archaeological site can be mapped to record its exact location within space. In fact, provenience is recorded even before the artifact is ever removed from the ground. This point is measured as *(x, y)* coordinates from a set point, called a datum. Archaeologists also record *z*, or depth, which relates to how old the artifact is (see chapter 10). Figure 7.1 demonstrates.

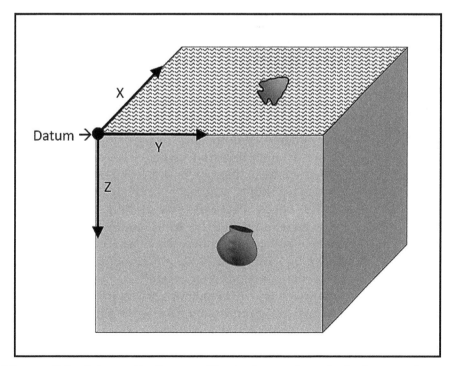

Figure 7.1. Schematic diagram illustrating archaeological provenience.

Association

Artifacts are often found alongside other artifacts (though sometimes they occur alone—what archaeologists call "isolated finds"). Oftentimes, they form an obvious pattern or relationship, such as a ring of rocks around a campfire. Or consider the site of Clovis, New Mexico. When it was discovered in the 1920s, a stone spear point was found lodged between the ribs of a species of bison that went extinct at the end of the last Ice Age. The association of the spear point and the bison proved beyond a reasonable doubt that humans had hunted the bison. It also settled a long-standing debate about how long humans had inhabited North America, establishing once and for all that people had been here at least since the end of the Ice Age. It was the context—the *association* in particular—between the bison skeleton and the artifact that allowed archaeologists to draw these conclusions. Consider the images in Figure 7.2—how might you interpret the identical spear point in each scenario shown?

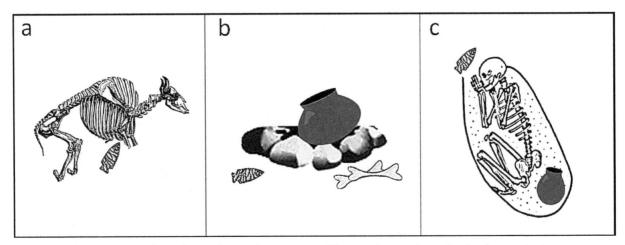

Figure 7.2. Three hypothetical scenarios illustrating archaeological association. Image (c) Courtesy Jeffrey Quilter from original drawings by Bernardino Ojeda.

Picture (a) is the scenario just described: the association of the point embedded in the bison skeleton is strong evidence that the animal was hunted intentionally, making the spear point just that—a spear point. Picture (b) shows a much different association—one in which the point is associated with cooking implements and food. Now the "spear" point is functioning more like a knife, perhaps to butcher the bone shown. Helping confirm this interpretation, archaeologists studying cut marks on bone have discovered they were produced by stone-cutting implements. Similarly, microscopic analysis of "spears" shows they have a distinct wear and polish pattern produced by cutting, rather than throwing. Thus, archaeologists often refer to projectile points more accurately as "projectile point/knives" (ppk). Finally, picture (c) shows the ppk in a burial context. In such a ritualistic context, the ppk may have multiple meanings: it may designate the deceased as a hunter, reflect the deceased's occupation as a toolmaker, or reflect the need for the deceased to have a tool in the afterlife. What other associations might you need to distinguish between these latter possibilities (see Worksheet 7.2)?

Matrix

The soil surrounding an artifact is the third and final aspect of context. This concept is somewhat less intuitive but no less important to making interpretations about people and human behavior. For example, imagine you are excavating a "site" on an island in large river (Figure 7.3). Several artifacts lie on the ground surface, so you and your crew set up your map grid and begin digging. As you go, you see more and more artifacts, but something seems off: you see several points dating to different time periods but lying in the same stratigraphic layer. Also, some of the artifacts appear worn, and somewhat rounded. Why might this be? The answer lies in the location and matrix of the site. Remember, you are on an island. Careful observation of the soil at the site shows that most of it is composed of rounded sand grains. This is typical of river sediments that have been carried downstream by water: as the grains bump each other, they become more rounded. If this archaeological "site" is composed of material that has been relocated from upstream, then the artifacts have too. Thus, while you have artifacts here, they are not in what archaeologists call *primary* (i.e., their original) context but rather have been transported from elsewhere and just happened to land here on the island's edge during a flood (what archaeologists call *secondary* context).

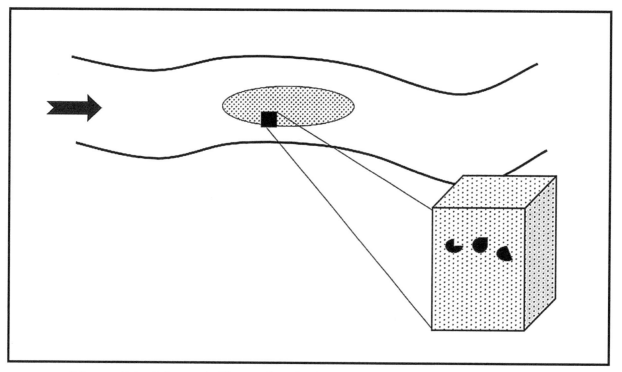

Figure 7.3. Schematic illustrating the importance of archaeological matrix.

Artifact Collecting

It is natural to want to pick up an artifact if we stumble upon it. Most people are genuinely intrigued by them and curious about the people who made them long ago. Unfortunately, when people remove artifacts without recording their provenience, association, or matrix, their context is lost forever and they have little or no scientific value left. This is why looting (i.e., "pothunting") artifacts is considered bad, and why it is illegal when it occurs on federal or public land. The object itself can give us some information, but most of the information archaeologists gather from a site comes from the context of those objects. If everybody were to visit a site and take one artifact each, there would soon be nothing left for us to study. But not only looters bear the responsibility of preserving artifacts' context: archaeology is ultimately a destructive science, and archaeologists can never put things back the same after they have been excavated. As a result, we destroy the context and could potentially lose vast amounts of information. This is why archaeologists are so tedious in their efforts to record and map *every*thing, even a simple stain in the soil, or a tiny speck of charcoal. Because you never know when it may be important to interpreting the site correctly and understanding how people lived in the past . . .

The Activity

This activity is designed to illustrate just how vital context is. Complete Worksheet 7.1 for the "artifact" your instructor gives you. These may be simulated artifacts, real artifacts, or a combination of both. Don't scuff at the "fake" artifacts. These, perhaps even more saliently than real artifacts can, make the point that, without context, interpreting the function and/or purpose of an artifact can be very much clouded by our own cultural biases and perceptions.

Suggestions for Further Exploration and Application

Your instructor may ask you to watch and/or read one of the following as part of an in-class discussion or individual reflection. Write your answers in the space provided in Worksheet 7.2.

- *Motel of the Mysteries* **(Macaulay 1979).** David Macaulay creates a wonderful spoof of Howard Carter's excavations of King Tutankhamun's tomb when he famously answered the question "What do you see?" by replying, "Things, wonderful things." In this short, fun read, Macaulay creates a hypothetical excavation of a motel room in the year 4022. Each "wonderful thing" he uncovers lacks its context and is misinterpreted in a comical yet surprisingly believable way. Originally written for junior readers, it has become a classic in our field, enjoyed by children and adults alike (adults—you'll truly appreciate the subtle puns and wit here . . . have fun with it!).
- **"Scholar Fights Looting in Egypt"** (*PBS NewsHour* **2014).** In the aftermath of Egypt's 2011 revolution and resulting political turmoil, the nation's treasured antiquities have come under increasing threat of looting and vandalism. This episode examines the emergency facing Egypt's rich archaeological heritage and one scholar's efforts to publicize the problem and save his country's heritage before it's too late.

Worksheet 7.1

1. Sketch your "artifact" from at least two directions (e.g., front and back or front and side). Oftentimes, the process of trying to reproduce an object's likeness—even if you are not an artist!—is helpful for making observations we might not otherwise make.

View 1	View 2

2. Describe your artifact using physical attributes such as size, weight *(light, heavy?)*, shape, color, and construction material(s):

Physical Attribute	
Size *(estimate or measure)* • length • width • thickness	
Weight	
Construction Material(s)	
Color	
Shape	

3. Based on the artifact's physical appearance *only*, what is your best guess for what this artifact is used for?

_____

_____

_____

_____

_____

_____

_____

4. Now get the "context" from your instructor . . . How do you interpret your artifact now?

_____

_____

_____

_____

_____

_____

_____

_____

5. How did having the context for your artifact help you interpret its function?

_____

_____

_____

_____

_____

_____

_____

_____

For Further Exploration and Application

Your instructor may have you do these questions as part of a class discussion or independently.

1. Refer to Figure 7.2c, which shows a projectile point/knife (ppk) in a burial context. In such a ritualistic context, the ppk may have multiple meanings: it may designate the deceased (male or female) as a successful hunter, reflect the deceased's occupation as a toolmaker, or reflect the need for the deceased to have a tool in the afterlife. What further associations might you need to distinguish between these latter possibilities?

_____

_____

_____

_____

_____

_____

_____

_____

_____

2. Watch "Scholar Fights Looting in Egypt," from an episode of *PBS NewsHour* (2014) on looting in Egypt. Why is looting a problem in Egypt, and why is it difficult to control?

_____

_____

_____

_____

_____

_____

_____

_____

_____

References

Macaulay, David. 1979. *Motel of the Mysteries*. New York: Houghton Mifflin Harcourt.
PBS NewsHour. 2014. "Scholar Fights Archeological Looting in Egypt." Video, 6:49. Uploaded 29 April. https://www.youtube.com/watch?v=TLx8DJczxgs. Accessed 4 June 2019.

CHAPTER 8

Button Classification

Classification

The process of classification is a fundamental analytical procedure employed in processual archaeology. Classification involves the sorting and grouping of copious quantities of artifacts into a smaller number of classes, or *types*, which have the ability to inform archaeologists about past lifeways. The resulting series of types is referred to as a *typology*. For example, imagine an archaeological excavation in which thousands, or even tens of thousands, of ceramic sherds are recovered. By themselves, the sherds are chaotic and overwhelming in their sheer quantity (Figure 8.1a). Before they can be studied in any meaningful way, they must be sorted into recurring types based on shared *physical attributes* such as color, surface decoration, and construction method (Figure 8.1b-c). Other common physical attributes include size, shape, and raw material (e.g., obsidian, chert, metal, etc.).

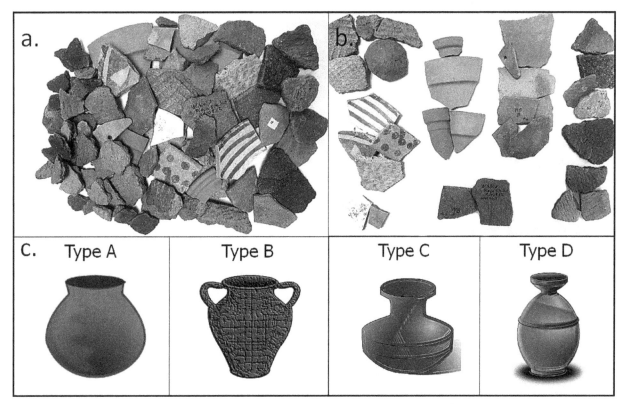

Figure 8.1. Hypothetical example illustrating the classification of ceramic sherds (a, b) into four distinct ceramic types (c).

Anthropologists also classify people, not just artifacts. Like ceramic sherds, the large quantity and great diversity of human cultures (in both time and space) has prompted archaeologists to construct cultural typologies as well. The most common in use today is Elman Service's (1962) "bands-tribes-chiefdom-states" typology, which groups human societies according to attributes such as population size, subsistence mode (i.e., how they get their food), settlement pattern (e.g., isolated village vs. network of cities) architecture type (i.e., small ephemeral grass huts vs. grandiose stone temples); and economic, sociopolitical, and religious organization (see Figure 8.2c). While this typology is not without problems (see also "For Further Exploration," Worksheet 8.1), it does help organize a large amount of diversity into a few manageable types, which is crucial for both communication and research.

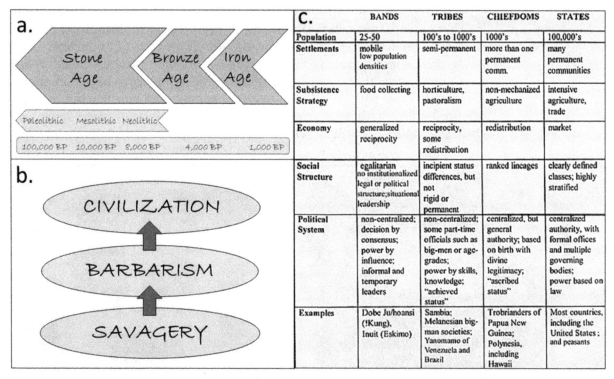

Figure 8.2. Two nineteenth-century typologies based on technological attributes: Thomsen (a), Morgan (b), and Service's twentieth-century typology in common use today (c).

Advantages and Disadvantages of Classification

Classification offers several advantages. First and foremost, it creates order out of chaos, thereby facilitating communication among professionals. It is certainly much easier to talk about a greater proportion of "Type B" pottery than this tongue twister: "cord-marked, grit-tempered pottery constructed from kaolinitic clay using the coil method characterized by a body wider than its spout and exhibiting stirrup handles on either side" (Yikes! What was that again?). Second, constructing typologies based on shared physical attributes enables us to create relative chronologies; one you are familiar with already is Christian Jürgensen Thomsen's (1836) famous "three-age" typology, which is still in use today (Figure 8.2a).

Despite these advantages, we must be careful when working with typologies, since there are several disadvantages as well. For example, look at Figure 8.2a again: this seems like a very convenient way to divide time, since we do generally see a shift from the use of stone, to bronze, to iron throughout prehistory. But are these types mutually exclusive? Consider the gunflints (stone) used in (metal) guns until about World War I—or onyx (stone) mortars and pestles used today in India and elsewhere (including many American chefs who feel stone is superior to other materials). This, then, is one of the main disadvantages of typologies: they tend to pigeonhole artifacts into one type when, in reality, they may have characteristics of more than one type.

Another set of problems is illustrated by anthropologist Lewis Henry Morgan's (1877) typology illustrated in Figure 8.2b. The first is obvious: Morgan's hierarchy is clearly a politically motivated typology designed to justify the mistreatment of cultures deemed "inferior" to Westerners, people who lived on land they wanted to exploit and colonize. Moreover, Morgan constructed this typology based on the attributes valued by Western cultures, such as agriculture, metallurgy, and written language. These are *etic* attributes that are not necessarily those valued by a band of hunter-gatherers or a tribe of mountain pastoralists for whom farming, metal tools, and written language have little if any value. Service's typology (Figure 8.2c) attempts to overcome some of these problems by using less subjective attributes and less derogatory type names, but it still suffers from the use of etic attributes (i.e., valued by those doing the classifying, not those being classified) and the (albeit inadvertent) creation of a progressive timeline in which societies are thought to evolve from less complex (bands) to more complex (states). We now know this is not true; in fact, many societies have done just the opposite and shifted from greater to *lesser* complexity over time because of changing climate, warfare, and resource (over)exploitation.

The Activity

This activity is designed to illustrate just how tricky, and etic, classification can be. Complete Worksheet 8.1 by arranging your bag of buttons into different classes based on gender, age, socioeconomic status, and function. For each, explain what physical attributes you used and why. For example, if you placed a small, pink, bunny-shaped button in the "child" type when classifying by "age," then you would write down the attributes of *color* (pink is feminine), *size* (children have small buttons for small fingers), and irregular *shape* (adults tend to have more circular buttons). These may be "fake" artifacts, but don't scuff. These, perhaps even more saliently than real artifacts can, illustrate the advantages and disadvantages of classification and that our typologies can be very much clouded by our own cultural biases and assumptions.

Suggestions for Further Exploration and Application

While this exercise may initially seem silly, remember that buttons are an important class of material culture that can shed much light on site function (e.g., sewing house, washroom, etc.), as well more esoteric themes such as gender roles and social ranking. Despite their utility, surprisingly little attention is given to the classification and analysis of buttons, but the first three suggested readings are nice treatments of buttons if you want to pursue this theme further.

- **"An Analysis of the Buttons from Three Historic Homes in Western Kentucky" (Rivers 1999).** Sara Rivers examines buttons from three sites in western Kentucky to better understand clothing trends and fashion preferences in the 19th century.
- **"Buttons, Beads, Thimbles, and . . .???" (PTAP 2010).** Settled by the English in 1727, the town on the Port Tobacco River soon became the second largest in Maryland. The blog provides regular updates on field and lab work, while this entry is on the buttons found.
- **"'Unrelenting Toil': Expanding Archaeological Interpretations of the Female Slave Experience" (Jordan 2005).** Elizabeth Jordan argues that clothing-related artifacts such as buttons should be viewed not merely as objects of personal adornment but also as the byproducts of women's labor. When considered as such, they can be used to explore the social, cultural, and economic significance of slave women's work.
- **"Ancient Cultures: The Aborigines" (KMPM 2013).** This five-minute video provides an overview of Australian Aboriginal culture, the "Dreamtime," and contemporary social problems stemming from colonization.

Worksheet 8.1

1. Your group will receive one bag of buttons, which you will classify into different typologies based on physical attributes (*size, color, shape, surface decoration, and raw material*).

Age	Gender
Function	**Socioeconomic Status (e.g., wealth)**

2. Refer to Figure 8.2, which illustrates three common typologies used to classify human societies, both based largely on technological attributes valued by Western cultures. What downfalls do you see in these typologies? How might they be used to push a political agenda and/or subjugate a particular group of people?

_____

_____

_____

_____

_____

_____

_____

_____

_____

3. Say you find a lot of buttons at a historic archaeological site: what might that indicate about the use of that site? What might we learn about culture by classifying and analyzing buttons? Look at some archaeological buttons from the Port Tobacco Archaeology Project (PTAP 2010). What do you think of the single-holed wooden buttons? How might they have been used?

_____

_____

_____

_____

_____

_____

_____

_____

_____

Worksheet 8.2

For Further Exploration and Application

Your instructor may have you do these questions as part of an in-class discussion or independent reflection. Use the back of this worksheet if you require more space.

1. Watch "Ancient Cultures: The Aborigine" (KM Plus Media 2013). Lewis Henry Morgan (1877) placed the Australian Aborigines in the "savagery" type, using his Western, etic technology attributes such as farming, metallurgy, and written language. What if the Aborigines were to create a typology of human societies—what emic attributes might they value instead?

_____

_____

_____

_____

_____

_____

_____

_____

2. Read either the Rivers (1999) or Jordan (2005) article on buttons. What do they find out about people and human behavior by including buttons in their archaeological analyses? What information would we lose about everyday people's lives if they hadn't looked at buttons (and similar classes of material culture in Jordan's article)?

_____

_____

_____

_____

_____

_____

_____

_____

_____

References

KMPM (KM Plus Media). 2013. "Ancient Cultures: The Aborigine." Video, 4:55. Uploaded 22 January. https://vimeo.com/57962965. Accessed 4 June 2019.

Jordan, Elizabeth. 2005. "'Unrelenting Toil': Expanding Archaeological Interpretations of the Female Slave Experience." *Slavery and Abolition* 26 (2): 217–232.

Morgan, Lewis Henry. 1877. *Ancient Society: Or, Researches in the Lines of Human Progress from Savagery, through Barbarism to Civilization*. New York: H. Holt.

PTAP (Port Tobacco Archaeological Project). 2010. "Buttons, Beads, Thimbles, and . . .???" 17 June. http://porttobacco.blogspot.com/2010/06/buttons-beads-thimbles-and.html. Accessed 4 June 2019.

Rivers, Sara. 1999. "An Analysis of the Buttons from Three Historic Homes in Western Kentucky." *Ohio Valley Historical Archaeology* 14: 29–35.

Service, Elman. 1962. *Primitive Social Organization*. New York: Random House.

Thomsen, Christian Jürgensen. 1836. "Kortfattet udsigt over mindesmærker og oldsager fra Nordens fortid." In *Ledetraad til nordisk Oldkyndighed*, 27–90. Copenhagen: S. L. Møllers.

CHAPTER 9

The (Site) Matrix

Site Formation Processes

In the 1980s, the archaeologist Michael Schiffer advocated for the study of something he called site formation processes. Site formation processes, sometimes more simply called formation processes, refer to the events that create, affect, and *transform* an archaeological site after its creation. Two classes, or types, of formation processes are recognized: culturally created process (C-transforms) and naturally created processes (N-transforms) (Schiffer 1987). Examples of C-transforms include purposeful and accidental discard of objects (i.e., trash), burning and demolition of structures, and even archaeological excavation itself (a point you'll discuss later with your class). N-transforms include catastrophic natural events such as earthquakes, floods, and landslides, as well as slow processes such as rodent burrowing and decomposition. This concept forces us to think about how sites are formed to begin with, how they are transformed over time, and how they are ultimately destroyed—all of which help us better understand human behavior and adaptation to their local environment.

Imagine a meandering river flowing through a floodplain. Along the river bend, where the current slows down, much sand and gravel are left behind. Over the centuries, so much is deposited that it becomes stable and a group of hunter-gatherers begin to fish there every spring. They camp there year after year, leaving behind campfires, stone tools, and fish bones. After a few decades, the river meanders slightly away, leaving the old sand bar high and dry—so much so that people begin to live here year-round, building a several houses and a plaza. Then, perhaps a century or so later, the climate becomes wetter and the river begins to flow more strongly and becomes wider, filling in the entire older channel. In the wettest years, the river floods repeatedly, forcing the people who once lived on the bar to abandon the site for higher ground; they still come to fish in the spring but then return to their village a mile away. The initial energy of the floodwaters may destroy some of the houses and even scour out the site so much that the top layer is removed altogether, erasing the evidence of the most recent village habitation. But an astute archaeologist who knows how to read the sediments (called a "geoarchaeologist") will be able to "see" the flood. The destruction of this uppermost layer may at first seem like a bad thing, but there is an upside: the sediments the flood lays down also act to a "seal" the remaining deposits and protect the site from further destruction such as rodent burrowing or looting. Additionally, even though some data have been lost, knowing a flood has done so is important to understanding why people settled there in the first place and why it was abandoned later—both of which are important for understanding how past people affect, and are affected by, their local environment. So, an understanding of formation processes is vital to accurate reconstructions of the past. The archaeologist Brian Fagan (1978) sums up formation processes this way: "The archaeological record that has come down to us is a sorry reflection of once vibrant, living cultures. From the moment a site was abandoned, or a dwelling burnt down, the forces of human activity and nature have acted on it."

The Activity

In this activity, you will explore the various processes that form and shape archaeological sites. You will do this by creating a matrix consisting of four cells: (1) cultural processes/behaviors that add material to sites, (2) cultural processes/behaviors that subtract (i.e., remove) material from sites, (3) natural processes that add material to sites, and (4) natural processes that subtract material from sites. The purpose of the "site matrix" is to create a mental rubric to help you remember the vast number of processes that occur to create and destroy sites, and that help archaeologists better understand human behavior and the natural environmental processes that contribute to people settling or abandoning a site.

Suggestions for Further Exploration and Application

Your instructor may assign one or more short videos as case studies to illustrate the concepts of the site matrix. Questions for each video appear on Worksheet 9.1 (back).

- **"Lost Cities of the Amazon" (NGS 2007).** This episode of *National Geographic Explorer* discusses how ancient people in the Amazon created a soil so fertile that it is still used today. The three-minute clip discussing these impressive soils (called *terra preta*) runs from 15:50 to 18:25. Or, you can watch the slightly longer 15-minute clip spliced together from **"The Secrets of El Dorado" (BBC 2002),** which additionally discusses how the *terra preta* was made and why it is of interest to today's farmers.
- **"Hunting for History through the Eyes of the Ice" (Yin 2018).** This short article, which includes a two-minute video, describes the emerging field of glacial archaeology and interviews European archaeologists about the effects of thawing glacial ice as it exposes sites to erosion and decay.
- **"Ultimate Tut" (PBS 2012).** This episode of *Secrets of the Dead* (from 1:31:00 to 1:46:00) describes and animates a surprising new geologic hypothesis for how King Tut's tomb remains the only unlooted tomb in Egypt's Valley of the Kings.

Worksheet 9.1

1. Think about some processes that might add to or take away from an archaeological site, both things that people do (C-transforms) or that nature does (N-transforms). Your instructor may ask you to do this individually or as part of a class activity.

	Cultural	Natural
+		
−		

2. Why can archaeology itself be considered a "cultural subtraction?" How can we avoid it?

_____

_____

_____

_____

_____

For Further Exploration and Application

Your instructor may have you do one or more of these questions as part of an in-class discussion or independent reflection.

1. Watch "Lost Cities of the Amazon" (NGS 2008) or "The Secret of El Dorado" (BBC 2002) What is *terra preta*? What kind of formation process is this? Why does an archaeological knowledge of *terra preta* have significance for today?

_____

_____

_____

_____

_____

2. Watch "Ultimate Tut" (PBS 2013). Why was Tut's tomb not looted, and what kind of transformation is it? How did that process prevent another, cultural, transformation from taking place centuries/millennia later?

_____

_____

_____

_____

_____

3. Read "Hunting for History Through the Eyes of the Ice" (Yin 2018) and watch the embedded two-minute video associated with it. How is global climate warming transforming the archaeological record? What kind of formation process is this? Would you argue this transformation is positive, negative, or both?

_____

_____

_____

_____

_____

References

BBC (British Broadcasting Corporation). 2002. "The Secret of El Dorado." *Horizon*, season 8, episode 10. Aired 19 December. https://www.youtube.com/watch?v=vUAEa4ORAkY. Uploaded by ReturnProject 1 December 2013. Accessed 4 June 2019.

Fagan, Brian M. 1978. *Quest for the Past: Great Discoveries in Archaeology*. Reading, MA: Addison-.

NGS (National Geographic Society). 2008. "Lost Cities of the Amazon." *National Geographic Explorer*, season 4, episode 14. Aired 20 November. https://www.dailymotion.com/video/x5ipo8h. Accessed 4 June 2019.

PBS (Public Broadcasting Service). 2013. "Ultimate Tut." *Secrets of the Dead*, season 12, episode 5. Aired 10 July. http://www.pbs.org/wnet/secrets/ultimate-tut-watch-the-full-episode/1049. Accessed 4 June 2019.

Schiffer, Michael. 1987. *Formation Processes of the Archaeological Record*. Albuquerque: University of New Mexico Press.

Yin, Sabrina Ho Yen. 2018. "Hunting for History through the Eyes of the Ice." *GlacierHub*, 6 February. http://glacierhub.org/2018/02/06/hunting-history-eyes-ice/. Accessed 4 June 2019.

CHAPTER 10

Body Mapping

Gridding and Mapping an Archaeological Site

As discussed in Chapter 7, once an archaeological site has been excavated, it is gone forever. As a result, archaeologists must carefully record exactly where all the artifacts, ecofacts, and features are located relative to one another in order to record their *archaeological context*, including provenience and association. Before any soil or artifacts are removed from a site, a site grid is created (Figure 10.1a). A datum point, or a fixed reference point from which all measurements are taken, is established and a rectangular grid is superimposed over the whole site. In Figure 10.1a, the site datum is N100 E100. Note that had it started at N0, any units laid out to the south would be negative; thus, it is common to start at 100 or 500 to avoid negative numbers and leave room for the archaeological grid to expand as excavations continue over time.

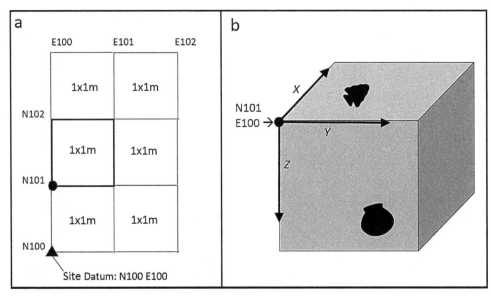

Figure 10.1. Example of gridding an archaeological site, in this case into six 1 × 1 meter units and oriented North (a) and mapping artifacts in three dimensions relative to the datum (b).

Each square within the grid is assigned a number. These squares are often referred to as *test units*. In Figure 10.1b, the test unit shown is designated as N101 E 100. In other words, it is one meter north of the site datum and zero meters to the east. This number, then, becomes a "local datum," which is tied into the site datum. Local datums can be in any corner; which one is used generally varies by region (e.g., in the Mid-Atlantic, it is common to use the northeast corner). Regardless of the corner used, such a system allows archaeologists to create a precise map of the site and to preserve the exact provenience and association of all the features and artifacts within each unit.

Piece Plotting

Once you have established a local datum, you can measure any artifact, ecofact, or feature located in your test unit relative to that point. For artifacts, we generally map the center point—a process called *piece plotting*. For example, in Figure 10.2a, the arrowhead pictured would be piece plotted as E100.48 (x-coordinate), N101.45 (y-coordinate). In other words, the center point is 45 centimeters north of datum (which is itself one meter from site datum, hence 101.45) and 48 centimeters east of datum. Remember, there are 100 centimeters in a meter. Features are a bit trickier to map at first glance, but the same principle applies. Rather than plotting the center point, note that in Figure 10.2a several points around the circumference of the oval feature are measured. From these four points, then, you can "sketch" in the true shape. Be careful: new archaeologists often do this very geometrically when they connect the dots, losing the sense of the shape in the process. Use the points as a guide but attempt to approximate the true shape to facilitate interpretation down the road. For example, if you mapped four points to denote a circular feature but drew it square when connecting the dots, then you drew it too literally (Figure 10.2b). A square would not indicate to another archaeologist that the feature is actually a house post; a circle, on the other hand, is a red flag to another archaeologist that it is a house post, especially if those circles form a pattern, such as you might expect of posts outlining the wall of a house (Figure 10.2c). The upshot? Archaeological context is half science, half art!

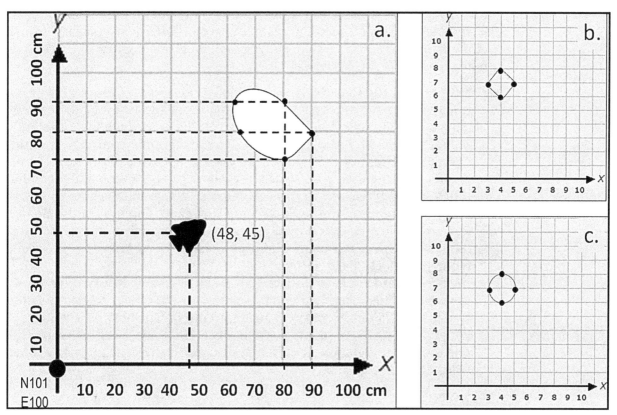

Figure 10.2. The (*x, y*) center coordinates for an arrowhead located in Test Unit N101 E100 (a), an example of a feature drawn too geometrically (b), and an example of a feature sketched well (c).

The Activity

In this activity, you will do two things. First, you will learn how to construct a square unit using a process called *triangulation*. Triangulation entails using the known length of a unit's sides to calculate the hypotenuse. Watch the first two and a half minutes of the University of Sydney Department of Archaeology's (2009) training video "Archaeological Methods: Setting up a 1m Grid Square." See if you can figure out which geometric formula you would use to determine the hypotenuse as shown. Your instructor will demonstrate this process for you. Second, you will learn how to map artifacts and features in two dimensions using the (x, y) coordinate system. On a real excavation, you would additionally map everything in three dimensions using an (x, y, z) coordinate system. The z dimension is simply the depth below the surface. If you are an archaeology major, you will learn how to do this when you take your archaeological field school. If your instructor opts to map in three dimensions, they will demonstrate how to set up a system for measuring depth using the local datum and a strung line level.

Suggestions for Further Exploration and Application

Your instructor may have you watch one or two short videos to illustrate applications of archaeological mapping. In the first video, mapping allows archaeologist to reconstruct changes over time at the colonial site of Jamestown, Virginia. The second video shows how important archaeological techniques, especially accurate mapping, are to forensic investigations and criminal investigations. Watch the video(s), and then answer the accompanying question(s) in Worksheet 10.2.

- **"FBI Hunts for Clandestine Burials"** *(6:30 minutes)*. This excellent introduction to the methods of forensic archaeology shows the "corpse" mapping techniques used in this activity. This video highlights the FBI's (2009) annual Recovery of Human Remains training course held at the University of Tennessee's famous Body Farm. Speaking of the Body Farm, if forensics interests you, watch the short, witty National Geographic (2016) video "Welcome to the Body Farm," which follows the comedian Francesca Fiorentini to the Texas State University Forensic Anthropology Research Facility to see how donated bodies help solve crimes. Beware, though . . . this is not for the faint of heart or weak-kneed! If you want more, just google "body farm"!
- **"A New Window into James Fort" (Jamestown Rediscover 2016)** *(4 minutes)*. This video is a good overview of 2016 field school students (College of William & Mary) at Historic Jamestown showing several cool artifacts and features, square test unit excavation, mapping with a transit, and drone photography. Feel free to explore this website, as many other video clips are available.

Worksheet 10.1

1. Calculate the hypotenuse for the excavation units shown. Label the lengths of both sides, as well as the hypotenuse. Show your math in the space provided.

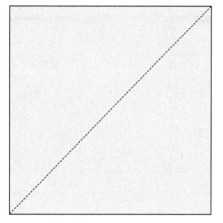

2 × 2 meter square

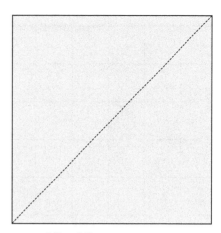

10 × 10 meter square

2. On the back of this worksheet, draw your "corpse." Be sure your map includes scale, units, and datum (and North arrow if you used a compass to lay in your unit). Remember to use these points to guide your drawing, rather than connecting the dots too literally.

3. List three reasons why archaeologists dig square units rather than round or irregular.

_____

_____

_____

4. Watch the "FBI Hunts for Clandestine Burials" (FBI 2009). Why does the FBI train agents in archaeological methods and mapping techniques?

_____

_____

_____

_____

Worksheet 10.2

1. Calculate the hypotenuse for the excavation units shown. Label the lengths of both sides, as well as the hypotenuse. Show your math in the space provided.

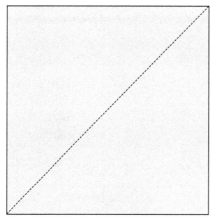

2 × 2 meter square

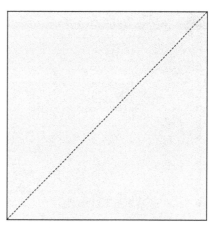

10 × 10 meter square

2. On the back of this worksheet, complete the feature by using the coordinate pairs listed below the map. Remember that while accuracy is important, you'll have to use some "artistic license" to soften the angles and reflect the features true shape rather than connecting the dots too literally.

3. List three reasons why archaeologists dig square units rather than round or irregular.

_____

_____

_____

4. Watch "FBI Hunts for Clandestine Burials" (FBI 2009). Why does the FBI train agents in archaeological methods and mapping techniques?

_____

_____

_____

_____

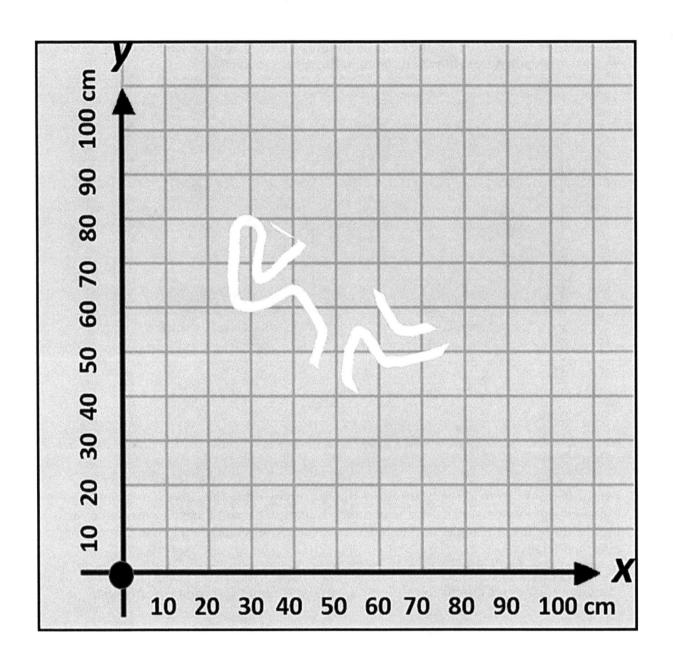

(x, y)	(73, 67)	(80, 60)
(35, 84)	(68, 67)	(84, 48)
(40, 86)	(64, 75)	(80, 48)
(46, 79)	(55, 75)	(60, 32)
(60, 82)	(60, 65)	(50, 29)
(70, 75)	(65, 55)	(45, 46)

References

FBI. 2009. "FBI Hunts for 'Clandestine Burials.'" Video, 6:31. Uploaded 9 October. https://www.youtube.com/watch?time_continue=5&v=-iaqynaRU6k. Accessed 4 June 2019.

Jamestown Rediscovery. 2016. "A New Window into James Fort." Video, 4:13. Uploaded 21 July. https://www.youtube.com/watch?v=3k9XVbytkfM. Accessed 4 June 2019.

National Geographic. 2016. "Welcome to the Body Former | Explorer." Video, 1:50. Uploaded 22 December. https://www.youtube.com/watch?v=8wDJINtov6U. Accessed 11 June 2019.

SFU (Simon Fraser University) Museum of Archaeology and Ethnology. 2010. "Investigating Forensics: Archaeological Process." Video, 1:37. http://www.sfu.museum/forensics/eng/pg_media-media_pg/archaeologie-archaeology/video/35/. Accessed 29 March 2019.

University of Sydney Department of Archaeology. 2009. "Archaeological Methods: Set Up a 1m Grid Square." Video, 5:36. Uploaded 30 September. https://www.youtube.com/watch?v=xNdFDzQzqPk. Accessed 11 June 2019.

MODULE 3

Frameworks for Measuring Time

CHAPTER 11

Human Stratigraphy

Stratigraphy

Because types of earth are recognizable by variation in textures, colors, and inclusions, archaeologists can recognize different layers (called *strata*) during excavation of a site. *Stratigraphy*, then, is the study of these strata and their relationship to one another. Stratigraphic principles allow archaeologists to relatively date each layer as being older or younger than another layer. If charcoal or other organic material is present, it can be used to absolutely date the layer (see chapter 16), but often all we have are the strata themselves. Stratigraphic relationships can also help archaeologists interpret how a site formed over time, through both cultural as well as natural processes, as discussed in chapter 9. Figure 11.1 is an example of stratigraphy from the prehistoric site of Dust Cave, located in northwestern Alabama and occupied from the Late Paleoindian to the Middle Archaic periods.

Law of Superposition and Cross-Cutting Relationships

The most fundamental principle of stratigraphic analysis is the *law of superposition*. This principle simply states that younger strata will overlie older strata. If strata are horizontal, placing the strata in order from oldest to youngest is quite simple. For example, in Figure 11.1, strata T4 is older than strata P5 because it was deposited first. Unfortunately, a host of cultural and natural transformations, such as those you read about in chapter 9, can significantly alter the ideal stratigraphic model. One of these processes is pit digging: humans dig into the ground to bury their dead, construct houses, put in storage pits, dig privies, or hide caches of goods in the ground. You can see several pits in Figure 11.1: features 128 and 292 are burial pits, features 130 and 339 are firepits where food was cooked, and feature 390 is a possible storage pit. These pits always cut across the older, original layers. Thus, the principle of *cross-cutting relationships* states that intrusions such as pits are always younger than the surrounding strata. For example, feature 390, the possible storage pit, cuts through strata R1, making it younger than that stratum.

Reverse Stratigraphy

Another issue that complicates the analysis of stratigraphy is *reverse stratigraphy*. This occurs when younger strata get moved or deformed such that they end up deeper than they were originally, below older strata. In Figure 11.1, you can see this represented well by strata D4. Follow this stratum to the left toward the cave wall. Notice that it dips way down, past E1, J1, and even K3. The artifacts in strata D4 date to the most recent occupation at the

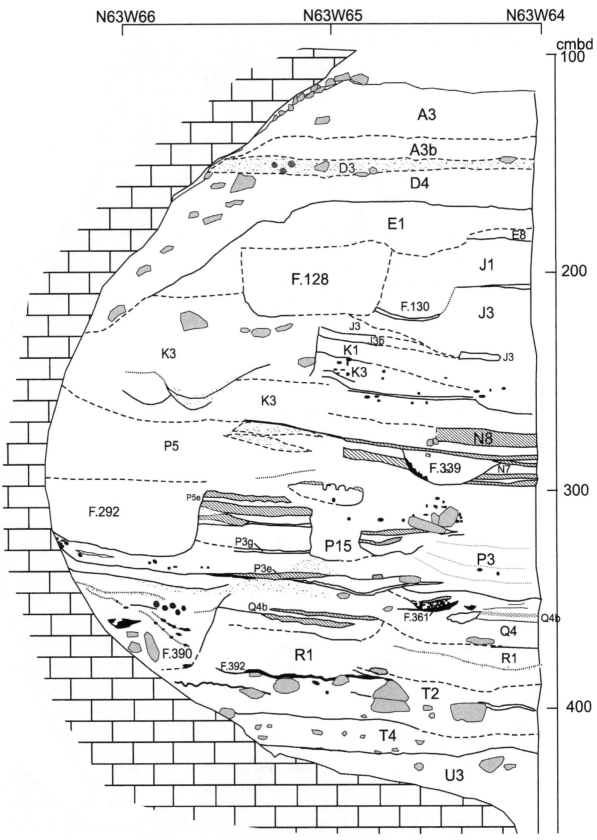

Figure 11.1. Example of stratigraphy from the archaeological site of Dust Cave, Alabama. Sherwood 2001, Figure 8.9.

cave, the Benton component (3600–4500 BCE), but the artifacts in strata K3 date to the period older than that, the Eva/Morrow Mountain component (6,400–5,200 BCE). Imagine digging an excavation unit in this far-left portion of the image—the artifacts from both time periods seemingly would be lying side by side. This phenomenon is common in caves and rock-shelters, where soil readily slides downslope into crevasses and low areas along the walls. Other examples that may create reversed strata include trees falling, bringing up older soil toward the surface, or earthquakes that fracture the strata enough to cause part of the strata to fall down or be pushed up relative to the other side. Cultural transformations that create reverse stratigraphy include pit digging, and people digging dirt from barrow pits and depositing it above the original ground surface to construct mounds or terraces.

Stratigraphic Unconformities

A final nuance to be aware of is the possibility that *unconformities* exist in the stratigraphic record. Unconformities represents gaps in time. These gaps can erase large time periods, even entire cultural components. For example, in Figure 11.1, the artifacts in strata U include points dating to the Late Paleoindian period, while those in strata R date to the Early Side Notched period. At many other sites in the region, Dalton points occur between these two periods, but at Dust Cave, significant flooding has eroded away some of the sediments dating to this time. Thus, this unconformity has erased the record, if it did exist. But these unconformities, while they may initially seem to be a bad thing, can tell us a lot about a site. At Dust Cave, we can see the unconformity in the flood sediments; floods may scour away a living surface, leaving a distinctive, sharp boundary rather than the gradual boundary created by continuously depositing sediments. Sediments above such a surface often "fine upward" as the sediments get smaller and smaller because of the floodwaters slowing down. Identifying this at Dust Cave tells us the site was extremely wet during this time, and probably not a very desirable place to live. These river sediments disappear by strata P and above, suggesting the site dried out significantly later in time. Indeed, geologic studies of the Tennessee River now demonstrate the river shifted southward over time, eventually moving far enough away from the cave to no longer flood it.

The Activity

In this activity, you will work together as a class to create your own "stratigraphy" out of a mess of random clothing. Your teacher will ask you to come to class prepared with an extra item of clothing; bring something you don't mind throwing on the floor (e.g., hoodie, jacket). The exercise will allow you to both create and analyze stratigraphy to apply the principles of superposition, cross cutting, reverse stratigraphy, and unconformities. Following your class discussion, answer the accompanying questions on Worksheet 11.1.

Suggestions for Further Exploration and Application

- For a more challenging stratigraphic exercise, try Worksheet 11.2,[1] which illustrates what archaeologists call a *stratigraphic profile* (i.e., you are looking at a vertical cut into the earth, as if you cut through a layer cake with a knife to reveal the layers). In this profile, you can see 26 strata (two of which—U and W—are features), two burials, a burial shaft (near the top of the profile; the item inside is a ceremonial burial urn), and the remains of a stone building (labeled "wall"). Things get complicated around the wall about partway up the profile shown. Your job is to place the strata in relative order from oldest to youngest, and then use the stratigraphy to help interpret the cultural and natural processes forming the site. Remember: "earlier" and "older" mean further in the past, and "younger" and "later" mean closer to the present.

- In lieu of readings, we suggest the 22-minute video **"In Vivid Color: Voices from Shiloh's Mound" (Tomlinson Brummer 2005)**, which illustrates the complex stratigraphy at Shiloh, a stunning Native American mound overlooking the Tennessee River at Shiloh National Park. Excavated by the National Park Service in the early 2000s, this mound's stratigraphy is dramatically changing archaeologists' views of Native American engineering and art. We no longer view mounds as the trim, grass-covered mounds we see in parks today but rather as striking, tiger-striped edifices that would have been visible from miles away. Questions on the video follow in Worksheet 11.1.

Worksheet 11.1

1. Imagine you plan to excavate the stratigraphically complex site created by your clothing. How might you go about it to best relatively date the site and reconstruct its formation over time? Would you place a few scattered 1 × 1 meter units? Larger units? Or would you trench it with a backhoe and/or connect any of the units? Remember: you need to represent not only the major strata but also those pesky microstratigraphic units and reverse stratigraphy.

_____

_____

_____

_____

_____

2. Watch "In Vivid Color: Voices from Shiloh's Mound" (Tomlinson Brummer 2005). What is the traditional view of what Mississippian mounds looked like, which you see today if you visit sites like Shiloh and Cahokia (in Missouri)? How has the stratigraphy changed our view of the mounds' meaning? Think particularly in terms of engineering (technomic) and symbolism (socio- and ideotechnic).

_____

_____

_____

_____

_____

3. Based on the stratigraphic profile on the back of this worksheet,[2] answer the following questions:

   a. Which ceramic vessel is youngest: 2, 3, or 4? _____ Which is the oldest: 4 or 5? _____

   b. Order the burials from oldest to youngest: _____, _____, _____, _____

   c. Which is older, burial Y or vessel 3? _____

   d. Was the wall built *before* or *after* burial Y was interred? _____

   e. Which ceramic vessel is the oldest: 6 or 7? Explain your answer: _____

   _____

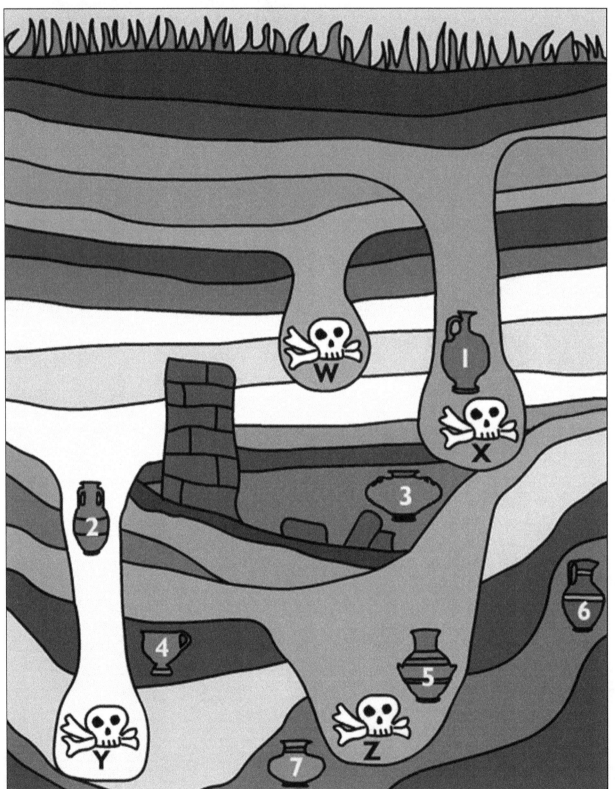

Worksheet 11.2

For Further Exploration and Application

Place the strata in relative order from oldest to youngest. Write your answers vertically in the left-hand margin with the oldest layer at the bottom. Include the burials, wall, and the burial shaft.

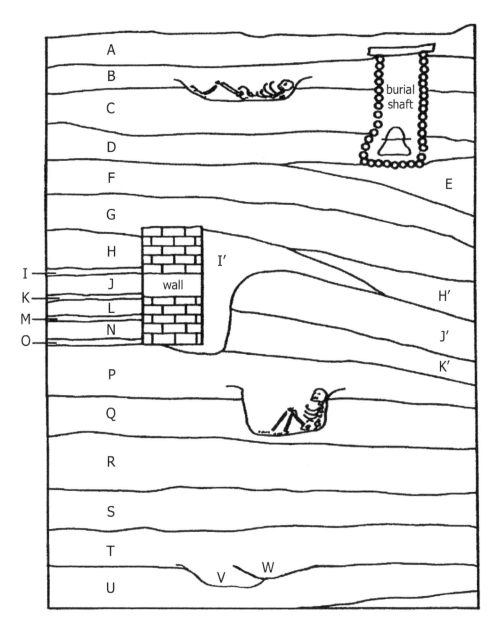

1. Explain what is happing around the wall. What are layers I, M, K, and O? How did I' form? Use the back of this worksheet if you need more space.

_____

_____

_____

_____

Notes

1. Used with permission from Patterson (1994).
2. Adapted with permission from Denbow (2012).

References

Denbow, James. 2012. "Lab I: Seriation and Stratigraphy." https://la.utexas.edu/users/den
bow/labs/lab1-strat.htm. Accessed 29 March 2019.

Patterson, Thomas. 1994. *The Theory and Practice of Archaeology: A Workbook.* 2nd ed. Upper
Saddle River, NJ: Prentice Hall.

Sherwood, Sarah C., and T. R. Kidder. 2011. "The DaVincis of Dirt: Geoarchaeological Perspectives on Native American Mound Building in the Mississippi River Basin." *Journal of
Anthropological Archaeology* 30 (1): 69–87.

Tomlinson Brummer, Cindy. 2005. "In Vivid Color: Voices from Shiloh's Mound." Video,
22:32. Archaeology Channel. http://www.archaeologychannel.org/video-guide/video-
guide-menu/video-guide-list/259-in-vivid-color-voices-from-shilohs-mound. Accessed 29
March 2019.

CHAPTER 12

Time Lines

Deep Time

To understand the human past, as well as our human evolution, archaeologists must think in much larger units of time than we are used to in day-to-day life. Sometimes, it is difficult to imagine further back than the number of years we have been alive, let alone thousands or millions of years. Yet, that is exactly what archaeologists have to do every day: evolutionary changes, and even many cultural changes, do not occur at a scale of days, months, or even years. Rather, they occur on the scale of centuries, millennia, and millions of years, all recorded in the layers of rock that are deposited over time as the geologic strata we see today. Scientists refer to this vast stretch of time as "deep time." As many have noted, deep time is nearly as incomprehensible to us as deep space; it is just something we humans have trouble wrapping our heads around. Will we ever truly comprehend such vastness? Probably not entirely, but this activity, which will scale Earth's 4.6-billion-year history to a roll of toilet paper (yep, go ahead . . . roll your eyes), is designed to develop a framework for appreciating the vastness of 4.6 billion years, and the extremely short fraction of which humans have occupied. Even the age of dinosaurs—which reigned supreme for more than 68 million years—only accounts for less than 2 percent of the Earth's history. Humans account for much, much less!

Deep time, or "geologic time," as it is often called, is broken into eons, eras, and epochs in a system called the *geologic time scale* (Figure 12.1). Eras are the primary unit of geologic time. The three eras are the Paleozoic (i.e., old era), Mesozoic (i.e., middle era), and Cenozoic (i.e., recent era). Geologists refer to the time before the Paleozoic—a huge stretch of time—as the Precambrian. Eras are subdivided into geologic *periods*, which are further subdivided into geologic *epochs*. Notice that more epochs are shown for the Cenozoic than the earlier two periods. This is because the closer we get to the present, the more complete and better preserved the geologic record, and therefore the greater our knowledge of the past. We currently live in the Cenozoic Era, Quaternary Period, Holocene Epoch, the latter of which began approximately 11,700 years ago following the Ice Age. Recently, some geologists and archaeologists have called for the designation of a new epoch within the Quaternary—the *Anthropocene*.

The Anthropocene

Those in favor of designating an Anthropocene epoch note that over the last few decades, and perhaps centuries, humans have become the dominant geologic force in shaping the planet. Moreover, they argue that these dramatic—and permanent—changes are starting to become evident in rock and soil strata. The name comes from *anthropos* meaning "man," and *cene* meaning "new." Not all scientists agree. Generally, geologic epochs are designated

Table 12.1. Simplified Version of Geologic Time Scale.

Era	Period	Epoch	Notable Events	Years before Present
Cenozoic	Quaternary	Holocene		12,000
		Pleistocene	Major extinction event at end; Ice Ages; hominins evolve	0.5 to 2 million
	Tertiary	Pliocene	Megafauna	13 million
		Miocene	Abundant grazing animals	25 million
		Oligocene	Whales appear	36 million
		Eocene	Mammals flourish	58 million
		Paleocene	First placental animals	63 million
Mesozoic	Cretaceous		Major extinction event at end; first flowering plants	135 million
	Jurassic		Age of Dinosaurs; birds appear	181 million
	Triassic		First dinosaurs, first conifers	230 million
Paleozoic	Permian		Major extinction event at end; Pangaea supercontinent forms	280 million
	Carboniferous	Pennsylvanian	Age of Reptiles; giant insects; major coal swamps form	310 million
		Mississippian	Reptiles appear; brachiopods	345 million
	Devonian		Age of Fishes; amphibians appear	405 million
	Silurian		First terrestrial plants/animals (e.g., corals, crinoids)	425 million
	Ordovician		First fishes; invertebrates abundant	500 million
	Cambrian		Age of Trilobites; major extinction event at end	600 million
Precambrian			Oldest dated algae / Oldest dated meteorite / Free oxygen in atmosphere forms	

only when a global stratigraphic marker, sometimes called a "golden spike," can be identified across the world and radiometrically dated to the same period. For example, the boundary between the Cretaceous and the Tertiary is visible in many places throughout the world in a layer of iridium produced when the comet that killed the dinosaurs hit in what is today the Gulf of Mexico. This boundary, which looks the same everywhere in the world and has been independently dated to 65 million years ago, is known as the "K-T boundary."[1] Some geologists rightly argue that no such "golden spike" yet exists. But others argue that since we are currently living in the Anthropocene, a stratigraphic layer has not yet formed. But they point to manmade materials now entering the modern soil (which will someday lithify into rock) and polar ice caps. Examples include tree pollen resulting from the massive deforestation of the world's forests, elevated levels of greenhouse gases produced from the burning of fossil fuels (such as carbon dioxide and methane) trapped in polar glaciers, radionuclides produced from the detonation of atomic bombs, fertilizers and pesticides generated from modern-day large-scale farming, and "plastiglomerate," a rock-like material (similar to the natural rock conglomerate) consisting largely of plastic, forming on our shorelines and in the oceans. And, of course, archaeologists say that someday our buildings will be part of a stratigraphic unit.

But even among those who propose making the Anthropocene an official geologic unit of time, there is disagreement over when in time it should begin. Many prefer 1945, the year the first atomic bomb was detonated. Others argue it should begin in the 1800s, when the Industrial Revolution and the subsequent burning of fossil fuels initiated the era of rising greenhouse gases that only continues to rise today. Still other archaeologists have argued that we take a longer view and recognize the extensive change catalyzed by prehistoric populations, including deforestation during the Agricultural Revolution, overkill of the Pleistocene megafauna (such as mammoth, mastodon, and bison). Regardless, the debate over just how real the Anthropocene is will likely continue for some time (pun intended!).

The Activity

Your instructor will conduct this activity in class and may ask for some volunteers to help. Alternatively, they may opt to have you do a more involved analogy in which you will scale geologic time to a running track (a good excuse to go outside) instead of the TP (Worksheet 12.1).

Suggestions for Further Exploration and Application

Your instructor may ask you to watch one or more of the following videos. If you have an interest in climate change issues, we recommend the last couple evaluating the Anthropocene period.

- **"An Anthropocene without Archaeology: Should We Care?" (Braje et al. 2014).** This article argues for formal designation of the Anthropocene as a geologic period.
- **"Becoming Human, Part 1: First Steps" (PBS 2011)** *(51 minutes)*. This *NOVA* episode examines the geologic and evolutionary factors that caused hominins to split from the other great apes.
- **"Humans Have Created Striking New Pattern in Earth's Energy Flow That Has Triggered a New Geologic Era" (Zolfagharifard 2016).** This article includes a three-minute video titled "Welcome to the Anthropocene."
- **"Signs of the 'Human Age'" (Fleur 2016).** This article discusses the controversial designation of the Anthropocene and highlights some of the culturally produced materials that are rapidly become part of the geologic record.

Worksheet 12.1

1. Did the toilet paper (or running track) analogy change your perceptions about geologic time? Why or why not?

_____

_____

2. Based on what you know about stratigraphy and the law of superposition, how can we prove dinosaurs and hominins were not contemporaneous?

_____

_____

For Further Exploration and Application

Your instructor may have you do these questions as part of an in-class discussion or independent reflection.

1. Complete the table on the back to scale geologic time to a running track.

2. Watch the videos and/or read the articles assigned by your teacher about the most recently proposed geologic epoch. How might we "see" the Anthropocene geologically? In other words, what kinds of physical evidence will be part of the geologic record in 1,000 years?

_____

_____

_____

_____

_____

3. Watch "Becoming Human, Part 1: First Steps" (PBS 2009). During which geologic era/epoch did hominins evolve? What geo-environmental processes helped shape our hominin evolution (namely, big brains), and how were these changes advantageous?

_____

_____

_____

_____

Geologic Period	Years before Present	Length of Time (millions of years)	Fraction of Geologic Time	Number of Meters
Holocene	0–12,000	0.01		
Pleistocene	12,000–1,800,000	2,000,000		
Tertiary	1,800,000–65,000,000	65,000,000		
Cretaceous	65,000,000–140,000,000	75,000,000		
Jurassic	140,000,000–208,000,000	68,000,000		
Triassic	208,000,000–245,000,000	38,000,000		
Permian	245,000,000–286,000,000	41,000,000		
Carboniferous	286,000,000–360,000,000	74,000,000		
Devonian	360,000,000–408,000,000	48,000,000		
Silurian	408,000,000–440,000,000	32,000,000		
Ordovician	440,000,000–510,000,000	70,000,000		
Cambrian	510,000,000–540,000,000	34,000,000		
Precambrian	4,600,000,000	4,056,000,000		
		Total	**100%**	**400 meters**

Note: Round to the nearest half-meter; total may exceed 400 meters due to rounding error.

Note

1. Geologists abbreviate the Cretaceous by the letter K (C is already taken by the Cambrian period), and the Tertiary by the letter T; thus, the K-T boundary represents the interface between the two.

References

Bradshaw, Steve, dir. 2016. *Anthropocene*. Documentary. Reading, PA: Bullfrog Films.

Braje, Todd, Jon M. Erlandson, C. Melvin Aikens, Tim Beach, Scott Fitzpatrick, Sara Gonzalez, Douglas J. Kennet et al. 2014. "An Anthropocene Without Archaeology: Should We Care?" *SAA Archaeological Record* 14 (1): 26–29.

Fleur, Nicholas. 2016. "Signs of the 'Human Age.'" *New York Times*, 11 January. https://www.nytimes.com/interactive/2016/01/11/science/anthropocene-epoch-definition.html. Accessed 5 June 2019.

PBS. 2009. "Becoming Human, Part 1: First Steps." *NOVA*, season 36, episode, 13. Aired 3 November. https://www.pbs.org/wgbh/nova/video/becoming-human-part-1. Accessed 5 June 2019.

Wenner, Jennifer M. 2018. "Toilet Paper Analogy for Geologic Time." *On the Cutting Edge Peer Reviewed Teaching Activities Collection*. Science Education Resource Center, Carleton College. Last modified 18 April. http://serc.carleton.edu/quantskills/activities/TPGeoTime.html. Accessed 5 June 2019.

Zolfagharifard, Elfie. 2016. "Humans Have Created Striking New Pattern in Earth's Energy Flow That Has Triggered a New Geologic Era." *Daily Mail*, 23 March. http://www.dailymail.co.uk/sciencetech/article-3506634/Humans-created-striking-new-pattern-Earth-s-energy-flow-triggered-new-geological-era.html. Accessed 5 June 2019.

CHAPTER 13

Childhood Battleship Curves

Seriation

Have you ever looked at old pictures of your parents and laughed at the clothes they were wearing, which seemed so out of style compared to today's fashion? Clothing styles, like so many other things in our culture, constantly change; what were rad bell-bottoms in the 1970s may be the laughingstock of the fashion world by 1980. The amazing "new" pants that Sonny and Cher rocked in the '70s predictably disappeared from closets and were eventually replaced by skinny jeans (hello, 1980s!). Sometimes, styles reappear, much to our chagrin. In fact, bell-bottoms have done just that—not once, but several times. Believe it or not, they first came into fashion in the 19th century when the British Navy adopted a "flared" bottom pant leg as its official uniform. They came back a century later in the late 1960s as part of the hippie counterculture—even wider than before. They reappeared a second time in the mid-1990s, this time as "boot" or "flare" cuts, but essentially the same style. They had a good run until the mid-2000s when they faded in popularity and "skinny jeans" came into vogue and continue to be quite popular today.

Archaeological styles are no different; ceramic styles come and go in popularity, as do projectile point types, architectural styles, and tombstone motifs. Archaeologists can use this phenomenon to relatively date sites. For exam-

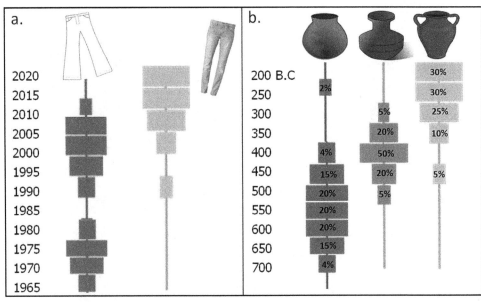

Figure 13.1. Battleship curves for flared and skinny jeans (a), and hypothetical curves and accompanying frequencies for archaeological ceramic vessels (b).

ple, we are often able to figure out the decade a picture was taken just based on the style of clothing or car in the image. Similarly, archaeologists often know what century they are dealing with just by looking at the design on a ceramic vessel. We can't get exact dates this way (i.e., absolute dates), but we can get relative dates and know which are younger and older than each other. Estimating the relative age of an archaeological stratum based on the changing popularity of artifact styles is called *seriation*.

Frequency Seriation

Seriation is a relative dating technique based on the proportional abundance (i.e., frequency) of a design style. For this reason, it is sometimes called *frequency seriation*. Essentially, the method is based on the principle that artifact styles gradually move through a range of popularity, beginning with a period of emerging popularity, a period of peak popularity, and a period of declining popularity. When looked at graphically, this popularity trend takes the shape of a battleship as seen from a bird's eye view: wide at the center, and narrower at each end of the "ship" (Figure 13.1). This graph is called a *battleship curve*. Take, for example, in Figure 13.1b, the hypothetical pot in the center: It was most popular in 400 BCE. Specifically, 50 percent of all pots of this style date to 400 BCE. They are clearly less popular half a century before and after, with only 20 percent of pots of this style dating to 350 BCE or 450 BCE. They are even less popular beyond that, with only 5 percent dating to 300 BC or 500 BCE.

While there are some assumptions surrounding seriation, which you will discuss in class, the technique is nevertheless commonly used by archaeologists. For example, in Figure 13.1a, bell-bottom pants came into style in the mid-1960s. Throughout this decade, they became more popular and more people wore bell-bottoms then straight-leg pants. During their second wave, the largest percentage of people wore them from about 1995 to 2000. Notice that both periods of popularity result in a "battleship" shape. In the mid-2000s, bell-bottoms became less popular, while skinny pants became more popular and the percentage of people wearing skinny pants increased. The resulting battleship curve is truncated because we are still in a period of popularity for this style.

The Plymouth Colony Project

Seriations are invaluable to archaeologists. One famous archaeological example is James Deetz's (1967) now classic Plymouth Colony Project in which he brilliantly seriated gravestones based on the popularity of the designs carved at the top (Figure 13.2). Since the gravestones have dates inscribed in them, Deetz realized he could create a seriation of Early Colonial motifs: the death's head motif occurred with the greatest frequency between 1720 and 1780, the cherub between 1780 and 1800, and the urn and willow between 1800 and 1820. Now imagine another cemetery, this one in which most of the dates are too eroded or broken to read. You could still *relatively* date it to within a couple decades since you know in what years the cherub motif was most popular. Thus, Deetz's seriation can be applied to other sites in the region, assuming that the trends in popularity were similar from region to region.

The Activity

This activity will help you understand frequency seriation by relating it to "artifacts" from your childhood. Your instructor will ask you to think of things that have changed in popularity over the course of your life, such as TV shows, clothing styles, or technology. For each one, think about when it first emerged. Did it become popular quickly and remain popular? Did it go out of fashion quickly? Or did it slowly gain in popularity and then decline after a few years or so? Did it come back in style at any point, like bell-bottoms? Your instructor will sketch these trends in popularity on the board to create some battleship curves like the kind archeologists use all the time. In doing so, you will soon see how these cures work, but, even more importantly, you will begin to discern some of the problems and assumptions inherent to their use. Enjoy your trip down memory lane!

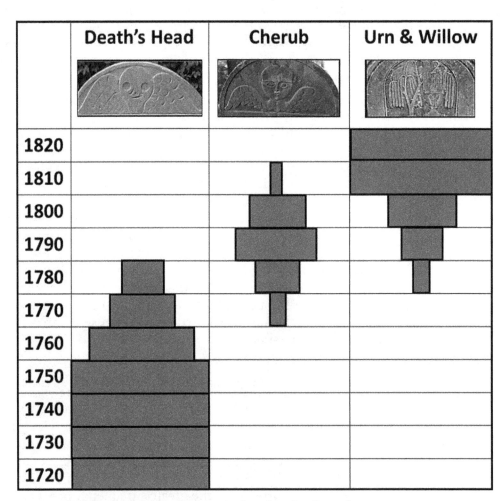

Figure 13.2. Deetz's seriation for the Stoneham cemetery in eastern Massachusetts.
From *Natural History*, March 1967,
© Natural History Magazine, Inc., 1967.

Worksheet 13.1

1. Duplicate the battleship curves your class created in the space below.

2. What assumptions do archaeologists need to be aware of when doing frequency seriation? List and explain at least two assumptions.

_____

_____

_____

For Further Exploration and Application

Complete the Seriation part of James Denbow's online lab "Seriation Stratigraphy." It will require some perseverance—be patient with it!

1. The ceramics from 10 undated sites are shown by vessel symbols. Each vessel symbol represents 20 vessels of that type found at the site. List the sites according to their relative chronology:

2. From the information given, is it possible to determine which site is the oldest? If so, which one? If not, explain why.

_____

_____

_____

References

Deetz, James, and Edwin Dethlefson. 1967. "The Plymouth Colony Project: Death's Head, Cherub, and Urn and Willow." Natural History 76 (3): 29–37. http://www.histarch.illinois .edu/plymouth/deathshead.html. Accessed 5 June 2019.

Denbow, James. 2012. "Lab I: Seriation and Stratigraphy." https://la.utexas.edu/users/denb ow/labs/lab1-strat.htm. Accessed 29 March 2019.

CHAPTER 14

Stirrup Bottle Seriation

Contextual Seriation

As discussed in chapter 13, seriation is based on the fact that styles come into popularity, peak, and then decline in popularity. The battleship curves you constructed in the last chapter illustrate a particular kind of seriation known as *frequency seriation*. In this chapter, we will explore a second kind of seriation known as *contextual seriation*. Contextual seriation is based on the rule of thumb that "like goes with like." In other words, artifacts that look more similar to one another stylistically are generally closer in age than artifact styles that are very different. For example, you can probably guess the decade just by looking at a picture of a car. Figure 14.1 shows the gradual change in style of the BMW 5 Series car; you can tell the cars that look more similar are closer in age. While there are many assumptions surrounding this rule of thumb, which are discussed later, the technique is nevertheless commonly employed, especially when seriating ceramics and lithics.

Figure 14.1. Evolution of the BMW 5 Series over time.

The Activity

1. The 12 pottery stirrup bottles illustrated on the following pages were excavated in a single cemetery near Cerro Prieta, Peru.[1] Radiocarbon measurement on textile fibers from the burials ranged from 3,800 ±200 years to 2,600 ±100 years, suggesting the cemetery was used over a period of about 1,000 years and that the stirrup bottles from different tombs might have different ages. Each excavated tomb contained a single stirrup spout bottle. The tomb containing bottle L had been dug into the shaft of a tomb

containing bottle B. The law of superposition states the materials deposited first are older than those deposited later; consequently, bottle B is older than bottle L.

2. A brief description of the 12 pottery bottles appears in Worksheet 14.1. Assuming the art style used in the cemetery was relatively homogenous at any given moment, and using the contextual seriation technique described earlier, your job is to arrange the stirrup spout bottles into a chronological sequence, beginning with the oldest.

3. Cut out the stirrup bottles in Figures 14.3–14.5 by tearing out the pages, folding them in quarters, and carefully ripping along the cresses. You should end up with 12 squares, each with a bottle on it.

4. Arrange the stirrup bottles into a chronological sequence, **beginning with the oldest bottle**. Carefully compare design elements such as surface decoration, rim style, and overall bottle shape (see Figure 14.2). Remember: bottle B is *older* than bottle L. Attach your sequence (with the youngest bottle on top of the pile) to Worksheet 14.1.

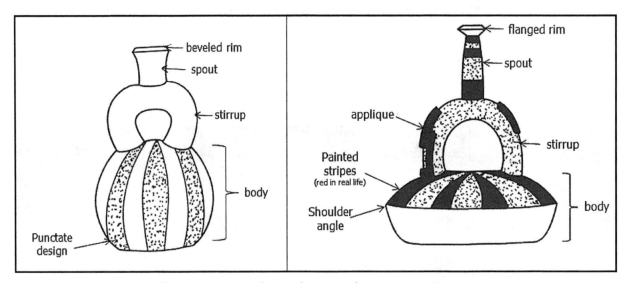

Figure 14.2. Stylistic elements for use in seriation.

Suggestions for Further Exploration and Application

- **"Grim Rites of the Moche" (Popson 2002).** This article summarizes recent archaeological finds at the ritual center of Moche, Peru, where macabre artwork depicted on stirrup-spouted bottles show ornate warrior priests slitting captives' throats, drinking their blood, and participating in acts of sodomy. In the absence of archaeological evidence, scholars believed these images were simply artistic hyperbole used by the elites to underscore their coercive power. But new evidence proves that the shocking scenes depicted in Moche art are faithful representations of actual behavior, if not records of specific events.

- **"Moche Burials Uncovered" (Donnan 2001).** This article includes a brief summary of the Moche, a field description of a tomb at the site of Dos Cabezas, and images to explore.

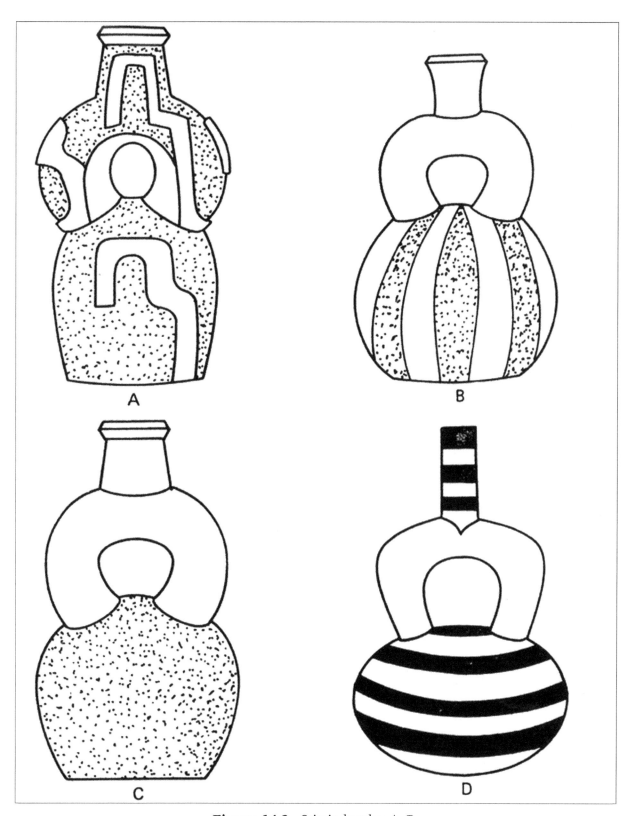

Figure 14.3. Stirrip bottles A–D.

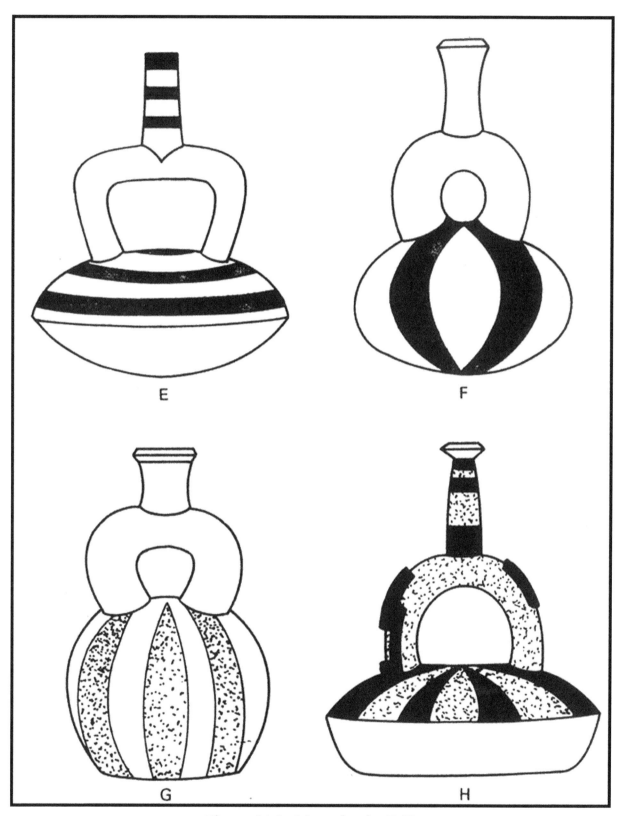

Figure 14.4. Stirrup bottles E–H.

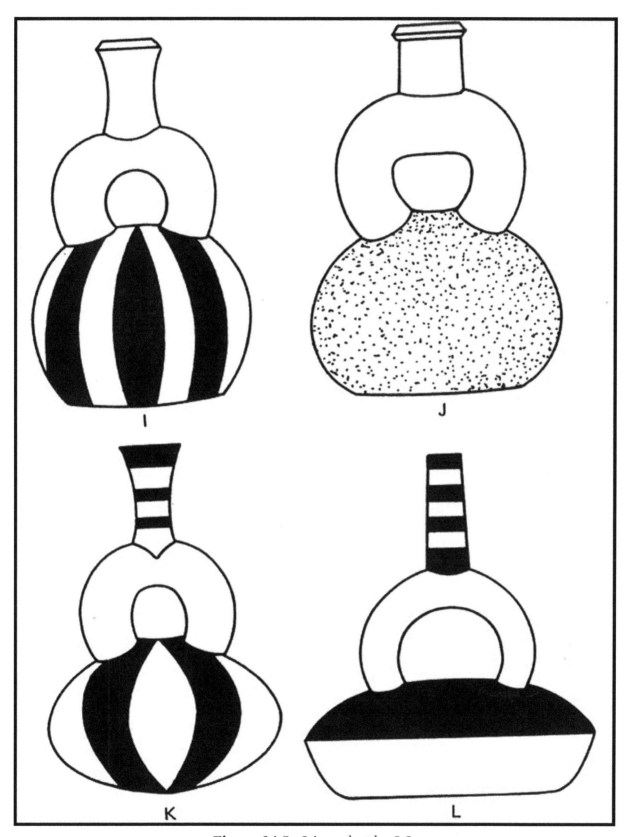

Figure 14.5. Stirrup bottles I–L.

Worksheet 14.1

1. Write your seriation sequence below from oldest to youngest:

   OLDEST   *YOUNGEST*

2. What assumptions did you make that prevented you from getting the correct sequence on your first try (or first couple of tries)?

   _____

   _____

   _____

   _____

   _____

   _____

For Further Exploration and Application

Your instructor may have you do these questions as part of an in-class discussion or independent reflection. This section uses the stratigraphy from chapter 11.

3. Using Table 14.1 as a guide, write the letter of the stirrup bottle that goes with a particular stratum in the stratigraphic profile on the reverse page. For example, bottle A sounds a lot like the description of the bottles found in strata Q. This will take some patience. *(Note: not all strata have matching bottles, and some strata will have more than one bottle present.)*

4. Overall, does the stratigraphy confirm the seriation of stirrup bottles? Explain your answer.

   _____

   _____

   _____

   _____

   _____

   _____

   _____

   _____

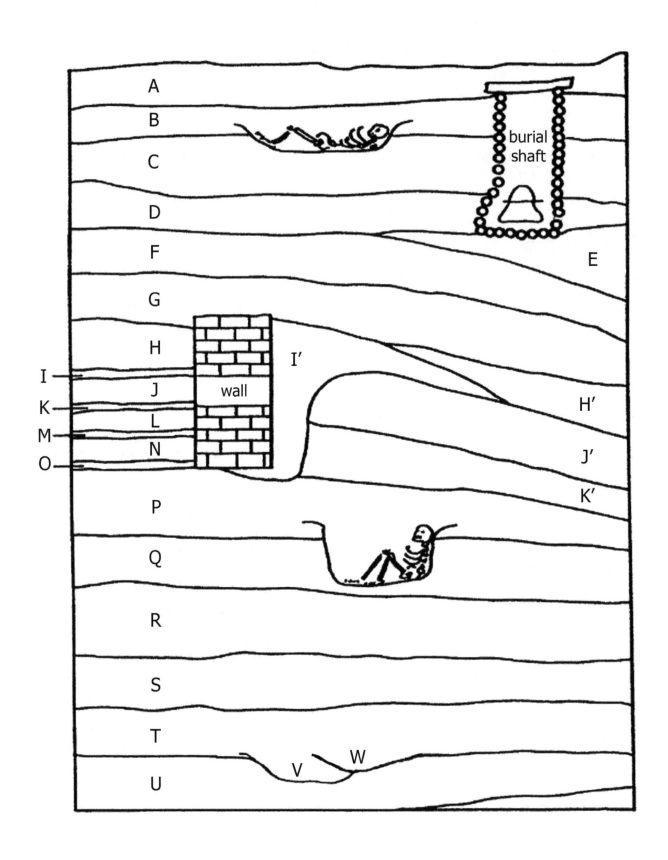

Table 14.1. Description of Material Culture Found in Each Stratum.

Stratum	Description
A	• Bottles with cupcake-shaped bodies, appliqué on stirrups, flanged rims, and tapering spouts
B	• Bottles with cupcake-shaped bodies, appliqué on stirrups, flanged rims, and tapering spouts
C	• Bottles with circumferential black-painted stripes, straight spouts, and no rim • Bottles with undecorated "triangular" stirrups and straight-sided, striped spouts
D	• Bottles with circumferential black-painted stripes, straight spouts, and no rim • Bottles with undecorated triangular-shaped stirrups and straight-sided, striped spouts
E	• Culturally sterile
F	• Bottles with circumferential black-painted stripes, straight spouts, and no rim • Bottles with undecorated triangular-shaped stirrups and straight-sided, striped spouts
G	• Bottles with undecorated triangular-shaped stirrups and straight-sided, striped spouts
H	• Bottles with vertical black painted bands and flat bottoms; • Bottles with concave-curved spouts (some striped), beveled rims, and rounded bottoms
H′	• Bottles with vertical black painted bands and flat bottoms; • Bottles with concave-curved spouts (not striped), beveled rims and rounded bottoms
I	• Micro-sized artifacts (less than 4mm) of pottery
I′	• Bottles with vertical bands of zoned punctate decoration *and* simple punctate, • Bottles with flanged *and* beveled rims
J	• Bottles with vertical painted bands, flat bottoms, concave-curved spouts, and beveled rims • Bottles with concave-curved spouts (not striped), beveled rims, and rounded bottoms
J′	• Bottles with vertical bands of zoned punctate decoration, flanged *and* beveled rims
K	• Micro-sized artifacts (less than 4mm) of pottery
K′	• Fragments of bottles with punctate decoration
L	• Bottles with vertical black-painted bands on base, flat bottoms, concave-curved spouts, and beveled rims
M	• Micro-sized artifacts (less than 4mm) of pottery
N	• Bottles with vertical painted bands, flat bottoms, concave-curved spouts, and beveled rims
O	• Micro-sized artifacts (less than 4mm) of pottery
P	• Bottles with punctate surface decoration on base and appliqué decoration • Bottles with conical bottle spouts, simple punctate bases, and flanged rims
Q	• Bottles with punctate surface decoration on base and appliqué decoration
R–U	• No ceramics • Obsidian points and fishhooks

Note

1. Used with permission from Patterson (1994).

References

Donnan, Christopher B. 2001. "Moche Burials Uncovered." *National Geographic Magazine* 199 (3): 58–73.

Patterson, Thomas. 1994. *The Theory and Practice of Archaeology: A Workbook.* 2nd ed. Upper Saddle River, NJ: Prentice Hall.

Popson, Colleen. 2002. "Grim Rites of the Moche." *Archaeology* 55 (2): 30–35. https://archive .archaeology.org/0203/abstracts/moche.html. Accessed 5 June 2019.

CHAPTER 15

Tree-Ring Match-up

Dendrochronology

Dendrochronology, sometimes called "tree-ring dating," is one of the most effective absolute dating methods archaeologists can use in temperate regions of the world. The method is based on the fact that trees in temperate and arctic regions are dormant during the winter and then grow the rest of the year. This creates a distinct ring of growth every year. The rings vary in thickness, color, and texture depending on that year's environmental conditions such as temperature and precipitation. This means one ring equals one year of growth. So, by counting and comparing the tree rings with numerous samples, dendrochronologists can determine the age of the tree when it was felled (Figure 15.1). Different trees of the same species will have the same pattern of rings for each year they are alive at the same time. For instance, in a year where there might have been a drought, the ring on each tree alive

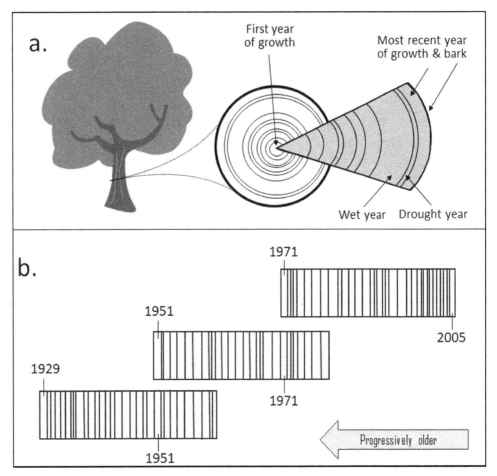

Figure 15.1. Growth of tree rings (a) and overlapping tree-ring sequences (b). Courtesy Crow Canyon Archaeological Center.

that year might be relatively narrow (i.e., not a lot of growth) as opposed to a year where there was optimal rain available (i.e., the ring might be thicker).

By matching up, or "cross-dating," the tree rings and connecting events where a date is known, such as the year the tree was cut down, sequences of rings associated with specific calendar dates can be constructed, sometimes far back into prehistory (Figure 15.2c). In some regions of the world, scientists have put together tree-ring sequences that go back for several thousands of years; these are called "master sequences." By matching wood samples from archaeology sites to regional "master sequences" archaeologists can tell how old a site is, sometimes to the specific year it was occupied. One region of the world where there is a significant master sequence is the Southwestern United States (Figure 15.2a–c). A. E. Douglass, an astronomer, was the first to pioneer tree-ring dating in the Southwest by creating master sequences from recently felled yellow pines near Flagstaff, Arizona, and preserved wooden house beams from prehistoric Pueblo structures. Assuming the Puebloans used the trees around the time they died, archaeologists can absolutely date a house structure. While tree-ring counting is scientifically sound, archaeologists do have to be careful about such assumptions—can you think of a scenario in which such an assumption might not work?

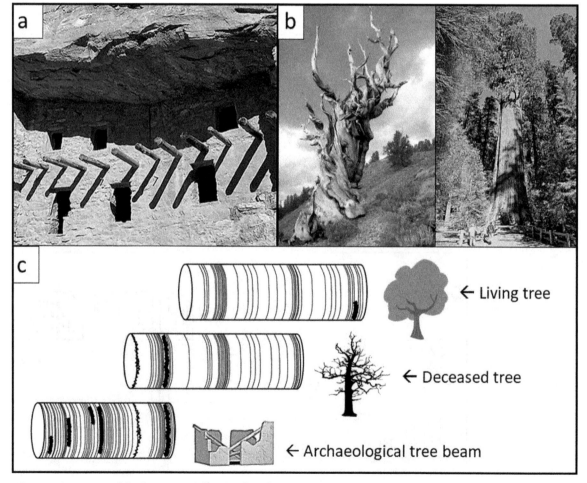

Figure 15.2. Pueblo house with wooden beams (a); example of a bristlecone pine (left) and Giant Sequoia (right) (b); and illustration of cross dating house beams to living and dead trees (c).

The Activity

Imagine you are an archaeologist working in the Southwestern United States. You have recently excavated five Pueblo house structures at one site and found that the structural beams have been well preserved. You are interested in knowing how old each structure is and the order the houses might have been built (i.e., are certain houses older than others?). You select one beam from each house to match up to a master sequence for the region to determine the specific cutting date of each beam (Figure 15.3). Assuming the inhabitants immediately used the cut beams when constructing their house, you will be able to determine the age of each house structure using dendrochronology. Working off the master sequence initially, match up the five wooden beams A–E, which represent five Pueblo house structures, respectively. You will need to cut them out with scissors and then tape them together once you have matched them correctly. Once they are matched, determine the cutting date for each wooden beam and the age of each house structure by counting the rings.

Tips

- Write the letter of the cross section (e.g., "A") on the back as you cut them out; this will really help keep track of them.
- Make sure the dot (representing the cutting date) is on the **left** so you don't accidentally match the sections upside down!
- Use tape "doughnuts" (at least initially) to make it easy to move a section if you make a mistake. Once you have it correct and are ready to count rings, then you may wish to tape the sequence together with flat tape.

Complete questions 1–3 on Worksheet 15.1. Don't forget to attach your taped together chronology from Worksheet 15.1 at the bottom of the page. Your instructor may ask you to complete questions 4 and 5 under "For Further Exploration and Application."

Suggestions for Further Exploration and Application

- **"The Secret of the Southwest Solved by Talkative Tree Rings" (Douglass 1929).** A. E. Douglass (1929) pioneered the science of tree rings in this *National Geographic* article, which includes impressive historic photographs.
- **"Tree Rings: Dendrochronology" (UCAR 2019).** This is a succinct web site prepared by the University Corporation for Atmospheric Research (UCAR) summarizing tree rings as well as other proxies for paleoclimate reconstruction such as oxygen isotopes, corals, and lake sediments.
- **"Tree Rings Do Tell Tales: Dendrochronology at Chaco Canyon" (Swanberg 2019).** Provides a nice summary of tree ring research conducted at Chaco Canyon National Historical Park which includes an excellent 2-minute video showing close-up footage of tree rings and tree beams from the prehistoric structures located in the Park.

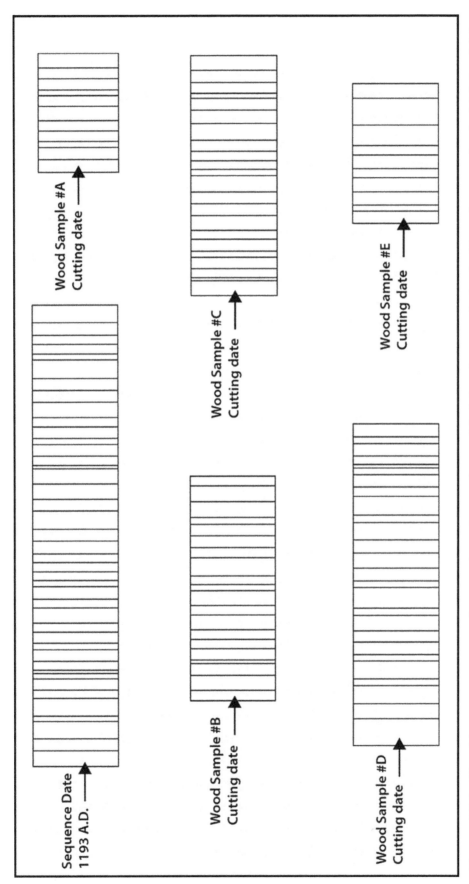

Figure 15.3. Use this page to cut out the tree rings. Remember to label the rings on the back side to keep track of which is which.

Worksheet 15.1

1. Attach your completed tree-ring sequence to the box at the bottom of this page.

2. What are the cutting dates for:

    Wood Beam A: _____   Wood Beam D: _____

    Wood Beam B: _____   Wood Beam E: _____

    Wood Beam C: _____

3. List the wood beams (and by association, the house structures they represent) in order from youngest to oldest.

    Youngest House   Oldest House

    _____   _____   _____   _____   _____

For Further Exploration and Application

Your instructor may have you do these questions as part of a class discussion or independently.

4. What is the complete date range represented by the wood beams?

    a. List from oldest ring* _____ to the youngest ring _____

    *Note: this is not the same as the "cut-date" ring

    b. For how many years was the site was occupied? _____

5. What might be some problems with applying dendrochronology to archaeological sites? *(Hint: Think about climate change, tree species, and how people collected house beams)*. Use the back of this worksheet if you need more space.

_____

_____

_____

_____

Attach tree ring sequence in this space.

Notes

1. Adapted with permission from Crow Canyon Archaeological Center (2019).
2. Sometimes droughts are extreme enough that trees fail to produce a growth ring at all. Other events may be recorded in tree rings as well, such as scars resulting from forest fire.

References

Crow Canyon Archaeological Center. 2019. "Dendrochronology." https://www.crowcanyon.org/index.php/dendrochronology. Accessed 18 May 2019.

Douglass, A. E. 1929. "The Secret of the Southwest Solved by Talkative Tree Rings." *National Geographic Magazine* 56 (6): 737–770.

UCAR (University Corporation for Atmospheric Research). 2019. "Tree Rings: Dendrochronology." https://scied.ucar.edu/tree-rings. Accessed 18 May 2019.

Swanberg, Susan. 2019. "Tree Rings Do Tell Tales: Dendrochronology at Chaco Canyon." Western National Parks Association. http://www.wnpa.org/research-item/tree-rings-do-tell-tales. Accessed 6 June 2019.

CHAPTER 16

"Smarties" Metric Dating

Radiometric Dating

As noted in chapter 11, scientists have calculated the age of Earth at a whopping 4.6 billion years, and the arrival of modern humans on this planet only about 150,000 years ago. But how can they be so sure of those ancient dates? A breakthrough came with the discovery of radioactivity in the early 1900s. Scientists discovered that rocks could be used as time capsules when studied atomically. Atoms of many chemical elements in rock exist in slightly different forms, known as *isotopes*. Isotopes are atoms of the same element that have different a number of neutrons than protons in their nucleus. Certain isotopes are unstable, so they spontaneously undergo a process of radioactive decay that transforms them into a new element. Lucky for us, this rate of decay is constant, so scientists can date a rock by measuring the amount of radioactive isotope remaining in a rock, allowing them to "see" way back in time. Let's look at this process in more detail using a common radiometric dating technique used by archaeologists: radiocarbon, or carbon-14, dating.

Radiocarbon

Usually, the carbon-12 atom has six protons and six neutrons; most of the carbon we breathe in is this common form. But carbon also has several rare isotopes, including carbon-14, which is formed in the upper atmosphere when cosmic rays bombard nitrogen atoms and convert them into carbon-14 atoms. Carbon-14 has six protons and eight neutrons in its nucleus, a configuration that makes it atomically unstable. As a result, the atom undergoes a process called *radioactive decay* in which it emits matter in the form of a beta particle, plus energy in the form of radiation (hence the name). The physics behind this process is not important for our needs, but essentially that emission results in a new atomic configuration with seven protons and seven neutrons in the nucleus; thus, it is no longer the element carbon (referred to as the original "parent" atom) but rather now the element nitrogen. Essentially, unstable radiocarbon decays into a stable new element, nitrogen, called the "daughter" atom (Figure 16.1). While organisms are alive, the carbon-14 does nothing; but at death, these radioactive atoms begin to decay.[1]

The Half-life

Although atoms decay spontaneously, it occurs constantly. As a result, the rate at which the decay occurs can be measured, which is what makes it so useful for dating objects. This rate is called the *half-life*—the amount of time it takes for any given number of parent atoms to decay into the daughter product. The length of a half-life varies depending on the element in question.

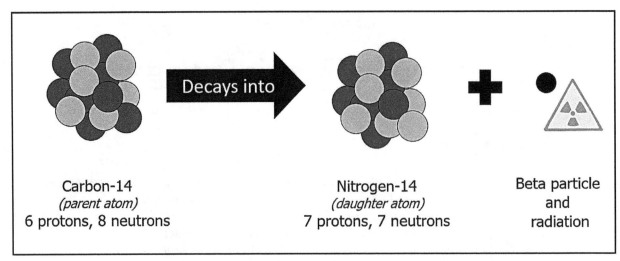

Figure 16.1 Schematic representation of radioactive decay of carbon-14.

For carbon-14, the half-life is 5,730 years. In other words, say you have 100 atoms to begin with: after one half-life has passed—that is, 5,730 years—50 atoms will have decayed and 50 radioactive atoms will be remaining. Thus, if we can count the number of radioactive atoms remaining in a sample, then we can determine how much time has elapsed. In contrast to the relatively fast decay rate of carbon-14, the half-life of potassium-40 (found in volcanic minerals) has a half-life of nearly 1.3 billion years! While this rate is almost incomprehensibly slow, it has the advantage of dating materials that are millions of years old rather than thousands. Table 16.1 illustrates the range of half-lives for different isotopes.

Table 16.1. Examples of Different Isotopes, Their Half-Lives, and Datable Materials.

Isotope		Half-Life (Years)	Datable Range (Years)	Datable Materials
Parent	*Daughter*			
Carbon-14	Nitrogen 14	5,730	400–50,000	Organics (e.g., wood, bone, charcoal)
Potassium-40	Argon 40	1.3 billion	100,000–4.5 billion	Volcanic rocks and ash
Rubidium-87	Strontium 87	47 billion	10 million–4.5 billion	Metamorphic rocks
Uranium-series[2]	Thorium-230, Lead 238	variable	variable	Corals and cave speleothems

Limitations of Radiocarbon

It is important to note that radiocarbon dating can only be used to date organic materials, that is, carbon-based materials such as wood charcoal, bone, peat, seeds, shell, and plant fibers like linen. Some famous examples include the Dead Sea Scrolls, dated to between 400 BCE and 300 CE and the Shroud of Turin, which, though once thought to be the covering Jesus was buried in, was independently dated by three independent laboratories to the Middle Ages.[3] Unfortunately, because it is limited to organics containing carbon, radiocarbon cannot be used to date fossils. Another limitation is that radiocarbon is restricted to measuring a date range of about 400 to 50,000 years (see Worksheet 16.1). While these limitations don't affect most archaeologists, they do affect paleoanthropologists who study fossilized remains of our ancient hominin ancestors such as Neanderthals and Australopithecines. An isotope that paleoanthropologists have been able to take advantage of is potassium-40, which works when dating minerals containing—you guessed it, potassium—such as volcanic materials like ash. A famous example of potassium-40 dating in a paleoanthropological context is Lucy, the fossilized skeleton of a bipedal *Australopithecus afarensis*. The bones themselves are fossilized (i.e., organics have been replaced by inorganic minerals) and therefore not datable by either radiocarbon or potassium-40, but they were recovered sandwiched between two volcanic ash strata, which could be potassium-argon dated. Using the law of superposition (discussed in chapter 11), then, Lucy was relatively dated to approximately four million years old.

Two final limitations of radiocarbon include potential contamination and the need to calibrate dates. Contamination often comes in the form of "older" or "younger" carbon mixing with a sample. Younger carbon can come from materials with very recent carbon in it, for example, the coals at the end of a cigarette. A lot of parent carbon remains: it is therefore chronologically younger than archaeological carbon and can skew results if mixed in. This is why archaeologists do not smoke on an archaeological site. Similarly, older carbon can also skew results in the opposite direction. Old carbon most often derives from coal seams near an archaeological site; because most coals formed during the Carboniferous geologic period (see chapter 11), very little parent carbon remains: it is therefore chronologically older than archaeological carbon and will make an archaeological deposit appear much older if mixed in. This is one reason we pay close attention to stratigraphy and sediments, so that we can identify any potential contaminating deposits. Another source of older carbon comes from a surprising source: the burning of fossil fuels. The copious output of carbon when fossil fuels are burned alters the ratio of carbon-12 to carbon-14 in the atmosphere, which is vital to determining age. This is one reason it is essential that radiocarbon dates be *calibrated*. Calibration curves going back tens of thousands of years have been constructed. Can you think of a way to construct such calibration curves using another absolute dating technique discussed in this book?

The Activity

This activity will use Smarties candy to illustrate the concept of a half-life and how it can be used to date an object. Yes, you will get to eat the candy, but wait until your teacher tells you to! Your instructor may have you complete Worksheet 16.1 and/or do some of the "For Further Exploration and Application" questions (Worksheet 16.2). If you want to watch a short video before class, *Scientific American* (2012) has straightforward one called "How Does Radiocarbon Dating Work?"

Suggestions for Further Exploration and Application

- **"Fossil Fuel Emissions Are Making Carbon Dating More Difficult" (Kaplan 2015).** This article discusses the concern that fossil fuel burning may endanger the effectiveness of radiocarbon dating.
- **"Why Shroud of Turin's Secrets Continue to Elude Science" (Viviano 2015).** This recent study argues that the original dates came from fibers used to repair damaged sections during the Middle Ages. His samples, from non-repaired areas, yielded a date between 300 BCE and 400 CE, once again calling into question the Shroud's secrets.

Worksheet 16.1

1. Complete the sketch below by coloring in the correct number of atoms that will have decayed (i.e., daughter elements) after each succeeding half-life. In the space below, indicate the number of years that have passed if the atoms are carbon-14 (half-life = 5,730 years).

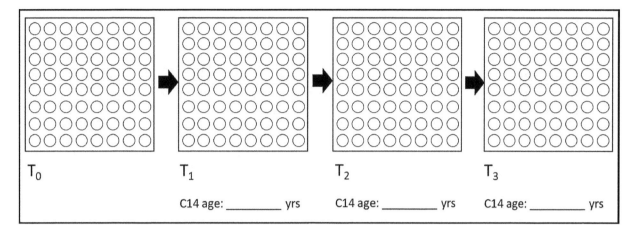

T_0

T_1

T_2

T_3

C14 age: _____ yrs   C14 age: _____ yrs   C14 age: _____ yrs

2. Complete the following graph using what you know about half-life and the data in question 1. Then determine the time elapsed (i.e., age) for each half life. Write the number in the blank space provided on the x-axis.

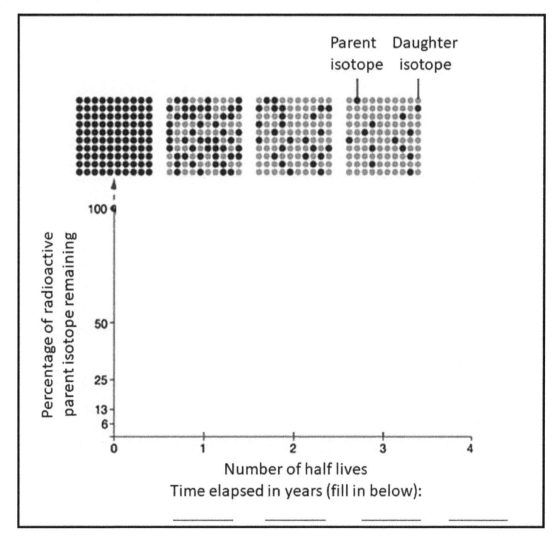

Parent   Daughter
isotope   isotope

Percentage of radioactive parent isotope remaining

100

50

25

13
6

0   1   2   3   4

Number of half lives

Time elapsed in years (fill in below):

_____   _____   _____

3. Look up the definition of a fossil, such as a dinosaur femur, if you don't already know how one forms. Why can't a fossil be radio*carbon* dated? There are two good reasons.

_____

_____

4. In the scenario below, does the relative stratigraphy support the potassium-argon date in Strata C? Why or why not? Write your answer to the right of the image:

Stratum A: charred seed C-14 dated to 50,000 yr BP

Stratum B: mineral rubidium-strontium dated to 5.2 mya

Stratum C: ash potassium-argon dated to 4.2 mya

Stream gulley cuts through strata A & B to reveal hominin footprints in stratum C, which is composed of volcanic ash

5. Radiocarbon dates are reported in years BP (before present). This means the date as reported is not a calendar age (e.g., BCE). Convert T3 (from question 1) to a calendar age BCE by subtracting the years elapsed from the "present." But note that because the present is constantly changing, archaeologists generally use a constant date of 1950, the year Willard Libby discovered the concept of radiometric decay. Show your work:

_____

_____

_____

6. Once your date is in calendar years, it still needs to be calibrated. We always denote these "cal. BCE." Go to *CalPal Online* (CalPal 2019), a free calibration service.[4] Calibrate your BCE dates above with an error range of +100 using the online software package. How do your dates differ, and why is calibration therefore so important?

_____

_____

_____

Worksheet 16.2

For Further Exploration and Application

Your instructor may have you do these questions as part of an in-class discussion or independent reflection.

1. Radiocarbon dating has lower and upper limits of 400 and about 50,000 years, respectively. Look at the graph from Worksheet 16.1 and see if you can figure out why. Keep in mind that the most common type of radiocarbon dating (accelerated mass spectroscopy, or AMS) counts *individual* atoms in a mass accelerator machine. Based on your conclusions, and what you know about when radioactive decay begins, explain why the comic below, similar to one which appears on a website attempting to debunk radiocarbon dating, is barking up the wrong tree.

Illustration created by Joseph Bomberger.

_____

_____

_____

2. The decay of carbon-14 is constant but also spontaneous. It is not therefore not possible to measure all the radioactivity in a given sample. Thus, radiocarbon dates are reported with error ranges.[5] For example, 11,460 ±200 years means the true age may actually exist between 11,260 and 11,660. Statistically speaking, this represents 1 "standard deviation" and is equivalent to a 68 percent chance that the true date is in that range. These odds are not great, so archaeologists often double the error range to 2 standard deviations, statistically equivalent to a 95 percent chance. Doubling the standard deviation means we also double the error range. So, in this example, there is a 95 percent chance the true date falls between 11,060 and 11,860 years BP. In the first scenario, the odds aren't as good that your date is correct, but it is more precise. In the second scenario, the odds are much higher that your date is correct, but it is less precise. Which do you prefer? Why?

_____

_____

_____

If instructed by your teacher, pick one of the following questions for the appropriate short article from the "For Further Reading and Application" section.

3. Read Viviano's (2015) "Why the Shroud of Turin's Secrets Continue to Elude Science." What argument does Viviano make regarding the veracity of the shroud? Assuming you could access it and test it any way you wanted (which of course you can't!), how would you recommend dating it? From where would you sample it? How many samples would you take? How many labs would run the samples?

_____

_____

_____

_____

_____

_____

_____

_____

4. Read Kaplan's (2015) "Fossil Fuel Emissions Are Making Carbon Dating More Difficult." Why are scientists so concerned about accelerated burning of fossil fuels, other than the obvious problems of climate warming and concomitant rising sea levels? How, specifically, might it ultimately affect archaeology? Is there a solution? If so, how can scientists control for it? (*Hint: Think about calibration and/or other absolute dating methods.*)

_____

_____

_____

_____

_____

_____

_____

_____

Notes

1. For minerals, radioactive atoms begin to decay after crystallization from lava into rocks.
2. There are many isotopes of uranium (U), which ultimately decay to lead (Pb) but with several intermediary daughter products, including thorium (Th).
3. For a more detailed description of the Shroud of Turin, and recent new findings calling the original studies into questions, see "Suggestions for Further Exploration and Application."
4. Notice that the input value must be in years BP and an error range included.
5. For more information, see Higham (2002).

References

CalPal (Cologne Radiocarbon Calibration & Paleoclimate Research Package). 2019. *CalPal Online*. Quickcal2007 ver. 1.5. http://www.calpal-online.de. Accessed 11 June 2019.

Higham, Thomas. 2002. "Age Calculation." *Radiocarbon Web-Info*, last modified 16 May. http://www.c14dating.com/agecalc.html. Accessed 11 June 2019.

Kaplan, Sarah. 2015. "Fossil Fuel Emissions Are Making Carbon Dating More Difficult." *Washington Post*, 22 July. https://www.washingtonpost.com/news/morning-mix/wp/2015/07/22/fossil-fuel-emissions-are-making-carbon-dating-more-difficult/?utm_term=.bfdc9528e0e3. Accessed 5 June 2019.

Levin, David. 2008. "Radiocarbon Dating." *NOVA*, 18 November. http://www.pbs.org/wgbh/nova/tech/radiocarbon-dating.html. Accessed 5 June 2019.

Scientific American. 2012. "How Does Radiocarbon Dating Work?" 30 November. https://www.scientificamerican.com/video/how-does-radiocarbon-dating-work-i2012-11-30. Accessed 5 June 2019.

Viviano, Frank. 2015. "Why Shroud of Turin's Secrets Continue to Elude Science." *National Geographic Magazine*, 17 April. http://news.nationalgeographic.com/2015/04/150417-shroud-turin-relics-jesus-catholic-church-religion-science. Accessed 5 June 2019.

MODULE 4

Exploring Archaeological Specialties

CHAPTER 17

Flaky Archaeology
Lithic Analysis

Lithic Analysis

Lithic material (i.e., stone tool debris) is one of the—if not *the*—most abundant (and oldest) material remains recovered from archaeological sites (Odell 2006). Because it is rock, it is highly durable and can be found unaltered even millions of years later. For these reasons, the study of lithics is one of the most common analyses undertaken by archaeologists. Lithic analysis consists of the study of both formal stone tools and the flaked debris resulting from tool manufacture. The analysis of formal tools such as arrowheads is often seen as the glamorous side of archaeology. But despite the wow factor of the finished product, archaeologists often learn more about human behavior and site use from the less glamorous flaked debris—called *debitage*, after the French word for "waste." The methods of analysis used depend on the questions being asked, but two common methods you will try your hand at in this activity are (1) flake analysis and (2) debitage analysis.

Flakes have several characteristics that distinguish them from naturally broken stones (Figure 17.1a). Rock surfaces are carefully prepared by those who make stone tools (i.e., flintknappers), be they modern or prehistoric. This results in a noticeable *platform* on the resulting flake, a somewhat flat surface left over from where core preparation occurred. When a core is struck with a harder material such as a granite hammerstone or antler billet, the force of the blow sends energy through the rock, creating a *bulb of percussion*, a cone-shaped bulge adjacent to the platform. The force may also cause a tiny flake to pop off, leaving behind an *eraillure scar*. Finally, the energy may

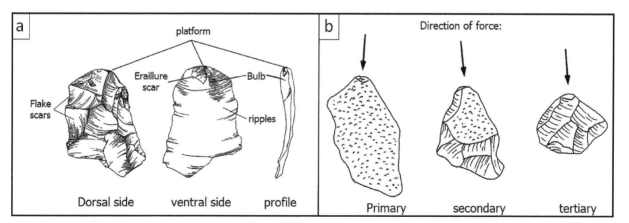

Figure 17.1. Typical features of a culturally modified flake (a) and schematic representation of primary, secondary, and tertiary flakes (b). Note that stippling indicates cortex.

also cause *compression rings* to form—sort of like ripples produced by tossing a stone into a puddle of water.

Lithic Reduction

The reduction process begins when a core of raw material is made smaller, or *reduced*, in the process of making a stone tool. Flintknappers use a rounded rock (i.e., hammerstone) or antler tine to strike flakes off one at a time. This is a very strategic and complex process, and not nearly as easy as it sounds. Your instructor may show the Cleveland Museum of Natural History's flint-knapping video; archaeologist Mark Kollecker makes it look easy, but it is something prehistoric knappers probably spent years apprenticed to a master to learn. During the reduction process, the original stone core gets smaller as material is removed. Initially, the flakes are very large and thick, and the weathered rind of the rock—called the *cortex*—covers most of the outer (i.e., *dorsal*) surface. As the process continues, the flakes become smaller and smaller, with fewer of them having cortex as the weathered rind is removed. Eventually, it is the right size, shape, and thickness to begin fine-tuning it into a final product. At this point, the tool prototype—or *biface*—is more fragile, and knappers must use a lighter tool such as a deer antler tine to carefully take off the smaller, thinner flakes. Finally, the knapper shapes the tool using a technique called *pressure flaking*—that is, pressing the tip of the tine against the tool to create a strong, serrated edge capable of scraping deer hide, drilling through leather, or penetrating the muscle of an animal. Now imagine looking at the ground and seeing all those waste flakes. This, then, is what archaeologists often find themselves studying . . . the tools are long gone, but the debitage remains.

Flake Analysis

Debitage can be separated into three major flake types: primary, secondary, and tertiary (Figure 17.1b). Primary flakes are defined as those flakes exhibiting cortex on a flake's entire dorsal surface. They are generally large flakes taken off during the early stages of core reduction, but occasionally smaller flakes have a lot of cortex too. Secondary flakes exhibit cortex on some portion of the dorsal surface, but not covering it. Secondary flakes are generally medium in size (though they come in a wide range), and numerous flake scares from previous knapping are visible on the dorsal surface as well. Finally, tertiary flakes have no cortex visible. These are generally small flakes (some quite tiny) that are chipped off during the late stages of biface completion, during the resharpening of tools or when a dull, worn tool is recycled, what archaeologists call "repurposed" (e.g., a biface recycled into a thumbnail scraper). Experimental flintknapping has demonstrated that each stage of reduction results in predicable proportions of the three types of flakes. As a general rule of thumb, we find the following proportions:

Early stage: > 25 percent primary flakes
Middle stage: < 25 percent primary flakes; 25–50 percent secondary flakes
Late stage: > 50 percent secondary & tertiary flakes

Debitage Analysis

Archaeologists who specialize in lithic analysis also measure the size of the resulting debitage. In general, as the reduction continues, several trends can be observed:

- The percentage of flakes smaller than 0.25 inches increases;
- There is a decrease in the percentage of flakes having cortex;
- The average weight of flakes decreases.

It's important to recognize that these are trends rather than absolute truths. For example, look at the pile of debitage Kollecker creates in his flintknapping demo. Even though he was working in the early stages of the reduction process, notice there are many small waste flakes (he even picks up a few). So, early-stage reduction can and does create quite a bit of small, tertiary flakes. This is why archeologists often use multiple methods of analysis (e.g., flake and debitage analysis) and often rely on the relative proportion of large, primary flakes to small tertiary flakes.

The Activity

In this activity you will examine the flakes in assemblages A, B, and C (Figures 17.2–17.4). First, determine if the flakes shown are primary, secondary, or tertiary, and record these numbers in Worksheet 17.1. *Note: The stippling (i.e., dotted pattern) indicates the presence of cortex.* Second, measure the flakes using the scale provided (to facilitate this, hold a blank sheet of paper up to the scale, and transfer the markings so that you can use it as a ruler). You don't have to measure them precisely, but rather simply need to determine which of the size grades shown in Worksheet 17.1 ("Debitage Analysis") the flake falls into. Convert this frequency data into proportions, and then graph the results before answering the questions that follow. Note that the three assemblages have a couple items in addition to lithic flakes:

- Assemblage A: deer antler tine used for pressure flaking;
- Assemblage B: broken granite hammerstone and whole deer antler billet;
- Assemblage C: three broken formal tools, including a projectile point (center left), thumbnail scraper (center top), and drill (center right).

Finally, complete the front of Worksheet 17.2 by using the combined data to infer activity areas within the site. Your instructor may ask you to do some or all of the "For Further Exploration and Application" section (back of Worksheet 17.2) as part of classroom discussion or reflective homework.

Suggestions for Further Exploration and Application

- **"Children of Prehistory: Stone Age Kids Left Their Mark on Cave Art and Stone Tools" (Bower 2007: 265–266).** The relevant section ("Knap Time") discusses how archaeologists might be able to discern adult toolmaking from children's.

- **"Flintknapping Demonstration" (CMNH 2011)** (*8 minutes*). The Cleveland Museum of Natural History youth programs coordinator Mark Kollecker demonstrates the stages of lithic reduction.
- **"What Makes Us Human?" (PBS 2013)** (*13 minutes*). This *NOVA ScienceNow* episode focuses on the new hypothesis that the ability to make complex tools set the cognitive foundation for language development in modern humans.
- **"Woman the Toolmaker" (Brant and Weedman 2002).** This ethnographic work among the Konso in Ethiopia shows that women are not only tool users but also expert tool*makers*, challenging the common stereotype that toolmaking is a male calling, a stereotype the authors argue derives from our Western "Flintstones" paradigm.

Assemblage A

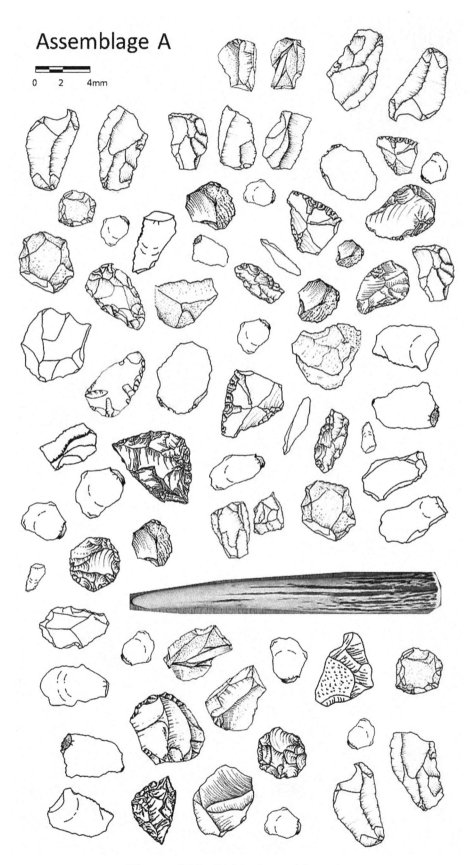

Figure 17.2. Lithic Assemblage A.

Assemblage B

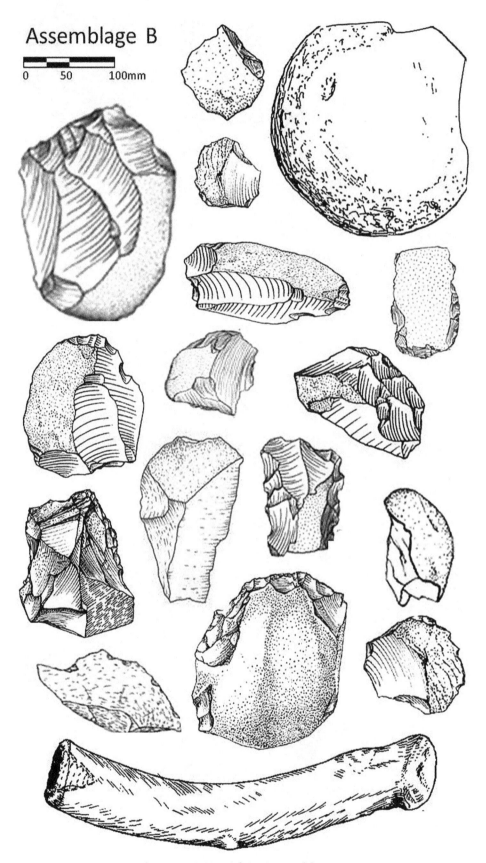

Figure 17.3. Lithic Assemblage B.

Assemblage C

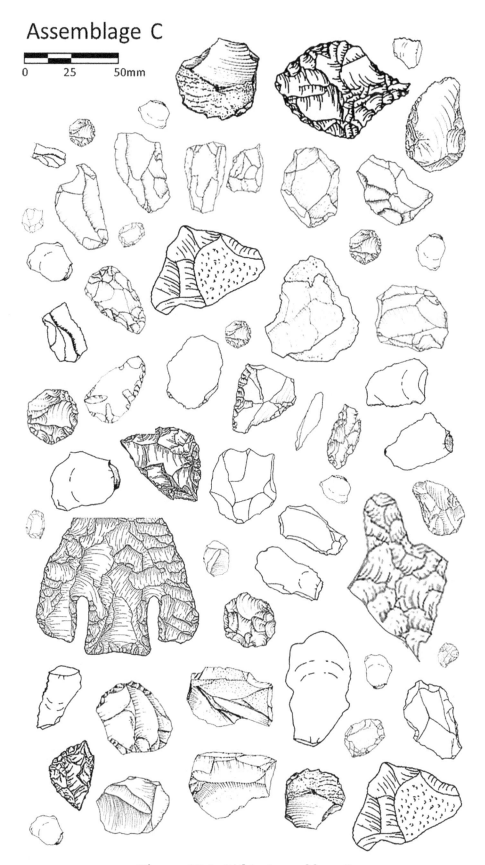

Figure 17.4. Lithic Assemblage C.

Worksheet 17.1

Flake Analysis

Record the number of primary, secondary, and tertiary flakes in each lithic assemblage, and then calculate the percent of total they comprise.

Assemblage	Primary Flakes		Secondary Flakes		Tertiary Flakes		Reduction Stage
	n=	%	n=	%	n=	%	
A							
B							
C							

1. Based on this flake analysis, what stage of reduction characterizes each assemblage? Explain your answer.

_____

_____

_____

_____

_____

_____

2. Do the lithic-related artifacts (e.g., antler tine) present in assemblages support your conclusion above?

_____

_____

_____

_____

_____

Debitage Analysis

Record the number of flakes in each size grade, and then calculate it as a percent of total per assemblage. Complete the graph below to visualize your data.

Assemblage	> 1" (> 25mm)		0.5–1" (12.5–25mm)		0.25–0.5" (6.25–12.5mm)		< 0.25" (< 6.25mm)		Reduction Stage
	n =	%	n =	%	n =	%	n =	%	
A									
B									
C									

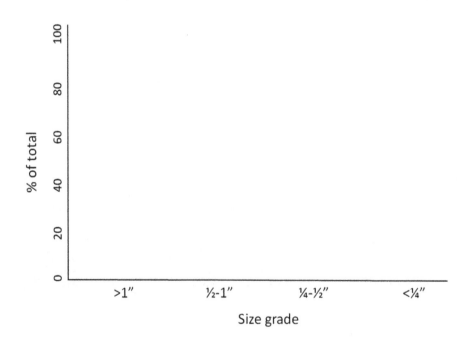

3. Based on your debitage analysis, what stage of reduction characterizes each assemblage? Explain your answer.

_____

_____

_____

Worksheet 17.2

1. Three activity areas are represented by assemblages A, B, and C: (1) a lithic quarry five kilometers from the village; (2) a non-elite domestic house midden (i.e., trash heap) just outside the village walls; and (3) a central firepit in a domestic house structure within the village walls. Details regarding the context for each is provided below. Using your flake and debitage analyses from Worksheet 17.1, and the context below, decide which assemblage belongs to which activity area.

Assemblage	Dominate Flake Type (circle up to two)	Dominant Flake Size (circle up to two)	Activity Area (circle one)
A	primary	> 1″	lithic quarry
	secondary	0.25″–1″	house midden
	tertiary	< 0.25″	central house fire
B	primary	> 1″	lithic quarry
	secondary	0.25 ″–1″	house midden
	tertiary	< 0.25″	central house fire
C	primary	> 1″	lithic quarry
	secondary	0.25″–1″	house midden
	tertiary	< 0.25″	central house fire

Archaeological Context

Assemblage A: In addition to the flakes shown, a deer antler tine was recovered (shown), as well as several carbonized fragments of bean, corn, black walnut, and wild grape seeds.

Assemblage B: In addition to the flakes shown, a whole deer antler billet and a broken hammerstone were recovered (shown). No other material culture was recovered.

Assemblage C: In addition to the debitage shown, three broken formal tools (a projectile point, thumbnail scraper, and drill) were recovered (shown), as well as several broken ceramic sherds, a clay pipe fragment, crumbling fire-cracked rock, and faunal remains with cut marks.

For Further Exploration and Application

Your instructor may have you do these questions as part of an in-class discussion or independent reflection.

2. Compare your flake and debitage analyses. Do the results corroborate (i.e., yield the same result) one another? If not, think of some reasons why.

_____

_____

_____

_____

3. For the mass analysis here, you used counts. How might have using *weight* altered the results?

_____

_____

_____

_____

4. Watch "What Makes Us Human" (PBS 2013) from minute 20 to 33. What hypothesis has been purported for the relationship between toolmaking and language development? Are you convinced? What other evidence might make you more likely to accept this hypothesis?

_____

_____

_____

5. Read "Knap Time" in "Children of Prehistory" (Bower 2007: 266). Explain how knapping skill and age might alter lithic assemblages, and therefore archaeologists' interpretations.

_____

_____

_____

_____

References

Bower, Chris. 2007. "Children of Prehistory: Stone Age Kids Left Their Mark on Cave Art and Stone Tools." *Science News* 171 (17): 264–266.

Brandt, Steven, and Kathryn Weedman. 2002. "Woman the Toolmaker." *Archaeology*, September/October.

CMNH (Cleveland Museum of Natural History). 2011. "Flintknapping Demonstration." Video, 8:15. Uploaded 4 January. https://www.youtube.com/watch?v=f2CcHYuOEsE.

Odell, George. 2006. *Lithic Analysis: Manuals in Archaeological Method, Theory, and Technique.* New York: Springer.

PBS. 2012. "What Makes Us Human?" *NOVA ScienceNow*, season 6, episode 1. Aired 10 October. https://www.youtube.com/watch?v=KSlS5MzRmBk. Accessed 5 June 2019.

CHAPTER 18

Pots and People
Ceramic Analysis

Ceramics Analysis

One of the most prolific artifacts found on archaeological sites is the pottery sherd. Pottery is a ceramic item made of fired clay. Clay can be shaped into figurines, but also vessels of all shapes and sizes, and then fired at high temperatures to turn them into ceramics. A broken piece of pottery is referred to as a *sherd* (Figure 18.1). Pottery sherds are so abundant at archaeological sites because ceramics are very durable and can last for thousands of years, whether buried in the ground or lying on the surface. Pottery sherds are very important to archaeologists in their study of past cultures because they can give archaeologists a plethora of information. Through extensive research, archaeologists have learned that pottery styles are distinctive to particular groups of people and that the styles change over time (see chapters 13, 14). This knowledge helps archaeologists figure out how old a site is, which group of people lived there, and what interaction—such as trade—they might have had with other people. Archaeologists also study vessel shapes and sizes to infer whether the pots were used for cooking, serving, or food storage. For example, a small-necked vessel probably stored liquids or very small (rather than large) seeds. Large open vessels such as bowls probably weren't used for storage, since they would be difficult to seal from moisture, rodents, and insects.

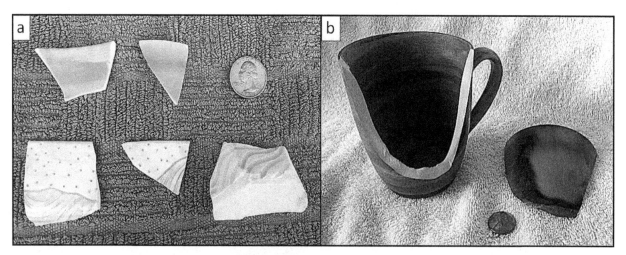

Figure 18.1. Body sherds (lower right) and rim sherds (a), and rim sherd and the cup from which it originated (b).

Determining Vessel Size

Because ancient pots are usually found broken into hundreds of sherds, it is tedious—and sometimes impossible—to refit and glue them back together. An alternative way to figure out how large a pot was is to calculate its original circumference. Rim sherds are used to do this because they often indicate how large the vessel opening was. For example, Figure 18.1b shows a cup with a missing piece and the corresponding sherd. If only the rim sherd had been recovered, we would have been able to determine the circumference of the vessel and presumed, based on the diameter, it was a cup and functioned as a container for serving beverages. We may not, however, have known it also had a handle unless other sherds were recovered as well.

Archaeologists use a *rim diameter chart* to reconstruct vessel circumference (Figure 18.4). To use the rim diameter chart, move the rim part of the sherd along the lines of the chart until the curve of the rim fits along one of the lines as shown in Figure 18.2. As you follow along the line, you will see what the diameter of the pot would have been when it was complete. You will want to make sure the rim is flush against the paper, not "tipped" too far forward or back. Note that sometimes it is easier to place the rim sherd adjacent to the x-axis rather than in the middle of the chart as shown. If you are using the paper cutouts, rather than real sherds, this latter method will be easier, since they are only two-dimensional.

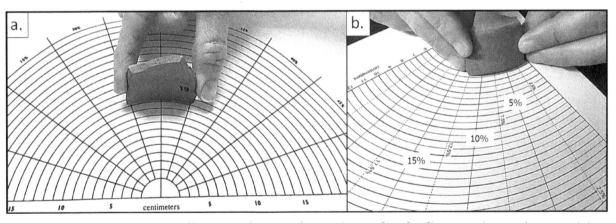

Figure 18.2. Using a rim diameter chart to determine a sherd's diameter in centimeters (a) and the proportion of original vessel (b).

Determining Vessel Type and Function

Archaeologists also measure the thickness of sherds. The thickness of a vessel, like the rim diameter, gives another clue about the function of the vessel. More robust (thicker-walled) vessels were often used for cooking and storage. Relative thickness of serving vessels may also indicate social status, with more gracile (i.e., thin-walled) vessels indicative of higher status, as they require a high level of specialization to create. You can often sort sherds into the following types and infer their functions:

- cup » drinking liquids
- dish/plate/platter » eating and/or serving food

- bowl » eating food
- pot » cooking, storing, and/or serving food
- jar » storing food
- vase » decoration/display

Determining the size of these vessels and identifying the shape can tell archaeologists a lot about how people lived. Noting the distribution of cooking versus serving versus storage vessels gives us an idea about the functions of the rooms or structures in which they were found. Knowing the size of pots and jars and calculating the storage capacity of these vessels gives insight as to how much food people could store. This knowledge gives us a method to estimate the population of the settlement. Additionally, vessels with small-necked openings probably were used to store liquids or small seeds. Vessels with wide openings probably were not used for storage, as they would be hard to seal and would spill easily.

The Activity

This activity will let you to experience the methods archaeologists use to analyze pottery sherds. You will measure the rim (or base) diameter and the thickness of each sherd in the assemblage you are given (or the cutouts in Figure 18.3 if your teacher is opting for the short version). If you are doing the long version, you will also be measuring sherd thickness and making inferences about the use of the vessels in your assemblage. Use the ruler in Figure 18.4 (rim diameter chart) to obtain your measurements, which will be in centimeters.

Suggestions for Further Exploration and Application

- **"The Beer Archaeologist: How Alcohol Shaped Civilization" (Ratner 2017).** This short article by Paul Ratner explains how chemical residues from ceramic wine glasses and fermentation vessels have helped reconstruct not only how old alcohol is but also the exact recipe of the barley beers made in ancient Mesopotamia and rice beers in ancient China. It includes two embedded videos interviewing Pat McGovern (biomolecular archaeologist at the University of Pennsylvania) and Sam Catagione (founder and president of Dogfish Head Craft Brewery).
- **"Pottery Traditions of India: Kutch" (Perryman 2010)** (*6:45 minutes*). This nice video documents traditional pottery production in western Gujarat, India. Topics covered include clay acquisition, preparation, and transport; throwing the pot on a hand-controlled pottery wheel; firing in a kiln; and the gendered division of labor.
- **"What Did They Eat?" (Reber 1999).** In this succinct article, Eleanora Reber shows how lipids and fatty acids from foods cooked in ceramic pots can be analyzed via gas chromatography to determine prehistoric diets.

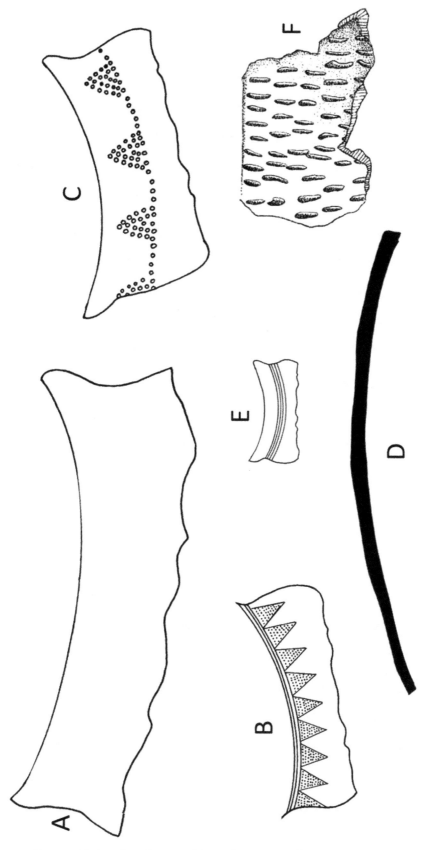

Figure 18.3. Sherd assemblage for use with Worksheet 18.1.

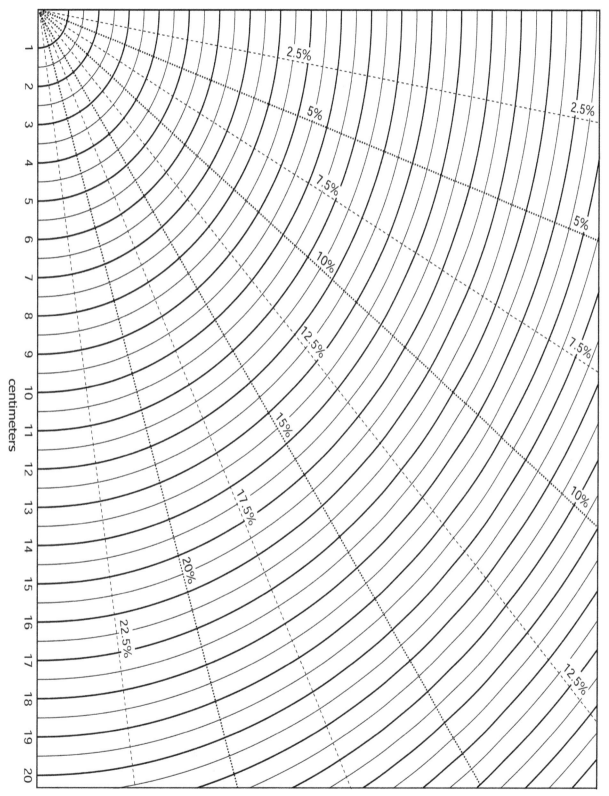

Figure 18.4. Rim chart (in centimeters) for measuring rim sherd diameter.
Note: Proportions refer to the percent of total vessel size sherd represents.

Worksheet 18.1

Record the rim diameter, thickness (for real sherds only), and type of vessel for each sherd in your assemblage (if using Figure 18.3, skip G–I). Then answer questions 1 and 2 below.

Sherd Letter	Rim Diameter (if applicable)	Sherd Thickness (in mm)	Vessel Type/Function
A			
B			
C			
D			
E			
F			
G			
H			
I			

1. Were there any sherds for which you could not record diameter? If so, why?

_____

_____

2. For the sherds you could determine the sizes for, note that this may only be the diameter size of the vessel *opening*. Below, sketch a pot in which the vessel opening might not accurately reflect the true size/shape of the vessel itself.

If you are using a real sherd assemblage, record the number of each type of sherd and divide by the total to give a percent of total for each vessel type. Then answer questions 3 and 4 below.

Type	Functional Typology	
	N (number) =	%
Totals:		
Unknown:		

3. What types of vessels do your sherds represent? What are the perceived functions of these vessels? On what did you base your conclusions?

_____

_____

_____

_____

_____

4. What is the significance of having outflaring rims versus those that curve in?

_____

_____

_____

_____

_____

Worksheet 18.2

For Further Exploration and Application

Your instructor may have you do these questions as part of an in-class discussion or independent reflection. Use the back of this worksheet if you need more space.

1. Compare the last two columns in your table on the front of Worksheet 18.1. (If you used the paper cutouts, record the following data: A, 8mm; B, 4mm; C, 4.5mm; D, 3mm; E, 3mm; and F, 7mm.) Is there a relationship between sherd thickness and vessel function? If so, what might this reflect?

_____

_____

_____

2. Look at your table on the back of Worksheet 18.1. Consider what it means if/when there are variations in the quantities of different types of vessels in different contexts. What does it mean to have a lot more serving vessels (platters)? Does this mean the inhabitants at this location entertained a lot? What does it mean to have many thick-walled vessels with wide openings? Does this represent a storage area?

_____

_____

_____

3. Read "What Did They Eat?" (Reber 1999) and/or "The Beer Archaeologist" (Ratner 2017). How can ceramics help us understand past diet and "paleo recipes?"

_____

_____

_____

4. Watch the six-minute video "Pottery Traditions of India: Kutch" (Perryman 2010). How could you tell the difference between sherds resulting from domestic (i.e., cooking) use and sherds used to cover pots during the firing process? (*Hint: think about their* context.)

_____

_____

_____

References

CBA (Council for British Archaeology). 2019. *Fabulous Finds: YAC Factsheet—Looking and Observing Games*. Accessed 29 March. http://www.yac-uk.org/userfiles/file/1429014915_Artefact_investigation.pdf. Accessed 5 June 2019.

Perryman, Jane. 2010. "Pottery Traditions of India: Kutch." Video, 6:45. Uploaded 27 October. https://www.youtube.com/watch?v=3_9A73UXETQ&feature=related. Accessed 5 June 2019.

Ratner, Paul. 2017. "The Beer Archaeologist: How Alcohol Shaped Our Civilization." *Big Think*, 17 August. https://bigthink.com/paul-ratner/how-alcohol-shaped-our-civilization-according-to-a-beer-archaeologist. Accessed 5 June 2019.

Reber, Eleanora. 1999. "What Did They Eat?" *Anthropology Newsletter* 40 (2). Reprinted in *Annual Editions: Archaeology*, 9th ed., chap. 23. New York: McGraw Hill.

CHAPTER 19

What's for Dinner?

Faunal Analysis

Zooarchaeology

Zooarchaeology is the analysis of animal bones found at archaeological sites. The study of animal, or *faunal*, remains enables researchers to better understand human and animal interactions in the past, and involves knowledge from biology, ecology, and other disciplines. While it might seem surprising, animal bones can tell us a great deal about how past societies lived. One of the more obvious things archaeologists can learn from bones is human diet and what foods were available to people in the past. Animals bones can also be used as a dating method. For example, if your assemblage includes bones of extinct megafauna (e.g., mammoth) from the Ice Age, you can hypothesize the site was occupied before those animals disappeared. Animal remains can provide insight into human behavior, such as (a) identifying whether people relied on the hunting and gathering of wild foods or on pasturing domesticated species; (b) locating activity areas (e.g., kill site or feasting area), within a site; (c) reconstructing ethic identity, such as a religious taboo against eating cow meat; and (d) differentiating among social status, for example, if certain animals or prime meat cuts were reserved for elite consumption. Faunal analysis consists of three primary tasks: (1) identifying species, (2) quantifying remains, and (3) assessing their context (Reitz 2008).

Identifying Species

Knowing the local ecology of an archaeological site gives researchers a place to start in identifying faunal remains. If, for example, the site is located in the Southwestern United States, it will not contain bones of arctic foxes or Saharan giraffes! It may, however, contain coyote, elk, turkey, and different varieties of deer and rabbit. It is important to remember the most abundant remains that will likely be found are generally the sturdier large, dense bones—what zooarchaeologists call macrofauna. Fragile bones such as fish bones often decay or get crushed beyond recognition because of a variety of cultural and natural transformations (see chapter 6). Thus, what is found at a site is only a fraction of what was originally present and may be biased toward the larger, better preserved animals. Zooarchaeologists use reference charts and comparative collections to help them identify bones to the species level, as well as the skeletal element each bone represents (e.g., skull, femur, rib, etc.). An example reference chart is shown in Figure 19.1. Other important data to collect include whether the bone belongs to the right or left side of the body, the portion of the bone present (complete, distal end, etc.), whether cut marks are present, and whether bone epiphyses[1] are fused (which reflect the age of an animal at death).

Quantifying Remains

To analyze their data, zooarchaeologists must first quantify it. The first step in doing this is to add up the *number of identified specimens* (NISP) for each bone type of each species. For example, in an assemblage of bowhead whale bones, one might find seven right ribs (NISP = 7) and four left scapulae (NISP = 4). Once these numbers are tallied, the *minimum number of individuals* (MNI) can be calculated. The MNI is the least number of individuals needed to account for all the identified bone of that taxon. The highest MNI value obtained is considered the minimum number of individuals from that taxon in that context (Reitz and Wing 2008). In the example in Table 19.1, 7 right ribs and 4 left scapulae (i.e., collarbone) were found. You might be tempted to say there are therefore 11 whales represented, but consider the following: a whale can have only 1 left scapula, so we know there must be a least 4 whales. And even though there are 7 right ribs, since a whale can have 13 ribs per side, we no idea if these 7 ribs are all from the same whale or 7 different whales. Thus, we say the minimum number of individuals, or the MNI, is 4, although we know it could quite possibly be more. Thus, the NISP by itself can be misleading, which is why zooarchaeologists also calculate MNI.

Table 19.1 NISP and MNI for Bowhead Whales.

Skeletal Element	# of elements in one animal	NISP	MNI
Right rib	13	7	1
Left scapula	1	4	4

Archaeological Context

Archaeologists frequently want to determine what activities occurred at a site, such as butchering, cooking, and feasting (such as during ceremonies) and where those activities occurred. Another thing zooarchaeologists do is determine how animal remains make it to a site. They figure this out by looking at the context of the bones—in other words, the association, provenience, and matrix (as discussed in chapter 7). They also look at modification to the bones, either natural or cultural. Evidence of cultural behavior includes modifications such as cut marks, which are made during the butchering and preparation of a carcass, and burning. Even the degree of burning can be ascertained: dark brown colors indicate low temperature burning, while white and bluish colors indicate much higher temperatures. Natural modifications include the tooth marks of gnawing rodents or scavenging dogs. Of course, natural and cultural modifications are not mutually exclusive. For example, humans might cut meat from the bones themselves and then throw the bones to their dogs. They may scoop these up later to be burned down and/or disposed of in the trash. This combination of activities would leave both cut marks and gnaw marks on the bones, as well as evidence of burning.

The Activity

This activity is designed for you to practice elements of faunal analysis. The animals found locally include elk, cottontail rabbits, and domestic turkeys. First, you will cut out the bones from each assemblage (A, B, and C) and determine the NISP and MNI. Then, you will examine the marks/modifications on the bones to make inferences cultural and natural formation processes. Finally, you will combine this information with an examination of the archaeological context for each assemblage to make inferences about site function, activity areas, and seasonality.

Suggestions for Exploration and Application

- **"Beyond the Temples, Ancient Animal Bones Reveal the Lives of the Mayan Working Class" (Livingston 2015).** Most of what archaeologists know about Mayan civilization relates to kings, queens, and their elaborate temples. To understand what life was like for the "99 percent," one researcher turned to ancient animal bones stored at the Florida Museum of Natural History.
- **"Bunnies Helped a Great Civilization in Ancient Mexico Thrive" (Gearin 2016).** This fascinating study by Conor Gearin examines the role cottontail and jackrabbit management played in the diet and life of residents at the huge pre-Hispanic city of Teotihuacan.

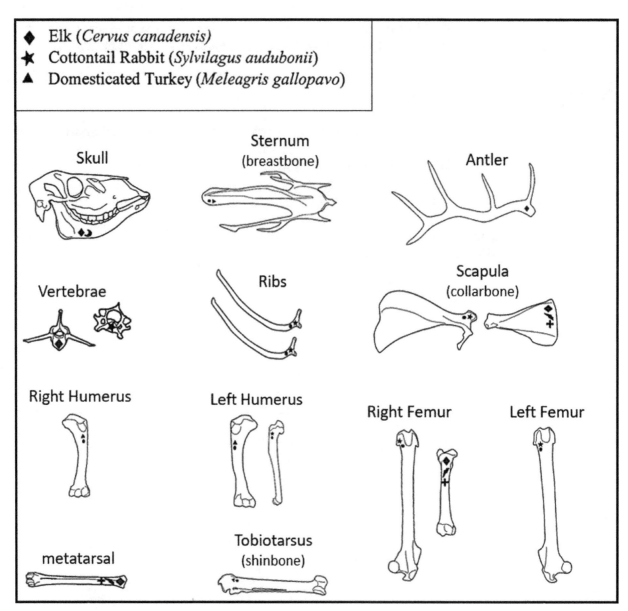

Figure 19.1. Skeletal element reference chart (not to scale).

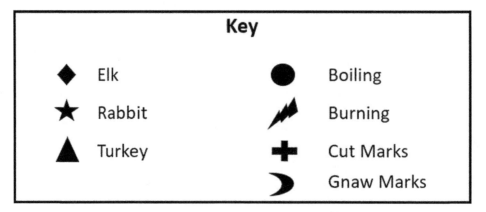

Figure 19.2. Key to symbols for Figure 19.1.

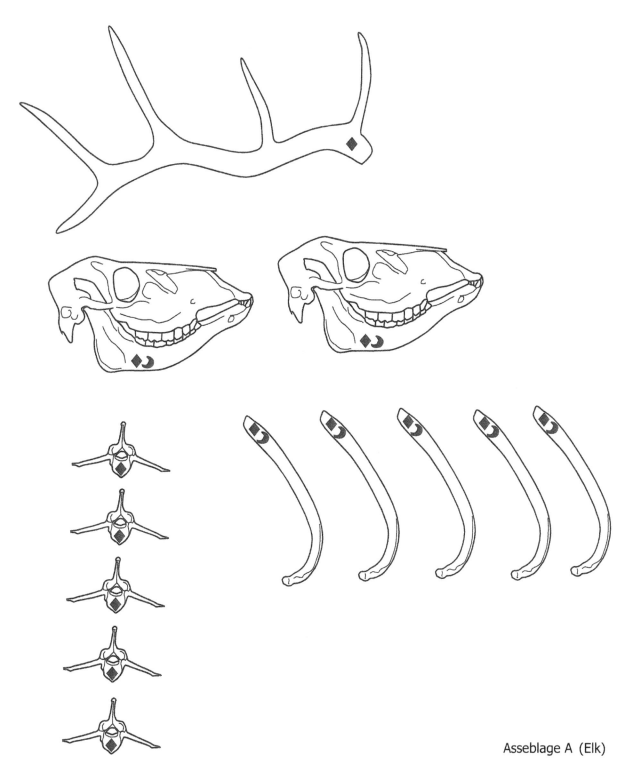

Asseblage A (Elk)

Figure 19.3. Cutouts for Faunal Assemblage A.

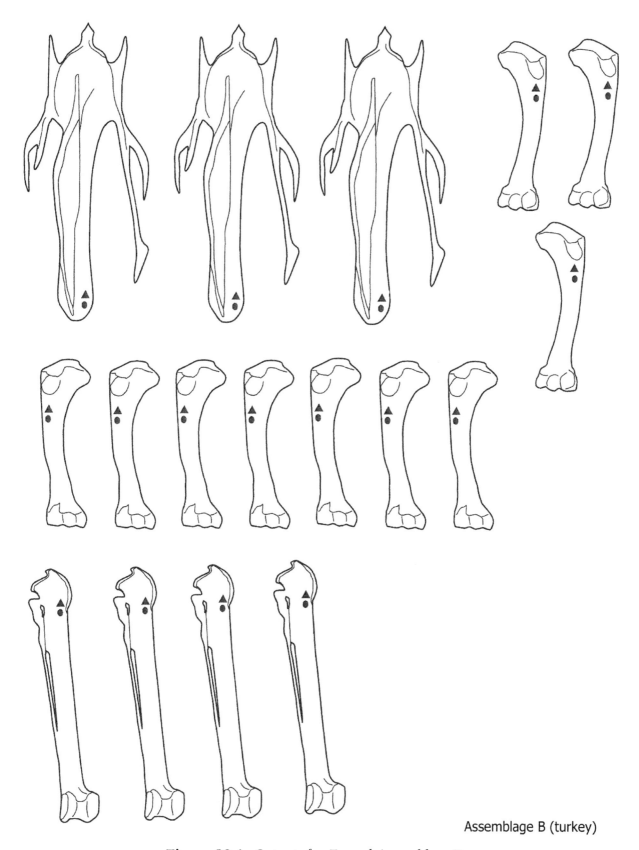

Assemblage B (turkey)

Figure 19.4. Cutouts for Faunal Assemblage B.

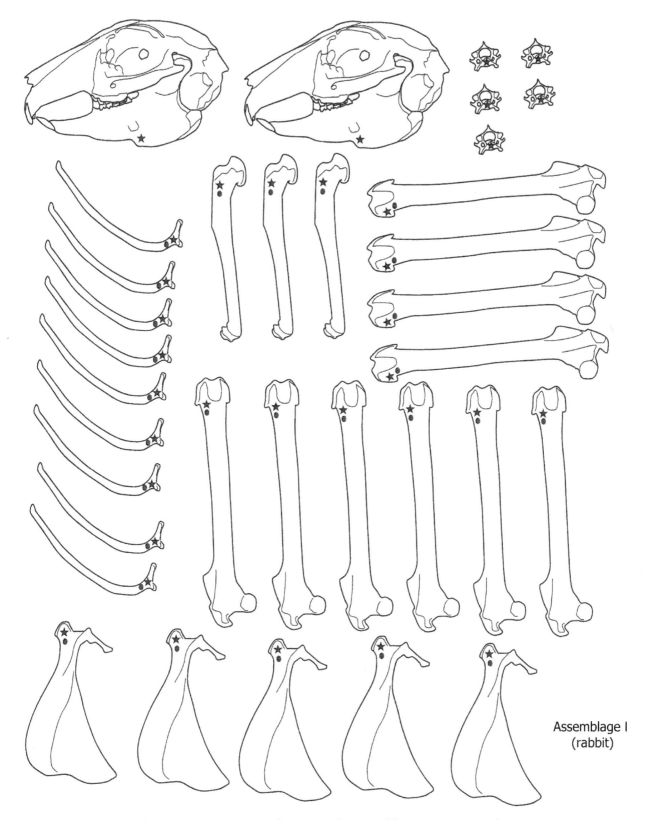

Figure 19.5. Cutouts for Faunal Assemblage B continued.

Assemblage I
(rabbit)

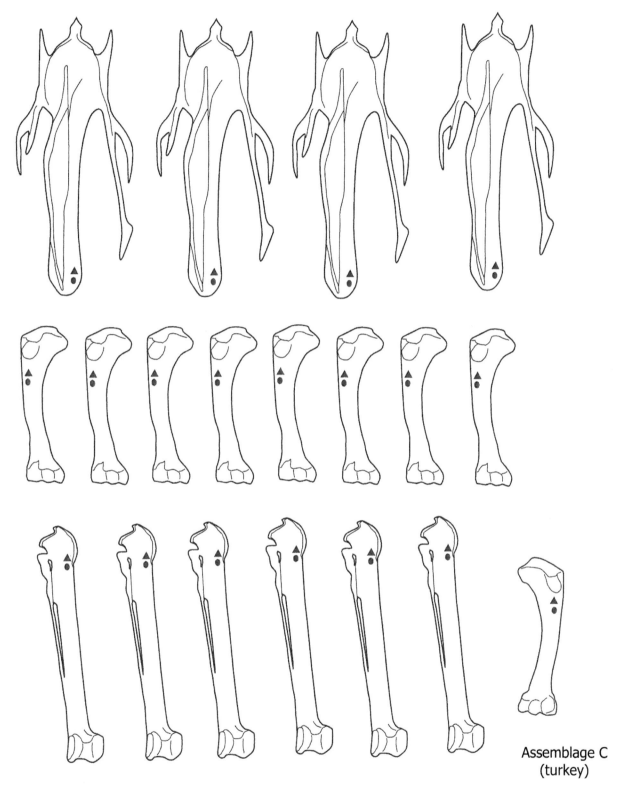

Figure 19.6. Cutouts for Faunal Assemblage C.

Assemblage C
(turkey)

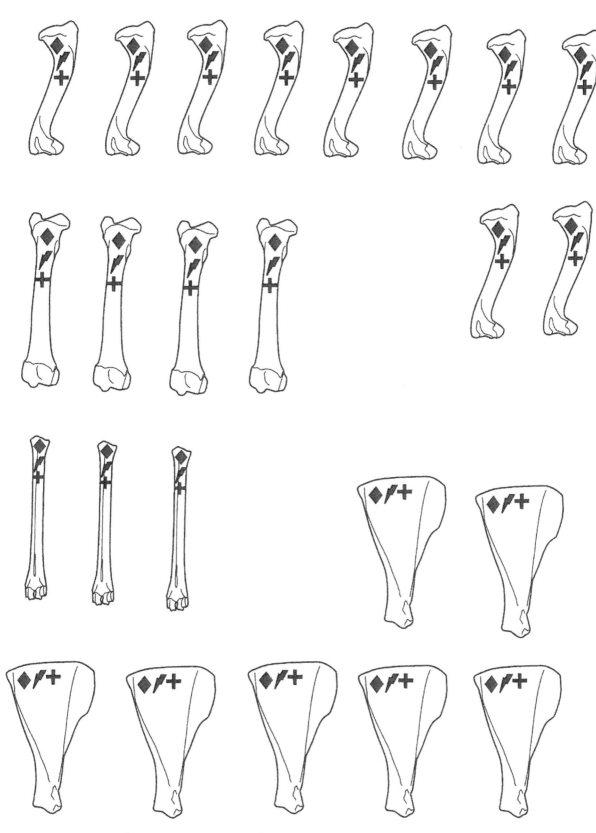

Figure 19.7. Cutouts for Faunal Assemblage C continued.

Worksheet 19.1

1. Cut out each bone (you can just cut around it to save time) from each assemblage provided in Figures 19.3–19.7. You may want to write the assemblage letter from which the bone originated in case the assemblages get mixed together during the activity.

2. Calculate the NISP and MNI and complete the table below. Use Figures 19.1 (the reference chart) and 19.2 (key) to help you identify skeletal elements. If you are unsure how many of a certain skeletal element an animal has (e.g., how many ribs a turkey has), you can Google it or ask your teacher.

Species	Bone Type	NISP	MNI *(for entire assemblage)*
Assemblage A			
Elk *(Cervus canadensis)*	Antler		
	Skull		
	Rib		
	Lumbar vertebra		
Assemblage B			
Cottontail rabbit *(Sylvilagus audubonii)*	Skull		
	Cervical vertebra		
	Left scapula		
	Left humerus		
	Rib		
	Right femur		
	Left femur		
Domestic turkey *(Meleagris gallopavo)*	Sternum		
	Right humerus		
	Left humerus		
	Right humerus		
Assemblage C			
Domestic turkey *(Meleagris gallopavo)*	Sternum		
	Right humerus		
	Left humerus		
	Right tobiotarus		
Elk *(Cervus canadensis)*	Right scapula		
	Left humerus		
	Right metatarsal		
	Right femur		

3. Three activity areas are represented by assemblages A, B, and C: (1) a butchering/kill site, (2) a non-elite domestic house midden (i.e., trash heap), and (3) a central plaza where elite feasting occurred. Details regarding the context are provided. Using Figure 19.1 and the context provided below, match the assemblage to the correct activity area.

Assemblage	Species Present (circle all that apply)	Bone Markings (circle all that apply)	Activity Area (circle one)
A	Wild rabbit Domestic turkey Wild elk	Gnaw marks Cut marks Boiling marks Burning	Kill site House midden Central plaza
B	Wild rabbit Domestic turkey Wild elk	Gnaw marks Cut marks Boiling marks Burning	Kill site House midden Central plaza
C	Wild rabbit Domestic turkey Wild elk	Gnaw marks Cut marks Boiling marks Burning	Kill site House midden Central plaza

Assemblage A: The faunal remains comprising this assemblage were found about a mile from the main village, in an area with no domestic structures, mounds, or other evidence of human habitation. A few scattered flint flakes and a chert scaping tool were found associated with the faunal remains. A broken spear point was also found.

Assemblage B: The faunal remains in this assemblage were excavated from a feature adjacent to one of the many small domestic house structures in the village, on the western edge of a large central plaza. Along with the faunal remains, other material culture found in the midden includes undecorated pottery sherds, tertiary flakes of local flint, and a used flint blade. A broken clay figurine fragment was also found.

Assemblage C: The faunal remains comprising this assemblage were recovered from charcoal-rich hearth features, including a large roasting pit (i.e., earth-covered cooking hearth) in the center of the site. Along with the bones, other elements found in the midden include finely decorated pottery sherds, a long knife of nonlocally occurring obsidian, and a few beads of jade, shell and copper.

Worksheet 19.2

For Further Exploration and Application

Your instructor may have you do these questions as part of an in-class discussion or independent reflection.

1. Assemblage A contained large elk antlers. If male elk start growing antlers in the spring and shed in the early winter, what can be said about the seasonality of Assemblage A? Based on this, what hypotheses can you make about other village events in relation to the seasons? What additional data would you use to support your hypothesis?

_____

_____

_____

_____

_____

_____

_____

_____

2. This exercise focused especially on animal bones that were thrown out after the meat attached to them was eaten. This is not the only context in which animal bones are found, however. In what other ways do you think animal bones might have been used in the past?

_____

_____

_____

_____

_____

_____

_____

_____

3. Read "How Bunnies Helped a Great Civilization in Ancient Mexico" (Gearin 2016). How can the chemistry of animal bones and the age of the animal help archaeologists?

_____

_____

_____

_____

_____

_____

_____

_____

_____

4. Read "Beyond the Temples, Ancient Animal Bones Reveal the Lives of the Mayan Working Class" (Livingston 2015). How can archaeologists use faunal remains to understand socioeconomic differences?

_____

_____

_____

_____

_____

_____

_____

_____

_____

_____

Notes

This chapter was contributed by Pascale Meehan, PhD Candidate at the University of Colorado Boulder.

1. Epiphyses are the end parts of long bones. These form separately from the shaft but fuse to it over the course of an individual's life. Knowing if epiphyses are fused, and which ones are fused, can help determine the age of an individual animal at death.

References

Gearin, Conor. 2016. "Bunnies Helped a Great Civilization in Ancient Mexico Thrive." *New Scientist*, 17 August 2016. https://www.newscientist.com/article/2101551-bunnies-helped-a-great-civilisation-in-ancient-mexico-thrive. Accessed 5 June 2019.

Livingston, Stephanie. 2015. "Beyond the Temples, Ancient Animal Bones Reveal the Lives of the Mayan Working Class." *UF News*, 29 October. http://news.ufl.edu/articles/2015/10/beyond-the-temples-ancient-bones-reveal-the-lives-of-the-mayan-working-class.html. Accessed 5 June 2019.

Reitz, Elizabeth J., and Elisabeth S. Wing. 2008. *Zooarchaeology*. Cambridge: Cambridge University Press.

CHAPTER 20

What's for Dinner?
Botanical Analysis

Paleoethnobotany

Paleoethnobotany is the archaeological specialty that studies plant, or *botanical*, remains of the past. By identifying the plant remains present at a site, archaeologists can learn many things, including what people ate (or didn't eat) as part of their diet (i.e., subsistence), the season a site was occupied (e.g., summer or fall), the origins of agriculture and domestication, and the medicinal use of plants. While plant remains are excellent indicators of this information, they do have limited preservation conditions, which should be kept in mind when studying them (Pearsall 2016). Plants preserve best when charred by fire, desiccated (i.e., dried), or waterlogged (i.e., saturated in water). Thus, cooked foods are more likely to preserve at archaeological sites than plants that have not been cooked. Similarly, very arid regions (e.g., deserts or a dry cave) or submerged sites (e.g., a lake or bog) tend to preserve a greater variety of plant types than sites that experience varying degrees of temperature and precipitation. Another factor to keep in mind is that some plant remains are simply hardier than others: a grape, for example, is soft and easily decomposed compared to something with a hard shell, such as a walnut. Grapes do have seeds, of course, but if you look closely at a grape seed, you will see it is tiny and soft—two factors that are not conducive to being preserved over centuries or millennia.

Flotation and Analysis of Plant Remains

Charred plant remains are usually recovered by a process called *flotation* (Figure 20.1a). The soil matrix is slowly added to agitated water. The soil, sand, and other heavy material, known as *heavy fraction* (Figure 20.1b), will sink to the bottom. The less dense organic material such as charred seeds, grains, and charcoal will tend to float to the surface. The material that floats to the top, called *light fraction* (Figure 20.1c), is diverted into a sieve with a mesh of about 1/32 inches (i.e., less than one millimeter). The light fraction is then dried and examined under a low power microscope at 10–20x magnification to make species identification; a collection of modern-day plants remains, called a *comparative collection*, is used to help accurately identify species. Once each species is identified, paleoethnobotanists then quantify the amount of plants from each species. Archaeologists use the following three measures to quantify plant remains for analysis.

Ubiquity: Ubiquity measures frequency of occurrence to quickly identify whether a certain species is present or absent in samples from a site. Generally, ubiquity is calculated as the percentage of samples in which a given plant species appears (though, for this activity, you will simply note presence/absence for each assemblage/strata). For example, if you had 10 samples in

Stratum A, and 8 of those samples had walnut present, then the ubiquity value for walnut would be 80 percent. If you had 10 samples in Stratum C, but only 2 contained walnut, then the ubiquity value would be 20 percent. Ubiquity is easy to calculate and can be very helpful to discern trends in plant use through time. That said, it is best used when comparing plants within one site, rather than across many sites, since different preservation environments (e.g., wet vs. dry) can account for differences in the frequency, and it may be those preservation differences that account for different ubiquity values, not differences in human behavior. Sometimes, as you will do in this activity, simple presence/absence is noted, rather than calculating ubiquity.

Percent frequency: Percent frequency is the percent of one species as a proportion of the total assemblage. So, for example, if a plant assemblage from a particular stratum had 1,000 plant remains, and 700 of them are domestic, wheat seeds, then 70 percent of the assemblage is comprised of wheat. Such a high percentage of domesticated cereals, rather than wild foods, likely indicates a sedentary, agricultural lifestyle, rather than one based on hunting and gathering. Note that rather than standardizing presence/absence values across all samples, percent frequency uses actual count data. For example, if the 1,000 plant remains are the summation of 10 samples, then those 700 wheat grains could be spread out over all 10 samples—in which case ubiquity is 100 percent—or, significantly, they may all come from one sample—in which case ubiquity is only 10 percent. Thus, the two measures are slightly different, and using both can provide a more nuanced interpretation of prehistoric diet.

Diversity: Diversity quantitatively evaluates the "richness" and "evenness" of a sample. Richness is the number of different types (i.e., species) that are represented, while evenness is the abundance of individuals (e.g., seeds, nutshells) within each species. If a sample is both rich and even, it is considered diverse—meaning the sample contains a wide range of plant species and there are many seeds (or nutshells) of each of those species. If, on the other hand, a sample is neither rich nor even, it is considered not diverse; in other words, there are few types represented, and very few individual seeds of each type. You will have an opportunity to work with diversity in the optional "For Further Exploration and Application" section.

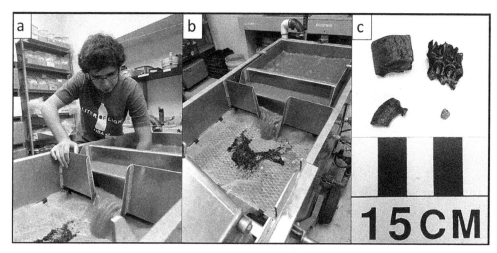

Figure 20.1. Archaeological floatation unit (a); light fraction (b); and photomicrographs (c) of wood charcoal (upper left), charred corn cob (upper right), hackberry seed (lower right), and charred nutshell (lower left).

The Activity

In this activity, you will examine the plant remains in three assemblages—A, B, and C—from a hypothetical cave site in North America. Because the cave is dry, the plants are well preserved. These correspond to Strata A, B, and C respectively, which is shown in Figure 20.2. You will compare the three assemblages (Figures 20.4–20.6) in terms of ubiquity, frequency, and (optionally) diversity to look at changes in human diet through time. A comparative collection (Figure 20.3) is provided to help you identify each species present in the assemblage. Your instructor may ask you to do some of the "For Further Exploration and Application" section as part of classroom discussion or reflective homework.

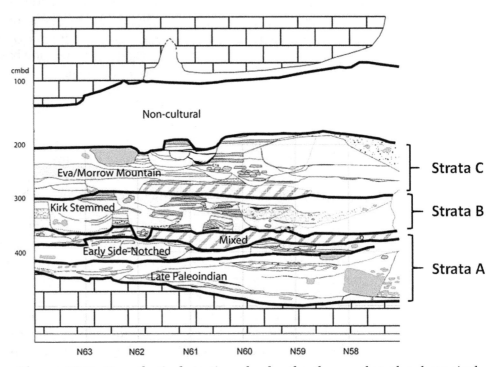

Figure 20.2. Hypothetical stratigraphy for the three paleoethnobotanical samples in this activity.

Suggestions for Further Exploration and Application

- **"Crops of Ancient Iowa" (OSA 2019).** This webpage, from the Iowa Office of the State Archeologist (OSA), goes into detail about many of the plant species used by Native Americans, including their nonfood value, such as medicine. There is also a nice page on how archaeologists differentiate between wild and cultivated seeds.
- **"The Worst Mistake in the History of the Human Race" (Diamond 1978).** Jared Diamond argues that humans' quality of life declines significantly following the "invention" of agriculture. He challenges our etic assumptions that farming is inherently superior to hunting and gathering. Definitely a new idea to chew on . . .

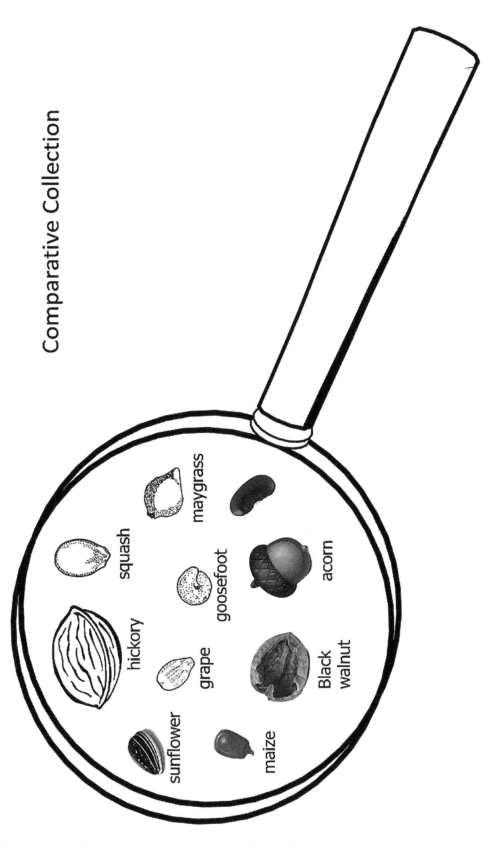

Figure 20.3. Comparative collection (note: goosefoot and maygrass are wild, starchy grasses that were eaten prehistorically in the Eastern Woodlands prior to the domestication of corn).

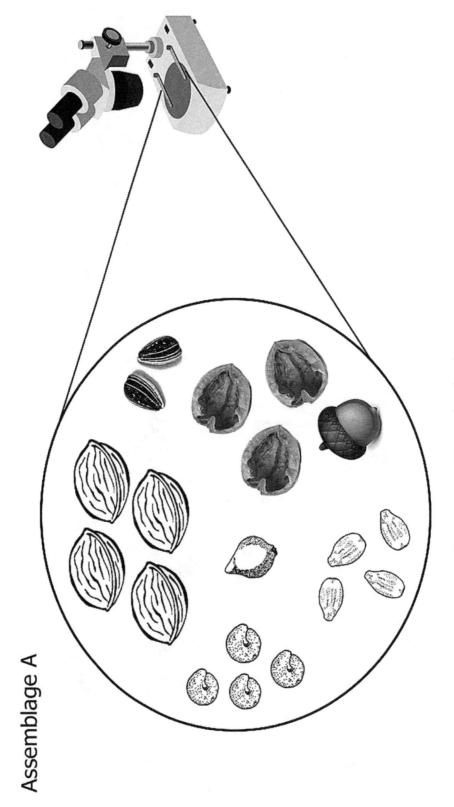

Assemblage A

not to scale; each image = 10x individuals

Figure 20.4. Botanical Assemblage A.

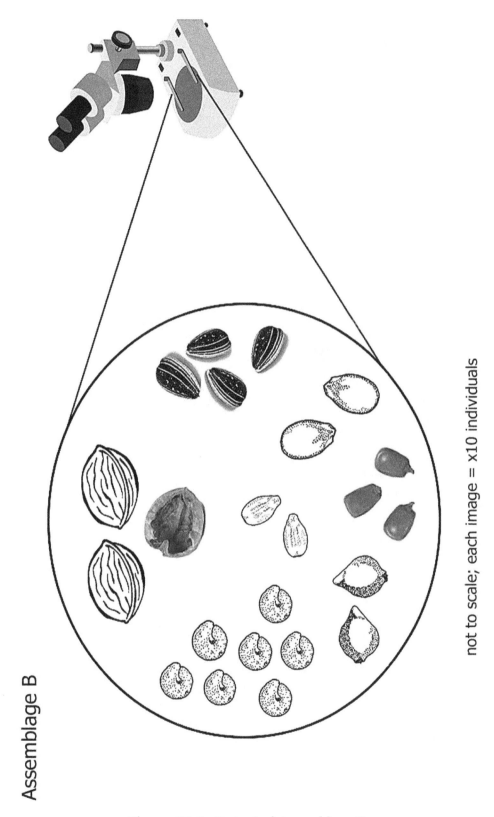

Figure 20.5. Botanical Assemblage B.

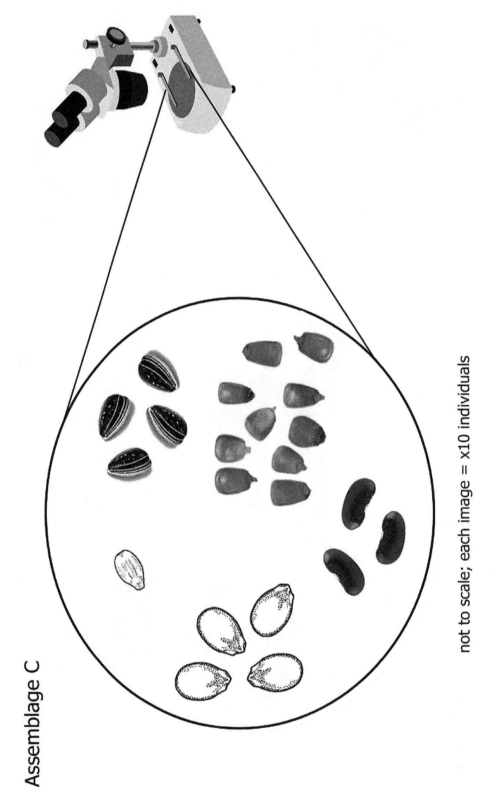

Assemblage C

not to scale; each image = x10 individuals

Figure 20.6. Botanical Assemblage C.

Worksheet 20.1

1. Using the comparative collection (Figure 20.3), identify the plant remains in each assemblage. Then complete the table below. On the left-hand side, note ubiquity for each assemblage by placing an "X" in the box if a taxon is present. On the right-hand side, calculate the percent frequency of each taxon in each assemblage. You will need a calculator to do this part.

Taxon	Ubiquity				Percent Frequency					
	A	B	C		A		B		C	
					n =	%	n =	%	n =	%
Hickory										
Black Walnut										
Acorn										
Grape										
Goosefoot										
Maygrass										
Sunflower										
Corn										
Bean										
Squash										
Totals						100%		100%		100%

1. Using the ubiquity and percent frequency values, describe the general trend in diet through time. Think about changes in mobility as well as diet. Are these changes gradual or sudden?

_____

_____

_____

2. What information do you get from the percent frequencies that is not immediately apparent in the ubiquity values?

_____

_____

_____

3. At first glance, there appears to be a significant increase in the use of corn during Strata C. But why do we need to be careful in making this interpretation? Think about the MNI concept you learned about in chapter 19 (and what a corn cob looks like!).

_____

_____

_____

4. Archaeologists can also determine when an archaeological site was occupied prehistorically by looking at the season in which various plant species ripen. Using the table below, determine when this site was occupied for time periods A, B, and C. Circle all that apply.

	May	June	July	Aug	Sept	Oct	Nov	Dec	Jan	Feb	Mar	Apr
Hickory					X	X	X					
Walnut						X	X					
Acorn					X	X	X	X				
Grape			X	X	X	X						
Goosefoot		X	X	X								
Maygrass	X	X										X
Sunflower			X	X	X	X						
Corn			X	X	X							
Bean				X	X							
Squash				X	X	X						

Strata A: SPRING   SUMMER   FALL   WINTER
Strata B: SPRING   SUMMER   FALL   WINTER
Strata C: SPRING   SUMMER   FALL   WINTER

Why might we need to be careful with this information? What natural or cultural processes might make a site appear to be shorter or longer lived than it actually was?

_____

_____

_____

5. Go to the OSA webpage "Crops of Ancient Iowa." Read about sunflower seeds and gourds . . . why do we need to be careful about assuming that all plants found at a site were consumed?

_____

_____

_____

Worksheet 20.2

For Further Exploration and Application

Your instructor may have you do these questions as part of an in-class discussion or independent reflection.

1. Using your table on the front of Worksheet 20.1, complete the table below to calculate the diversity index for Assemblages A and C. An example of how to calculate diversity can be found in Worksheet 20.3.

Species	Stratum A			Stratum C		
	n	**% N**	**n-1**	**n**	**% N**	**n-1**
Hickory						
Walnut						
Acorn						
Grape						
Goosefoot						
Maygrass						
Sunflower						
Corn						
Beans						
Squash						
Total (N)		100%			100%	

2. Using the equation below and the instructions on Worksheet 20.3, calculate the Diversity index (D) for Assemblages A and C. Show your work on the back of this page. Is this relatively high or low?

$$D = \frac{\Sigma \, n(n-1)}{N(N-1)}$$

Assemblage A: D = _____

Assemblage C: D = _____

3. During what time period (i.e., what strata) was diet the most diverse? How does the shift from gathering wild foods to farming domesticated grains have on diet diversity?

_____

_____

_____

4. Go to "Crops of Ancient Iowa" (OSA 2019). Read about cultivation and domestication . . . how can we tell if a seed is wild or domesticated?

_____

_____

_____

_____

5. Read "The Worst Mistake in the History of the Human Race" by Jared Diamond (1978). What are some of the (unexpected) downsides to adopting an agricultural diet?

_____

_____

_____

_____

Extra Work Space for #1:

Worksheet 20.3

You will use *Simpson's Diversity Index* to determine how diverse your plant assemblage is. The indices range from 0 to 1, with 0 representing the highest diversity and 1 representing no diversity. In other words, *the smaller D is, the greater the diversity.*

Example

Species	n	% N	n-1
Rat	9	20	8
Mouse	4	9	3
Shrew *(common or water)*	2	4	1
Vole	31	67	30
Mole	0	0	−1
Other *(e.g., bird)*	0	0	−1
Total (N)	46	100%	0

$$D = \frac{\Sigma \, n(n-1)}{N(N-1)}$$

Note: Σ means to sum, or add together.

$$D = \frac{9(8) + 2(1) + 31(30) + 0(-1) + 0(-1)}{46(46-1)}$$

$$D = \frac{72 + 12 + 2 + 930 + 0 + 0}{46(45)}$$

$$D = \frac{1016}{2070}$$

D = 0.49. This result indicates moderate diversity. This sample is fairly *rich*, in that several taxa are represented, but it is not very *even* since nearly all the individuals were of one species, rather than even distributed across all the species.

References

Diamond, Jared. 1978. "The Worst Mistake in the History of the Human Race." *Discover Magazine* 8 (5): 64–66. http://discovermagazine.com/1987/may/02-the-worst-mistake-in-the-history-of-the-human-race. Accessed 5 June 2019.

OSA (Office of the State Archaeologist). 2019. "Crops of Ancient Iowa." https://archaeology.uiowa.edu/crops-ancient-iowa. Accessed 29 March 2019.

Pearsall, Deborah M. 2016. *Paleoethnobotany: A Handbook of Procedures*. New York: Routledge.

CHAPTER 21

"Bone"-afide Archaeology?
Mortuary Analysis

Mortuary Analysis

Mortuary means related to the burial of the dead. Archaeologists can learn a great deal about past people's behavior and religious belief systems from the way they bury their dead. To do this, we analyze the material evidence of the rituals surrounding death and burial. The material evidence of mortuary contexts differs from the material culture archaeologists usually study in a key way: it was deliberately placed there in a manner that held meanings for the people who put it there, rather than being discarded or lost, as is often the case at archaeological sites. One of the fundamental ideas behind mortuary analysis is that people's individual and group identities, and their roles and positions in society, will be expressed or reflected in the rituals of their death and burial. These rituals include (1) treatment and positioning of the body, (2) objects buried with the body (called *grave goods*), (3) location of the grave (e.g., under a house floor on in a cemetery), and (4) aboveground elements such as monuments, tombs, and grave markers.

Ritual Activity

Human burials are always the product of ritual. How a people buried their dead tells us most directly about mortuary rituals and customs. These rituals and customs include:

- the treatment of the dead: should the dead be buried naked or dressed? Facing north or south? Lying on their backs (extended) or in the fetal position (flexed)?
- the choice of offerings appropriate to accompany the dead (grave goods)

The choice of grave goods can tell us which objects a society considered valuable. Or, grave goods may reflect a person's gender and/or occupation, with the individual buried with the objects they used most during life. A fisherman might be buried with hooks and nets, a hunter with a favorite spear, or a child with a special toy. For example, at the Peruvian site of Paloma, a gourd was found next to the skeleton of an infant; inside the gourd were tiny shells and cactus spines, indicating it was probably a baby rattle (Wilford 1981). The choice of grave goods can also tell us which items or materials an ancient people treated as ritual objects, important in making symbolic interpretations about the deceased to those still living. At the Archaic hunter-gatherer site of Dust Cave, dog burials were excavated in association with human burials. Although neither canine nor human had grave goods, the dogs were discovered to have arthritis, which Renee Walker says indicates the dogs were used as pack animals to help carry heavy loads (Walker et al.

2005). If so, then the burial of the two together may reflect a special relationship between hunter and dog, or that they died together in a hunting accident.

Social Organization

How an individual is treated in death can also express something about the individual's place in society, such as wealth (poor vs. rich) or social status (commoner vs. elite). In some societies (e.g., Aborigines), there are few—in any—wealth differences among families because equality is highly valued by them. In contrast, hierarchical societies (e.g., Egypt) have privileged "high-status" families that are better off than other families (they have more money, nicer things, more power). Archaeologists know that many societies carry over these wealth and status differences during life into the treatment of the dead. The dead from a wealthy, greatly respected, or high-status family is likely to receive a more elaborate burial and to be accompanied in death by more (or more valuable) grave goods than an individual from a poor or low status family. *But be careful!* Elaborate treatment in death may also reflect special circumstances of death, instead of great wealth or high status. An individual who died tragically or heroically may have a more elaborate burial than other individuals who died in more routine ways (e.g., the elaborate funerals for the heroic emergency responders after the historic 9/11 terrorist attacks on the World Trade Center). One or two elaborate graves are not necessarily convincing evidence that some members in a community were of higher social status than the others.

The Activity

This exercise is adapted from the archaeologist Jeffrey Quilter's (1989) book *Life and Death at Paloma: Society and Mortuary Practices in a Preceramic Peruvian Village.* We have changed some characteristics from the original for the purposes of this activity, but the backdrop remains unchanged. Paloma (meaning "dove" in Spanish) is a preceramic, Late Archaic village located near Lima, Peru, which dates to about 5700–2800 BCE, predating the Inca Empire by thousands of years. It is known that the site was a sedentary fishing village and that the residents hunted and ate shark, as well as many kinds of fish and shellfish. Because of the region's arid climate, artifacts, foods, and even human remains are remarkably well preserved. Archaeologists have found willow roof poles and woven grasses and cane that covered the inhabitants' dugout houses. In a depression in the floor of one house were the remains of a fish dinner, and next to it, in another depression, were bone fish hooks and 50 feet of cord fishing line. Clamshells worn from digging, stone projectile points, fishnets, and coarse textiles were also uncovered, but no ceramics (hence why we call it a "preceramic" site; gourds likely served as containers).

Archaeologists have excavated more than 220 skeletons from 56 houses, including infants, miscarried fetuses, and whole families. A sample of 12 of these burials are reproduced here (Figures 21.1–21.4). The burials, usually placed in graves only two feet deep, were interred around the inside walls of a house or sometimes outside the houses. Fortunately, the burials experienced little to no disturbance over the years, making it an ideal location for mortuary analyses. *Tip:* You will find in helpful to cut out the individual burials so that you can easily group them (e.g., by sex or burial position). This will allow you to easily move burials into groups and help you visualize some of the important mortuary trends.

Suggestions for Further Exploration and Application

- **"The Great Inca Rebellion" (PBS 2007).** This probing story of archeological discovery begins in a cemetery crammed with skeletons that offer tantalizing clues about a fierce sixteenth-century battle between warriors of the collapsing Inca Empire and Spanish invaders. Now, the long-accepted account of a swift Spanish conquest of the Inca—achieved with guns, steel, and horses—is being replaced by a more complete story based on surprising new evidence, including what may be the first gunshot wound in the Americas.
- **"With Climate Swing, a Culture Bloomed in the Americas" (Joyce 2008).** This *All Things Considered* podcast episode interviews archaeologists working at the preceramic Peruvian region of Norte Chico and discusses the effect climate change—specifically the arrival of El Niño—altered the fishing lifestyle of preceramic villagers in coastal South America.

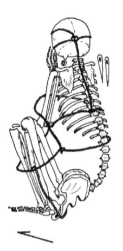

← Burial 10
Age: 34
Sex: Female
Location: Above a house floor
Grave Goods: Two textile tools next to right shoulder, a bead in the neck area, a (camelid?) fur skin, wrapping of straw, and a junco mat were all tied over the body with decorative rope tied to form a square. A necklace of barnacle shells, beads and another of unspecified shell beads with one stone bead. Red coloring noted on soil near the skull.

Burial 54 →
Age: Fetus
Sex: Indeterminate
Location: Under a house floor
Grave Goods: Burial had a covering of straw and a straw pit lining.

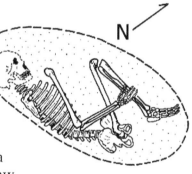

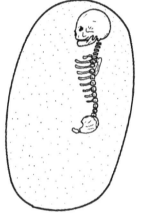

Burial 87
Age: 16
Sex: Female
Location: Unknown
Grave Goods: Straw pit lining only.

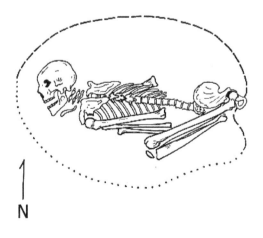

← Burial 110
Age: 20
Sex: Female
Location: In a hearth/trash dump
Grave Goods: Small piece of cordage over the neck area, another underneath the pelvis, strands of junco and a wad of the same material was near the inside of the right thigh. Gourd fragments at the base of the left shoulder. A small cap-like piece of fine junco textile was on the back of the skull, probably held in place by a small string. The grave was not lined, and the neck appeared to be broken at the base of the cervical vertebra. The left arm was bent with the hand in front of the chest and the fingers were in a gripping position.

Figure 21.1 Burial descriptions for burials 10, 54, 87, and 110.
Courtesy Jeffrey Quilter from original drawings by Bernardino Ojeda.

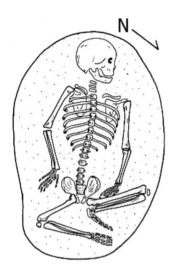

← Burial 115
Age: 2 mo.
Sex: Female?
Location: Under a house floor
Grave Goods: Feathers and wool (?) on skull, a thin string bound the skeleton and the burial was in a twined cradle or carrying strap. The pit was lined with a layer of junco and there was a large amount of roofing material and straw found above the burial, suggesting that the house had been destroyed, perhaps deliberately.

Burial 138 →
Age: 2
Sex: Female?
Location: Over a house floor
Grave Goods:
Fine looped material on the skull, braided cordage around the shoulders, ribs, and below the pelvis. Three

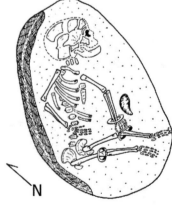

stone pendants, barnacle shell beads, and crab claws in the neck area appear to have been part of a necklace. There may have been an animal skin on the skeleton with fine textile wrapping it. There was also straw and a junco pit lining.

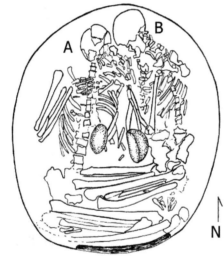

Burial 142 A, B →
Age: A 21; B 47
Sex: Male
Location: Not associated with house
Grave Goods: A hardwood stick was found in the southern end of the grave. A split mano or two manos were found on top of the central part of the burials. 142A had ropes associated and held a flat but sharp-edged rock in the right hand near the chest. 142B had fragments of two twined textiles and some twisted rope with knots, as well as what appeared to be wool on top of the skull. A calcite crystal was found near the feat of 142A in matting and cactus fruits were on top of the mat near his right shoulder. A small, circular basin-shaped pit was found in the southeast side of the burial which was filled with straw and midden and was about 20 cm in diameter and 30 cm deep.

Burial 152 →
Age: 2 mo.
Sex: Female?
Location: Under a house floor
Grave Goods: A mussel shell offering near the lower left arm, a bracelet on the left wrists, and two knee bands of cordage. Junco matting at edge of grave. The skeleton appeared to rest on a cradlelike object consisting of mat and wool, and there was blue powder on the skull.

Figure 21.2. Burial descriptions for burials 115, 138, 142, and 152. Courtesy Jeffrey Quilter from original drawings by Bernardino Ojeda.

Burial 159 →
Age: 17
Sex: Male
Location: Not associated with house
Grave Goods: An elaborate cane structure covered the grave. The grid-like framework was tied with junco cord. A=cord knots; B=rocks on cane poles; C=junco mat; D=mano; E=straw border; F=cane poles with ends in ground; G=bunch of straw; H=camelid (?) wool; I=mussel shell offering with

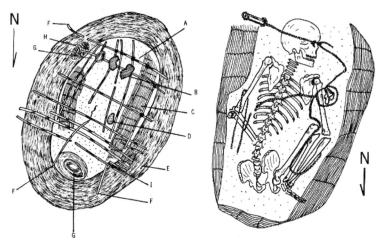

wool and a roll of junco. Gourd bowl found in upper fill. Large feathers, hair, and a bead strung on a quill were found in side of the pit. The skull was just south of B, a sea mammal bone was entangled in rope on the upper right arm and a wedge-shaped rock was under the left elbow. The entire left leg was missing and there are cut marks on the pelvis. This individual appears to have been the victim of a shark attack.

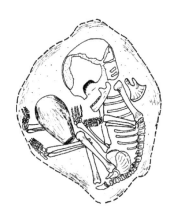

← Burial 202
Age: 6 mo.
Sex: Male
Location: Under a house floor
Grave Goods: Grass-lined pit and matting; textile found around the skull, possibly wrapping it. A gourd and wooden stick found have been suggested to be the remains of a rattle. Red pigment was found along the back and rimming the mandible.

Burial 224 →
Age: 32–38
Sex: Female
Location: No associated house
Grave Goods: Body wrapped in a map secured with rope and packed with junco. A gourd covered the skull and a grinding stone lay on the abdomen. Two unworked stones were on top of the mat, and a bone pendant was on the rib cage. The grave was below a concentration of mussel shells.

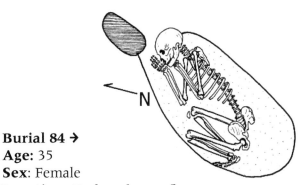

Burial 84 →
Age: 35
Sex: Female
Location: Under a house floor
Grave Goods: A grinding stone above head and a bone textile tool and five limpet shell beads near throat area. The pit was lined with straw and junco.

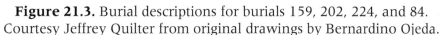

Figure 21.3. Burial descriptions for burials 159, 202, 224, and 84. Courtesy Jeffrey Quilter from original drawings by Bernardino Ojeda.

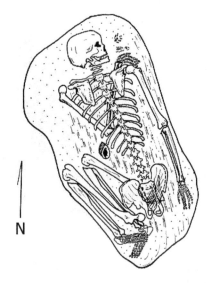

← **Burial 119**
Age: 30–34
Sex: Female
Location: No associated house
Grave Goods: Cordage around the sacrum, burnt shell in the stomach area, anchovy bones in front of the face, and straw lining the pit and on the pelvis. A pillar of "saltire" (sodium nitrate, a food preservative) was above the skull, suggesting it had been poured into the grave.

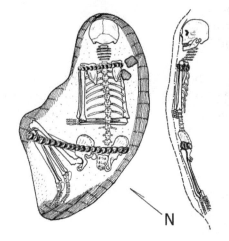

← **Burial 65**
Age: 30–34
Sex: Female
Location: Associated with house floor
Grave Goods: A braided rope bound the shoulders and scapulae, and another bound the pelvis and knees. A fine textile was in the head/should region and burnt rocks on a mat near the shoulder.

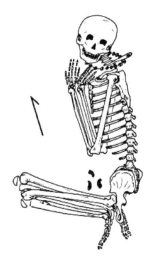

← **Burial 15**
Age: 30–34
Sex: Male
Location: Unknown provenience
Grave Goods: A bone textile tool and 15 shell beads (probably from a necklace) found near the throat. Lying on a mat of crushed junco. Botanical remains reported near the abdominal area.

Burial 220 →
Age: 30–34
Sex: Male
Location: Possibly associated with house
Grave Goods: The grave was both lined and covered with a fine mat, over which lay mussel shells and stones (right). There was a fine twined cap on the head covered with junco. Nine mussel shells were placed around the body. Gourd fragments were near the pelvis and skull. Two sticks were placed as if radiating from the skull and there were small pique shells on the upper mat covering the grave.

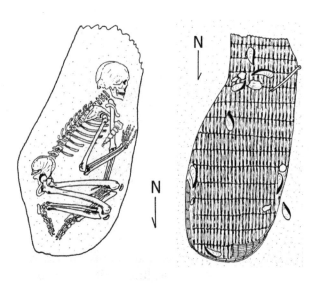

Figure 21.4. Burial descriptions for burials 119, 65, 15, and 220. Courtesy Jeffrey Quilter from original drawings by Bernardino Ojeda.

Worksheet 21.1

1. Tally the totals for each category in the top half of the table below, and then convert these numbers to percents in the bottom half of the table.

Sex	Fetus	New-born	Child		Juvenile	Adult				Old Adult		Total
			1–5	6–11	12–19	20–24	25–29	30–34	35–39	40–45	46–50	
Male	0	2	3	4	7	13	19	8	5	9	9	
Female	0	3	5	3	1	6	12	21	12	9	7	
Indeter-minate	9	11	10	9	2	0	0	1	0	0	0	
Total												200
Sex	Fetus	New-born	Child		Juvenile	Adult				Old Adult		Total
			1–5	6–11	12–19	20–24	25–29	30–34	35–39	40–45	46–50	
Male												
Female												
Indeter-minate												
Total												100%

2. Draw a bar graph on the back using the percents calculated above; you will have two bars per age range: one for male, another for female. Use this graph to answer Question 1 in Worksheet 21.2.

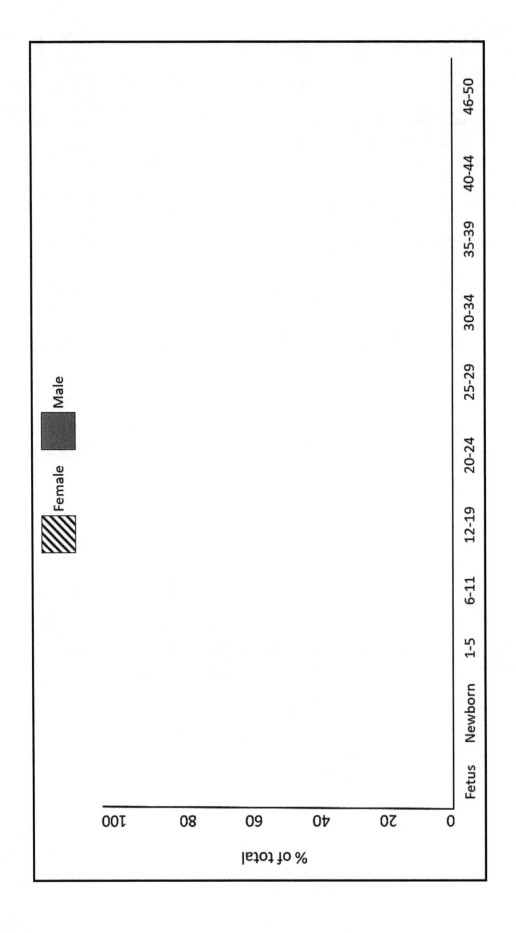

Worksheet 21.2

1. **Age and Sex Differences**: Based on the graph you made in Worksheet 21.1, are males and females equally represented or are their differences? If so, what might create such differences, (e.g., infanticide, warfare, and/or death during childbirth)? Keep in mind, there are roughly 50 percent male births, and 50 percent female births in a given population.

_____

_____

_____

_____

_____

_____

_____

_____

_____

2. **Ritual Activity:** Using the mortuary data (Figures 21.1–21.4), what is a "typical" Paloma burial in terms of placement, direction the body is laid out in, and grave goods? Are the grave goods ritual objects or "tool kits" the dead would have used during their lifetime? Do these objects suggest a belief in an "afterlife" similar to daily life in Paloma? Finally, does the placement of graves suggest anything about family relationships and community identity?

_____

_____

_____

_____

_____

_____

_____

_____

3. **Wealth and Status Differences:** Compare burials of the same age and sex to one another. Are there any differences in burials of males of the same age? Women of the same age? Children of the same age? What might some of these differences suggest about wealth and status in Paloma?

_____

_____

_____

_____

_____

4. **Gender Differences:** Are men's graves different from women's? Consider placement, positioning, and grave goods in filling in the circles below. Similarly, are multiple burials treated differently from individual burials? If so, how? What might these differences—if any—imply about gender roles and/or gender identity at Paloma?

_____

_____

_____

_____

_____

Worksheet 21.3

For Further Exploration and Application

Your instructor may have you do these questions as an in-class discussion or individual reflection.

1. Why are there so many "indeterminate sex" individuals in the fetus, newborn, and child age cohorts?

_____

_____

_____

_____

_____

_____

2. What additional information would you want to further explore this data set? Consider other kinds of data sets (e.g., DNA), sample size, and excavation strategies.

_____

_____

_____

_____

_____

_____

3. There are three types of marriage residence patterns: *matrilocal*, when a man goes to live with his wife's family in her village; *patrilocal*, when a woman goes to live with her husband's family in his village; and neolocal, when the newly married couple established a house of their own (e.g., as generally characterizes the United States). Look carefully at where men, women, and children are buried. Do you see any evidence for one of the marriage residency patterns above?

_____

_____

_____

_____

_____

4a. Watch "The Great Inca Rebellion" (PBS 2007). Describe the stratigraphic positioning, and context (*provenience* and *association*) of the Puruchuco burials. What does this lead the team to believe?

_____

_____

_____

_____

_____

4b. Explain how the forensic and mortuary evidence rewrites the story of the Spanish "conquest" of the Inca Empire. How do these data provide the emic perspective lacking in the Spaniards' etic accounts of what happened at Puruchuco?

_____

_____

_____

_____

_____

_____

5. Listen to the *All Things Considered* podcast episode "With Climate Swing, a Culture Bloomed in the Americas" (Joyce 2008). Based on what you heard, how might you expect burials to change over time?

_____

_____

_____

_____

_____

_____

References

Joyce, Christopher. 2008. "With Climate Swing, a Culture Bloomed in the Americas." *All Things Considered*, 11 February. http://www.npr.org/templates/story/story.php?storyId=18888119. Accessed 5 June 2019.

Quilter, Jeffrey. 1989. *Life and Death at Paloma: Society and Mortuary Practices in a Preceramic Peruvian Village*. Des Moines: University of Iowa Press.

PBS. 2007. "The Great Inca Rebellion." *NOVA*, season 34, episode 10. Aired 19 June. https://www.youtube.com/watch?v=Y1QsHJRdIJU. Accessed 5 June 2019.

Walker, R. B. D. F. Morey, and J. H. Relethford. 2005. "Early and Mid-Holocene Dogs in Southeastern North America: Examples from Dust Cave." *Southeastern Archaeology* 24 (1): 83–92.

Wilford, John Nobel. 1981. "Peru Yields Evidence of Oldest Village in Hemisphere." *New York Times*, 28 April.

MODULE 5

Interpretation and Explanation in Archaeology

CHAPTER 22

Campus Garbology
Processual Archaeology

Ethnoarchaeology

An important archaeological specialty is ethnoarchaeology, a methodological framework emerging out of the Processual Archaeology movement (see chapter 1). Ethnoarchaeology is the study of living groups of people using archaeological methods and perspectives. Like cultural anthropologists, ethnoarchaeologists study and live with contemporary groups of people, immersing themselves in a new language and culture in the process. But unlike cultural anthropologists, ethnoarchaeologists are keenly interested in the material culture that gets left behind (be it artifacts, ecofacts, or features) and in what patterns. Not only do they take pictures and record everything they see, but also they often meticulously excavate the site once the inhabitants leave or move to a new area, sometimes weeks or even months later. This allows them to study how human behavior creates the archaeological record and how natural processes of site formation (such as wind, rain, and animal scavenging) affect the distribution of material remains left behind. Ethnoarchaeologists are specifically interested in three broad categories of study:

(1) *Learning how artifacts functioned in the past.* For a long time, archaeologists found stone flakes at archaeological sites that looked like shapeless debris left over while making "real" tools such as projectile points (Figure 22.1a). Given their lack of uniform shape and size, it is easy to see why these flakes were initially overlooked and considered waste. Eventually, archaeologists using microscopes identified wear and polish on the edges, revealing that they had been used to cut and alter materials such as bone and hide. Yet, even after this realization, the flakes' use was attributed to men, a logical extension of the widespread "man the toolmaker" stereotype that persisted well into the 1990s (Gero 1991). Ethnoarchaeological fieldwork over the past few decades has called this stereotype into question by documenting women using *and making* stone flakes. For example, among the Konso of Ethiopia, Kathryn Weedman Arthur (2010) has demonstrated that women not only produce these flakes to scrape animal hides but also craft them from specially selected raw stone and using a specialized method that ensures a tool that is sharp enough to scrape hide well yet sturdy enough not to break during use. Such ethnoarchaeological research has given archaeologists an entirely different view of this previously underappreciated artifact by showing not only are they true tools but also that women manufacture them and control their production.

(2) *Creating analogies from modern societies to interpret past human behavior.* Some behaviors are intrinsically human, and the patterning of material remains they leave behind can be surprisingly similar. For example, Lewis Binford (1978) noticed that Nunamuit foragers in Alaska created a distinct pattern of debris during shared meals. As they ate caribou around a central fire, crumbs and small bits of bone tended to fall around their feet; no one much worried about these bits, leaving them where they fell—an area Binford dubbed the "drop zone." However, larger items such as large bones and empty cans of soda and sardines were tossed away from the hearth—a zone Binford called the "toss zone." When asked why they did this, they replied somewhat condescendingly that no one wants to sit down on a sharp bone! Binford, and others since him, have observed this same discard pattern when groups make stone tools around a fire: tiny flakes of stone debris are left to fall around their feet without concern, while large, sharp pieces are intentionally tossed away, either in front of or behind them (Figure 22.1b). In both cases, tossing larger materials away helps keep the main activity area free of cumbersome, and sometimes dangerous, debris. Assuming such an area is abandoned, covered with dirt soon thereafter, and left undisturbed by animals, it would preserve as two distinct zones. An archaeologist looking at such a pattern without knowing the sociocultural setting in which it formed might assume drop and toss zones represent two distinct activities, when in reality it represents only different sized materials resulting from the *same* activity.

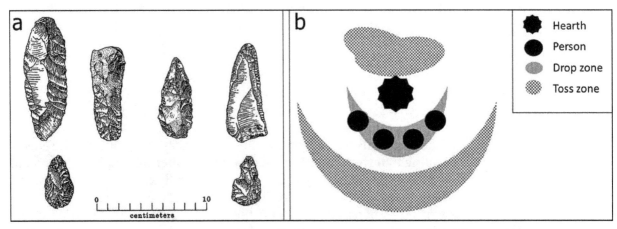

Figure 22.1. Representative expedient flakes from the archaeological site of Dust Cave in northwestern Alabama (a), and schematic representation of Binford's drop-toss zone (b).

(3) *Exploring past cultures' interaction with their environments to help solve contemporary environmental problems.* Perhaps the best example of this endeavor is William Rathje's famous "Garbage Project," which began in the 1970s. Despite the (good-natured) teasing he has taken over the decades about being a "garbologist," his work is an important ethnoarchaeological study of American waste disposal and discard habits. Rathje and his archaeology students went about their work in two key ways. First, they systematically (and stratigraphically) excavated the Tucson, Arizona, landfill to quantify changes in material culture through time. Second, they exten-

sively interviewed and surveyed Tucson residents. This enabled them to compare what people *said* they consumed (and threw out) with what they *actually* did. The results are extensively detailed in the book *Rubbish! The Archaeology of Garbage* (Rathje and Murphy 2001). We will discuss two observations that bear directly on the use of archaeological record. First, Tucson residents noted on their surveys that they consumed an average of one to two alcoholic drinks per week. But when they excavated the landfill layer dating to the time of the survey, the number of alcohol containers recovered was nearly triple the self-reported amount. The lesson here is that people do not always self-report accurately, be it intentionally or unintentionally. In this case, the artifacts proved to be a more objective and reliable estimate of human behavior, just as we saw with the Ephrata Cloister in chapter 6. A second example compared the amount of waste created by Anglo-Americans versus Mexican Americans. Rathje demonstrated that Anglo-Americans created significantly more waste and that this was the direct result of buying a wider variety of ingredients that often could not be reused the next day; as a result, they got discarded. Mexican Americans, on the other hand, tended to cook meals with a much smaller range of ingredients—ones, moreover, that could be used in nearly every recipe: "What isn't used in tacos today can be used in burritos tomorrow" (Rice 1998: 33). Today, even more so than the 1970s, Americans continue to invent new ways to dispose of our waste, either through incineration, dumping, or recycling. But Rathje's findings suggest simple behavioral modifications can eliminate waste before it is ever created, rather than trying to dispose of it on the other end. Given that Americans' annual waste increased 50 percent from 600 kilograms per capita in 1980 to nearly 900 kilograms in 2005 (McTaggart 2015: 17), this knowledge could be crucial to solving one of western society's largest environmental dilemmas.

Ethnographic Analogies

Ethnoarchaeology is a wonderful tool for gaining an emic perspective on the past. However, we must be careful in making analogies across time and space, especially when those dimensions are vast. It can be particularly tempting, even for seasoned archaeologists, to draw analogies between modern-day foragers and prehistoric foragers—sometimes going as far back as tens of thousands of years. For example, in an attempt to explain why prehistoric hunter-gatherers painted vivid images of Ice Age "megafauna" (e.g., horses, bison) on the ceiling of caves such as Lascaux Cave in France and Altamira Cave in Spain, archaeologists have often turned to contemporary rock-painting cultures such as the !Kung San of central Africa or the Australian Aborigines as analogies. But extending ethnoarchaeological analogies back more than 30,000 years is tenuous at best. Although both prehistoric and modern foragers generally share a wide suite of characteristics, including a hunting and gathering mode of subsistence, low population densities, and high mobility, we now know from extensive ethnographic research among the world's few remaining foragers that they vary widely in supernatural beliefs, language, and cultural behaviors. Ice Age hunters, African foragers, and Australian Aborigines undoubtedly paint for different reasons; we should therefore exercise caution when making comparisons. But, if viewed as a tool for developing testable hypotheses about the past rather than uncritically assuming cultural continuity between groups living in vastly different times and geographic spaces, then we can use ethnoarchaeology to its fullest potential.

The Activity

This activity is designed to illustrate how useful ethnoarchaeology can be in understanding the types and patterns of material culture that human societies leave behind on a daily basis. To illustrate this point, we will look at garbage found on your campus. Complete the worksheet for three artifacts or ecofacts that you find on campus. Your instructor will provide a campus map for you to record provenience. Once your classmates have done the same, you will examine the resulting patterns to make inferences about campus behaviors and activity areas.

Suggestions for Further Exploration and Application

- **"Ethnoarchaeology" (BSU 2015).** In this three-minute video, Pei-Lin Yu describes her job as an ethnoarchaeologist and demonstrates a cool "thingamajig" used by the Pumé people of Venezuela—an object that looks very much like a needle, but not the kind you would think. Its actual use is surprising (hint: it's not for the squeamish!) and highlights the important role ethnoarchaeology plays in providing context for unknown material culture.
- **"Rubbish!" (Rathje 1989).** Rathje's now classic "garbology" project involved systematic excavation of modern garbage to examine the discard patterns of Americans. His results, published in the *Atlantic Monthly*, highlight not only the nature of American waste but also the fact that material culture does not lie—and may even contradict—what people record. This is precisely the role of ethnoarchaeology: empirically examining the type and patterning of refuse from an archaeological perspective.
- **"A Tale of Garbage" (McTaggart's 2015).** This article by Ian McTaggart discusses the role of garbology in understanding how the types and patterning of material culture can shed light on the human societies we study. In this way, it is an applied version of the campus garbology activity. Finally, this article looks forward as well as backward in time: how archaeology can help inform public policy and make contemporary society more sustainable as populations continue to grow and produce more and more waste.

Worksheet 22.1

1. Collect or record three "artifacts" (i.e., trash) from around campus. Fill out the table below using the attribute codes provided below, and code the provenience on the map on the back.

	Artifact 1	Artifact 2	Artifact 3
Artifact Description			
Provenience *(i.e., where located?)*			
Association *(i.e., what artifacts, ecofacts or features nearby?)*			
Raw Material *(use codes 1–7 below)*			
Technology *(place codes 1–7 on map on backs)*			

Attribute Codes (list all that apply)

Raw Material	*Technology*
1. PLASTIC	1. FOOD/CONSUMABLE
2. PAPER	2. HOUSEHOLD
3. GLASS	3. SCHOOL
4. METAL	4. BEAUTY/HEALTH
5. WOOD	5. LAWN/YARD WORK
6. BONE	6. PET CARE
7. OTHER	7. OTHER

2. What trends do you see in artifact patterning? How would you be able to interpret these spaces even if you were unaware of the buildings' function? Also, what trends do you see, if any, in raw material predominance? What might this say about cultural behavior?

_____

_____

_____

_____

_____

_____

_____

3. Do you see any artifacts "out of place"? Are there spaces you feel should have an abundance of material culture (perhaps of a certain kind) but don't? What natural and/or cultural site formation process might account for this?

_____

_____

_____

_____

_____

_____

_____

4. Watch "Ethnoarchaeology" (BSU 2015). How did ethnoarchaeology allow the "thingamajig" described to be correctly interpreted? What lesson does that teach us?

_____

_____

_____

_____

_____

_____

_____

Worksheet 22.2

For Further Exploration and Application

Your instructor may have you do these questions as part of an in-class discussion or independent reflection.

1. Watch *Woman the Toolmaker: Hide Working and Tool Use in Konso, Ethiopia* (Belkin et al. 2008). How is this an example of ethnoarchaeology? What do the archaeologists learn from observing them that they would not know if without studying the Konso personally? How can we identify gendered division of labor and space using the patterning of material culture?

_____

_____

_____

_____

_____

_____

_____

_____

_____

2. Watch *The Potters of Buur Heybe, Somalia* (Belkin and Brandt 2006). How is this an example of ethnoarchaeology? What do the archaeologists learn from observing them that they would not know if without studying the Buur Heybe personally? How can we identify gendered division of labor and space using the patterning of material culture?

_____

_____

_____

_____

_____

_____

_____

_____

References

Arthur, Kathryn Weedman. 2010. "Feminine Knowledge and Skill Reconsidered: Women and Flaked Stone Tools." *American Anthropologist* 112 (2): 228–243.

Belkin, Tara, Steven Brandt, and Kathryn Weedman. 2008. *Woman the Toolmaker: Hide-working and Stone Tool Use in Konso, Ethiopia.* DVD. Left Coast Press.

Belkin, Tara, and Steven Brandt. 2006. *The Potters of Buur Heybe, Somalia.* DVD. Left Coast Press.

———. 2008. "The Potters of Buur Heybe, Somalia." *African Diaspora Archaeology Newsletter* 11 (3): art. 24.

Binford, Lewis. 1978. *Nunamiut Ethnoarchaeology: A Case Study in Archaeological Formation Processes.* New York: Academic Press.

BSU (Boise State University). 2015. "Ethnoarchaeology." Video, 2:55. Uploaded 17 December. https://www.youtube.com/watch?v=wj3rX8Nqv3c. Accessed 5 June 2019.

Gero, Joan M. 1991. "Genderlithics: Women's Roles in Stone Tool Production." In *Engendering Archaeology: Women and Prehistory*, edited by Joan M. Gero and Margaret W. Conkey, 163–193. New York: Wiley-Blackwell.

McTaggart, Ian. 2015. "A Tale of Garbage." *Earth Common Journal* 5 (1): 15–22. http://www.inquiriesjournal.com/articles/1331/a-tale-of-garbage. Accessed 5 June 2019.

Rathje, William L. 1989. "Rubbish." *Atlantic Monthly* 264 (6): 99–109.

Rathje, William L., and Cullen Murphy. 2001. *Rubbish! The Archaeology of Garbage.* Tucson: University of Arizona Press.

Rice, Patricia C. 1998. *Doing Archaeology: A Hands-on Laboratory Manual.* New York: Mayfield Publishing Company.

CHAPTER 23

Bringing Home the Bacon
Post-processual Archaeology

Introduction

While most chapters in this laboratory manual focus on concepts and techniques inherent to processual archaeology, this chapter and the next introduce you to post-processual archaeology, a theoretical perspective interested in themes such as ideology, gender, and something called *human agency*. Post-processual archaeology began in the 1980s in Europe as a critique of processual archaeology and gradually took root in the United States by the 1990s and 2000s. While processualists argued that cultural processes (i.e., human behavior) could only be reconstructed through rigorous use of the scientific method (see chapter 1), post-processualists felt the "old school" overfocused on hypothesis testing, material culture, and quantitative analysis. Post-processualists further (and more pessimistically) argued that all archaeologists, whether they admit it or not, impose their world views and cultural biases on the archaeological record and that the application of the scientific method and statistical analyses cannot prevent this, despite the best intentions of archaeologists.

As an alternative approach, post-processualists emphasized the need to consider the unique historical context of each culture, as well as the important role of the individual as agents of change within society—what they referred to as *human agency*. This emphasis on agency and individualism catalyzed the study of new themes in archaeology, themes that processual archaeology often eschewed because they are difficult to approach scientifically. These themes include gender, symbolism, and ideology. While processualists argued it is not possible to study these themes objectively through the scientific method, post-processualists argue such topics are crucial to understanding the past. They argue that by using approaches such as ethnographic analogy and ethnoarchaeology (see chapter 22), not only could such themes be explored, but also archaeologists can better understand past cultures as collections of *individuals*, not simply artifacts. Today, many archaeologists recognize that both schools of thought raise valid concerns. Importantly, even those advocating more of a quantitative approach now value the concepts of ideology, agency, and gender that post-processualists advocate as essential to a holistic approach to understanding past human societies. Similarly, post-processualists have begun to explore ways of studying these humanist themes in more quantitative ways and using material evidence without relying solely on analogy. This activity will allow you to explore the post-processual theme of gender by using processual quantitative approaches.

Gender Archaeology

Gender archaeology emerged as a subfield of archaeology during the 1980s on the heels of the women's rights movement. Originally called "feminist archaeology," advocates and practitioners of this approach correctly pointed out that if we fail to study women in the past, archaeologists are missing approximately 50 percent of human populations, and that the past cannot be accurately reconstructed given such an immense bias. Today, gender is conceived of much more broadly and considers the wide range of genders (not just biological sex) that exist today as well as in the past. This includes men, women, children, and nonbinary genders. The latter have been particularly overlooked by Western archaeologists following a paradigm of binary gender—that is, a simple distinction between male and female. Such a simplistic dichotomy is not made in all cultures. Many Native American cultures, for example, recognize other genders, which they collectively call "two-spirits."[1] Two-spirits embody the essence of both male and female; traditionally, they have been regarded as having special roles in society because of this unique quality. For example, among some Native Californian groups, two-spirits often served as undertakers because they were believed to possess supernatural gifts and serve as spiritual intermediaries between the physical and spiritual worlds. Two-spirits, then, are good examples of both complex gender dynamics and individual human agency.

The Activity

This activity examines the prevalence, and effects of, gender stereotypes in interpretations of the past. It has two parts. First, you will collect data by distributing a survey to friends and family to evaluate stereotypes non-archaeologists have about the gendered use of artifacts. These data are then compiled and graphed in class to investigate public perceptions of gender in the past. For example, the public nearly always associates projectile points and arrowheads as "male" and nutting stones and pottery as "female," attributions that reflect our Western notions of men "bringing home the bacon" and women "tending home and hearth." Although these attributions do not reflect the cultural norms in many non-Western societies, Americans generally still perceive gender roles the way they have traditionally been portrayed in popular media such as the *Flintstones* (Figure 23.1a). These assumptions, then, heavily influence our interpretations of the past (Figure 23.1b), albeit sometimes unconsciously.

Figure 23.1. Examples of Western gender stereotypes in the *Flintstones* cartoon (a) and reconstructions of our hominin ancestors (b).
Image (a) Courtesy Everett Collection.

Suggestions for Further Exploration and Application

- **"The Aboriginals' Female Hunter Society" (LF 2012)** (*2:32 minutes*). You'll be impressed with the feisty fare these women bring down—it's not for the timid!
- **"Agta Forager Women in the Philippines" (Griffin 1985).** This article is somewhat dated but still accurately describes male and female hunting and gathering and engages women's issues resulting from Westernization.
- **"New Women of the Ice Age" (Pringle 1998).** Recent research is changing our image of prehistoric gender; there is good reason to believe Ice Age women played a host of powerful roles—from plant collectors and weavers to hunters and spiritual leaders.
- **"The 'Two-Spirit' People of Indigenous North America" (Williams 2010).** This is a good overview of the concept of two-spirit among native North Americans, as well as the gender fluidity and complementarity associated with male and female hunting and gathering tasks.

Worksheet 23.1

Instructions to Participants

Please check the appropriate column based on whether you associate the following artifacts with male or female use.

	Artifact	Male	Female
	Arrowhead		
	Hoe		
	Ceramic Vessel		
	Earspools (large circularring worn in earlobe)		
	Bone Fishhook		
	Grinding Stone		
	Bone Needle		
	Worlf-tooth Pendant (worn around neck)		
	Cave Art		
	Scraper (used for curing animal hides)		

Worksheet 23.2

Instructions to Participants

Please check the appropriate column based on whether you associate the following artifacts with male or female use.

	Artifact	Male	Female
	Arrowhead		
	Hoe		
	Ceramic Vessel		
	Earspools (large circularring worn in earlobe)		
	Bone Fishhook		
	Grinding Stone		
	Bone Needle		
	Worlf-tooth Pendant (worn around neck)		
	Cave Art		
	Scraper (used for curing animal hides)		

Worksheet 23.3

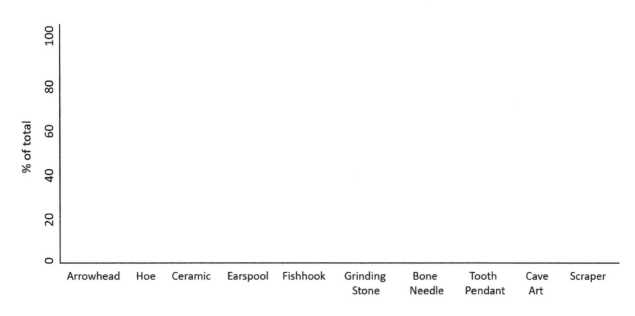

1. Use the master tally (provided by your teacher) to graph the survey participants' responses. What trends do you see? Which artifacts did participants tend to attribute to male activity in the past? To female activity? Where do these gender stereotypes come from?

_____

_____

_____

_____

_____

_____

2. Watch "The Aboriginal's Female Hunter Society" (LF 2012). What does it take for a man or women to earn the title of "good hunter"? Do men and women hunt the same prey?

_____

_____

_____

_____

_____

_____

For Further Exploration and Application

Your instructor may have you do these questions as part of an in-class discussion or individual reflection.

1. Read Bion Griffin's (1985) "Agta Forager Women in the Philippines." Describe women's hunting. In what way do women use human *agency*, and how is that agency being eroded by increasing globalization and interaction with Westerners in mainstream Philippines?

_____

_____

_____

_____

_____

2. Read Heather Pringle's (1998) "New Woman of the Ice Age." What material and/or ethnographic evidence is provided to support the hypothesis that Paleolithic women likely played a host of powerful and important roles, from plant collectors to weavers, and from hunters to spiritual leaders?

_____

_____

_____

_____

_____

3. Why do you think we tend to say women "gather" rabbits with nets or use fire to flush out monitor lizards, yet men "hunt" when collecting honey from a beehive or mussels from a riverbank?

_____

_____

_____

_____

_____

_____

Note

1. The term two-spirit is not interchangeable with "gay," "transgender," or "LGBTQIA." Two-spirit differs from most Western definitions of sexuality and gender identity in that it is not so much about whom one is sexually interested in or how one personally identifies but rather as a reflection of the inner spirit, or character. Not all Nations have rigid gender roles, but among those that do, there are at least four genders: feminine woman, masculine woman, feminine man, masculine man.

References

Griffin, Bion. 1985. "Agta Forager Women in the Philippines." *Cultural Survival Quarterly Magazine*, June. https://www.culturalsurvival.org/publications/cultural-survival-quarterly/agta-forager-women-philippines. Accessed 5 June 2019.

LF (Leakey Foundation). 2012. "The Aboriginals' Female Hunter Society." Video, 2:33. Uploaded by Fora TV, 16 May. https://www.dailymotion.com/video/xqvt3d. Accessed 5 June 2019.

Pringle, Heather. 1998. "New Women of the Ice Age." *Discover Magazine*, 1 April, 62–69. http://discovermagazine.com/1998/apr/newwomenoftheice1430. Accessed 5 June 2019.

Williams, Walter L. 2010. "The 'Two-Spirit' People of Indigenous North Americans." *The Guardian*, 11 October. https://www.theguardian.com/music/2010/oct/11/two-spirit-people-north-america. Accessed 5 June 2019.

CHAPTER 24

Lend Me Your Hand
Post-processual Archaeology

Paleolithic Cave Art

This chapter examines gendered assumptions about the famous cave art from well-known Upper Paleolithic (ca. 40,000–10,000 years ago) sites in Europe, such as Lascaux, Rouffignac, and Altamira caves. While images of Ice Age megafauna (e.g., oxen, horses, and mammoth) are perhaps the best-known Paleolithic art (Figure 24.1c), the caves also feature handprints (a) and "finger flutes" (b). Recent research has questioned previous interpretations about not only *what* these paintings reflect but also *who* painted them. Researchers such as Bruce Bower, Olga Soffer, and Jessica Cooney argue many the handprints were made by women and that the finger flutes are primarily the product of children, perhaps as young as toddlers (see King 2011). Why does knowing the gender or age of the painter matter? If you are a post-processual archaeologist, it matters a great deal. As Jennifer Huget (2006) writes, "Children may be present in a shadowy way, sitting at their parents' feet around the campfire or trailing along as part of a group migrating to follow game. They are rendered as passive beings, excluded from *active agency* (emphasis ours) . . . It is just as it once was with our portrayal of ancient women."

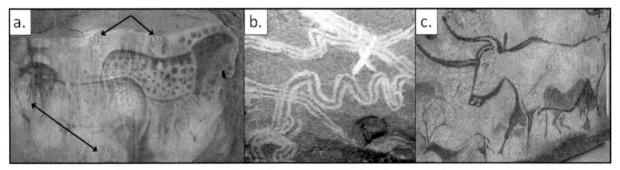

Figure 24.1. Examples of Paleolithic cave handprints (a), finger flutes (b), and megafauna (c).

Context of the Art

The context in which the cave art is found is just as illuminating as the paintings themselves. If you watched "The Day Pictures Were Born" (BBC 2005) in chapter 5, you'll remember the megafauna pictures were once believed to represent hunting magic; that is, early hunters depicted the images of animals they hunted and hoped to kill. But when researchers compared the depicted animals to the bones of animals eaten, they were surprised to learn they were quite different. They were drawing bison, oxen, and horses, but they were eating goat and other small animals. The *provenience* of the images was also puzzling. They were located in the far reaches of the "dark zone," which receives no light and is quite difficult to access. The question immediately arose: why go through all this trouble (and possible danger) to get to these far reaches of the caves, where presumably few people would ever see the pictures? This suggested they represented far more than just depictions of a hopeful hunt. And, what's more, the images were associated with curious dots, lines, and other geometric shapes overlying the images (through radiometric dating, we know they are contemporaneous with the animal drawings). If you watched the video, you'll remember this context prompted researchers to reinterpret the images as Paleolithic artists painting what they saw in hallucinations brought on by light deprivation—something one can't avoid in a cave! People went back to these areas to bring about the hallucinations, perhaps as part of trances designed to connect with the spirit world and their ancestors, something many modern-day band-level societies such as the !Kung San do. So, an ideotechnic meaning for these images seemed to be implied when considering the images' context. But . . .

. . . what of the handprints and finger flutes? Most of these images are in not the dark zone but rather the light zone, easily accessible to people of all ages. And they are not associated with the dots, lines, and so on that the megafauna were associated with. The question, then, is, what do these images represent? What is their meaning? Do they have a technomic, sociotechnic, or ideotechnic meaning? And, just as important, *who* drew them? Contrary to popular belief, and past archaeological interpretations, recent research has argued that their creators were not just men. Rather, women, teens, and children as young as toddlers may have been responsible for them. Your task in this activity is to evaluate the methodology underlying this new research, and—assuming it is correct—develop testable hypotheses for interpreting their elusive meaning.

The Activity

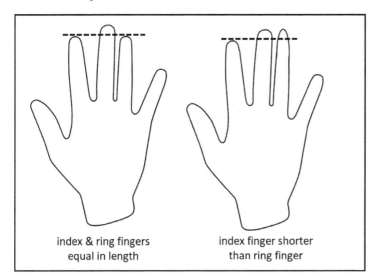

index & ring fingers
equal in length

index finger shorter
than ring finger

Figure 24.2. Schematic representation of female (left) and male (right) hands based on the ratio of the length of the index finger to the length of the ring finger.

This activity examines the prevalence and effects of gender stereotypes in our interpretations of the past. It involves sketching your hand and comparing the length of several of your fingers (Worksheet 24.1). Alternatively, your teacher may have you stencil your hands the way it would have been done 30,000 years ago, in order to explore the symbolism and agency behind the enigmatic cave art. Specifically, you will compare the length of your index and ring fingers the same way archaeologists have done to determine who made the handprints hauntingly preserved in these ancient caves. Your instructor may ask you to do some of the questions in the "For Further Exploration and Application" section for group or individual reflection.

Suggestions for Further Exploration and Application

- **"Children of Prehistory: Stone Age Kids Left Their Marks on Cave Art and Stone Tools" (Bower 2007).** Bruce Bower argues cave art in the form of "finger flutes" is likely produced by small children who were lifted to the cave ceiling by older children or adults.
- **"The Child Artists of Prehistory" (King 2011).** This is a shorter version of Bruce Bower's premise written by the biological anthropologist Barbara King, who emphasizes that both women and children in prehistory had agency and that our image of Paleolithic "man" as a spear-throwing male needs to change to reflect reality.
- **"Finger Forecasts" (Huget 2006).** In this article, Jennifer Huget (2006) explores the implications of finger ratios outside of archaeology, implicating its correspondence with everything from athletic prowess, to susceptibility to disease, to ethnic background. Most importantly, it raises the important caveat that "digit ratio is not a great tool for making predictions about individuals; it's more useful at assessing probabilities for groups of people," something archaeologists using finger ratios to sex Paleolithic handprints need to remember as well.
- **"The Day Pictures Were Born" (BBC 2005)** *(54 minutes)*. The famous prehistoric cave paintings were originally interpreted only from a technomic point of view, but recent research suggests an ideotechnic interpretation instead, one in which the prehistoric artists were experiencing powerful hallucinations. (*Note: Stop watching when the Altamira case study is over, approximately minute 46.*)

Worksheet 24.1

1. Use a pencil to outline one of your hands in the box below. Alternatively, your teacher may have you stencil your hand using finger paints.

2. Research has shown that men's ring fingers (the fourth digit) are usually longer than their index fingers (the second digit) (Figure 24.2). In contrast, women's second and fourth fingers are generally equal in length. Does your index to ring finger ratio better reflect a male or female hand (remember, there is *much* variation among people!) or neither? What about your other hand . . . do both hands exhibit the same pattern?

_____

_____

_____

_____

_____

For Further Exploration and Application

Your instructor may choose to have you do some of these questions as part of an in-class discussion or individual reflection.

1. Do modern sex differences in finger ratio necessarily reflect those of the past? Do modern hands necessarily reflect the same range of variation in prehistoric hands from 30,000 years ago? Brainstorm some reasons why finger ratios might vary through time.

_____

_____

_____

_____

_____

_____

2. Read "Children of Prehistory." In what way does Bower's (2007) argument make you rethink the events occurring in Paleolithic caves and the types of people engaged in those activities?

_____

_____

_____

_____

_____

3. What level of meaning (i.e., technomic, sociotechnic, or ideotechnic) would you attribute to the megafauna, the handprints, and the finger flutes? Consider not just the object painted but also the provenience, association, and gender of the paintings.

_____

_____

_____

_____

References

BBC. 2005. "The Day Pictures Were Born." *How Art Made the World*, season 1, episode 2. http://www.pbs.org/howartmadetheworld/series/buy. Accessed 5 June 2019.

Bower, Bruce. 2007. "Children of Prehistory: Stone Age Kids Left Their Marks on Cave Art and Stone Tools." *Science News* 171 (17): 264–266.

Huget, Jennifer. 2006. "Finger Forecasts." *Washington Post*, 17 October. http://www.washingtonpost.com/wp-dyn/content/article/2006/10/16/AR2006101600941.html. Accessed 5 June 2019.

King, Barbara. 2011. "The Child Artists of Prehistory." *13.7: Cosmos and Culture*, 6 October. http://www.npr.org/sections/13.7/2011/10/06/141042561/the-child-artists-of-prehistory.

CHAPTER 25

Optimally Foraging Money
Behavioral Ecology

Optimal Foraging Theory

Optimal foraging theory (OFT) derives from the field of evolutionary ecology and was first applied to avian (i.e., bird) foraging behavior. OFT models predict how animals behave when searching for food. Although obtaining food provides animals with the energy necessary for survival, searching for and capturing food expends both energy and time. Thus, animals seek (albeit unconsciously) to gain the most benefit for the lowest cost so that they can maximize their fitness. OFT helps predict the best strategy that an animal can use to achieve this goal. We can break OFT down into four basic factors that influence foraging decisions: needs, time, energy, and reward. Needs refer to those things that organisms require to survive, such as sufficient calories, protein, vitamins, minerals, and so on. Time, of course, is the amount of time spent meetings these needs. Energy is what organisms expend, in terms of calories, fat, etc., in the process of obtaining food. Finally, reward is the energy netted by organisms after accounting for the energy expended—analogous to what your net paycheck is after accounting for taxes.

If you have a cat or a dog, chances are you have seen them hunt optimally. If your pet is anything like my cat Chloe, she loves to eat. She especially likes to "hunt" dry kibble, which I place around the house in hidden spots, some easy to reach, others requiring more effort (I usually put the biggest, tastiest treats in these harder spots). Almost without fail, she seeks out the easiest to find first and may ignore the hard-to-reach ones. She's pretty lazy in this respect. But after a power nap in which she reenergizes, she's off to get those skipped rewards. She clearly nets more calories than she expends because, as our veterinarian gently put it, she's "chunky for her frame."

Optimally Foraging and Humans

An example of OFT applied to human cultures can be found among the !Kung, a San group who today live in the Kalahari Desert of Namibia, Botswana, and Angola. The !Kung are perhaps most famous to most Westerners as speakers of the "click" languages, which use several "clicking" sounds in their speech that are unfamiliar (and quite hard to reproduce) to most Westerners. Today, the !Kung eat a mostly plant-based diet, supplemented by some meat. One plant food that is prevalent during much of the year is the mongongo but. Mongongo nuts are an excellent source of protein (28 percent by weight) and energy (654 calories per 100 grams), as well as important nutrients such as magnesium (for more information, see Tu 1999). Thus, it would seem that the nuts more than adequately meet human nutritional needs, with minimal time and energy expended to reap a reward. Despite their nutritional value, and the fact that nuts literally cover the ground ankle-deep in some parts of the year, they account for only about half their daily caloric intake. But what is not readily apparent is that once collection time, processing efforts, and cooking time[1] are figured into the picture, mongongo nuts are actually one of the "lower-ranked" foods in the !Kung diet (Bettinger 2015). In other words, the reward (in energy gained) is lessened by the necessary time and effort (in energy expended). In fact, before recent times, the nuts were eaten even less than they are today. Only recently have they been relied on more heavily because other, more attractive, food resources are no longer available in the food-poor desert lands that Western cultures have forced the !Kung onto. Thus, while mongongo nuts may superficially seem to be the optimal food, further study shows they require more energy than they give back relative to other plant foods.

The Activity

Your teacher will give a demo to help make OFT more intuitive to understand that will conform perfectly to the expectations of OFT. *But* (big but) various factors can cause animals to deviate from optimal foraging. For example, the risk of predation may force the animal to select less profitable food items in a relatively safe location, rather than opting for the energetically most efficient feeding strategy. This is particularly true for humans, for whom cultural decisions and preferences may outweigh foraging interests. In fact, it turns out that several cultural factors may come into play and prevent them from foraging as optimally as they might if culture didn't exist. You will explore some of these cultural factors in this class demonstration and discussion.

Suggestions for Further Exploration and Application

- **"A Case for Eating Bugs" (PBS 2017)** (*4:28 minutes*). Entomophagy—eating bugs!—is something an estimated two billion worldwide do, in nearly 80 percent of the world's nations. But Westerners in general, and Americans in particular, are squeamish about eating bugs, despite its health and environmental benefits, because of our fiercely ingrained food taboo against eating insects. This video makes the case for it. Keep an open mind: even if you don't ever try it, think about the case it makes for insects truly being an optimal food for contemporary society.
- **"Real Men Don't Eat Deer" (Milton 1997).** While Katherine Milton was not writing about OFT per se, the content lends itself well as a critique of evolutionary models. As she states, "You are what you eat, the saying goes. But what you don't eat says a lot too." In this article, she relates the story of her fieldwork among the Ma't of Brazil, who refuse to eat a perfectly healthy deer that has been shot. Myriad reasons are suggested for why they won't eat it. The author herself does and later feels ill and wonders if she shouldn't have eaten it after all . . .

Worksheet 25.1

1. In what way is the coin activity like optimal foraging theory? What does OFT fail to consider? Give several examples of things that might void the predictions of OFT.

_____

_____

_____

_____

_____

_____

2. Look at the figure below, even if you didn't do this activity in class. The star represents a hunter-gatherer base camp, and the circles represent the distance they must travel from base camp; as they use resources within each circle, the must travel farther and farther as time goes by to get food. Based on this, why do you think hunter-gathers change base campus frequently? Frame your answer within a behavioral ecological perspective (i.e., OFT).

(b) Illustration created by Joseph Bomberger.

_____

_____

_____

_____

_____

_____

For Further Exploration and Application

Your instructor may have you do these questions as part of an in-class discussion or independent reflection.

1. Use optimal foraging theory to describe either (1) a trip to the grocery store or (2) trick-or-treating. Be sure to consider the four factors in foraging decisions: needs, time, energy, and reward. Consider some scenarios that might decrease the "optimal" foraging.

_____

_____

_____

_____

_____

_____

2. Read "Real Men Don't Eat Deer." What does Milton (1997) suggest is the reason why the Ma't don't eat deer, even though it is perfectly edible and nutritious? Does this explanation have any implications for OFT?

_____

_____

_____

_____

_____

_____

3. Food taboos (foods not eaten) and food rituals (foods traditionally eaten) are powerful forces of culture. Just as you saw with the Ma't—we have our own dietary rituals and taboos that give us a sense of cultural identity. Give an example from your own cultural background, country, and/or family heritage.

_____

_____

_____

_____

_____

Note

1. Dry fruits are usually steamed first to soften the skins. After peeling, the fruits are cooked in water until the flesh separates from the hard, inner nuts. The pulp is eaten, and the nuts saved to be roasted later. During roasting, direct contact with the fire is avoided, using sand to distribute the heat evenly. Once dry, the outer shell cracks easily, revealing the nut, encased within a soft, inner shell. The nuts are either eaten intact or pounded as ingredients in other dishes (Lee 1968). Roasted nuts can be store for long periods of time.

References

Bettinger, Robert L., Raven Garvey, and Shannon Tushingham. 2015. *Hunter-Gatherers: Archaeological and Evolutionary Theory*. New York: Springer.

Lee, Robert Borshay. 1968. "What Hunters Do For a Living, or, How to Make Out on Scarce Resources." In *Man the Hunter*, 30–48. Chicago: Aldine Published.

Milton, Katherine. 1997. "Real Men Don't Eat Deer." *Discover Magazine* 18: 46–53. http://discovermagazine.com/1997/jun/realmendonteatde1151. Accessed 5 June 2019.

PBS. 2017. "A Case for Eating Bugs." *Gross Science*, season 2, episode 34. Aired 20 June. https://www.pbs.org/video/the-case-for-eating-bugs-zbrxai. Accessed 5 June 2019.

Tu, Jean-Louis. 1999. "Is Cooked Food Poison? Looking at the Science on Raw vs. Cooked Foods." Part 3G. *Beyond Vegetarianism*. http://www.beyondveg.com/tu-j-l/raw-cooked/raw-cooked-3g.shtml. Accessed 2 April 2019.

CHAPTER 26

Tree of Life
Human Ecology

Dendrochronology

In chapter 15, you learned how to use tree rings as an absolute dating technique. This technique has the benefit of great accuracy in regions conducive to wood preservation, such as the American Southwest. But tree rings allow archaeologists to do much more than just date sites. As you now know, rings of new growth form within the trunk as trees grow. Fortunately for scientists who study past climates, called *archaeoclimatologists*, the width of these rings is dependent on temperature and rainfall. The amount that a tree grows each season is indicated by the size and color of the annual rings, which you can see in the cross section of the tree trunk (Figure 26.1a). A wide tree ring indicates wet and cool weather, which allows trees to grow rapidly. A thin ring is produced in dry and hot conditions, when tree growth is slower. A dark ring marks growth during late summer, and a light-colored ring indicates growth during spring. Finally, tree rings can also provide evidence of natural catastrophes such as floods, droughts, insect plagues, and forest fires. For example, a severe fire may create a fire scar (Figure 26.1b), which of course can be dated absolutely by where it falls in the ring chronology. They also record major climate patterns such as El Niño, The Little Ice Age, and the Great Dust Bowl, all of which are now known to have impacted human populations in myriad ways, both good and bad. While most living trees hold records of climate dating back no more than a few hundred years, tree trunks

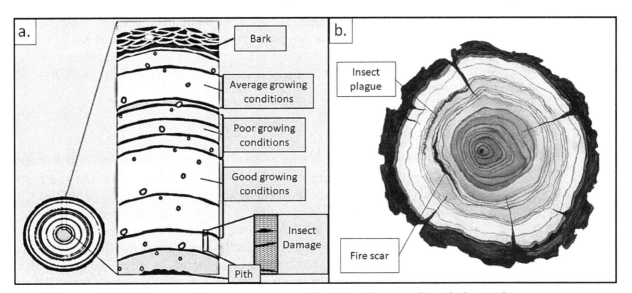

Figure 26.1 Climate effects on tree growth (a) and examples of physical appearance of natural disasters such as insect plagues and forest fires (b).

from archaeological sites allow scientists to determine what climate was like thousands of years ago.

Human Ecology

Archaeology viewed through the framework of *human ecology* emphasizes the dynamic interactions between human societies and their environments. While this approach to interpreting the past is sometimes criticized as being too environmentally deterministic (i.e., attributing all human change to environmental changes and catastrophes), it is never-the-less an important framework for interpreting the past, for as we can easily observe even today, changes in our physical environment, climate, and landscapes certainly do affect us. Human ecology is both a theoretical and methodological framework. Methodologically, archaeologists utilize a variety of techniques from multiple disciplines to reconstruct past environments, including climate, vegetation, and landforms. These include methods borrowed from geology (e.g., geomorphology and geochemistry), biology (e.g., zoology and dendrochronology), and climatology (e.g., isotope analysis and computer modeling). This chapter will focus on the ability of dendrochronology to provide not just absolute dates, but also data about past climates and natural disasters that influenced the everyday lives of past human populations.

The Activity

You have recently been hired to work in an archaeological laboratory at the University of Arizona's Laboratory for Tree-Ring Research (LTRR)[1] to analyze tree core samples from three significant preservation projects the lab has been contracted to consult on. It is hoped that both sites will be approved for listing on the National Register of Historic Places (NRHP). Your analysis will include determining the year the tree was cut to build the structures and locating significant climactic events that may bear on the site's significance for warranted listing on the NRHP (see also chapter 33). The knowledge gained will also add greatly to archaeologists' knowledge of the human ecology represented in each of the preservation projects. Read the scenarios below carefully and use the tree cores in Figures 26.2–26.4 to answer the questions in Worksheets 26.1 and 26.2.

Preservation Project 1

Sally Müllenberger and her family moved across the country to southeastern Colorado for new opportunities in the developing west following the Dust Bowl catastrophe. Her father, a soil scientist, has just been hired by the Civilian Conservation Corp (CCC) to bring the latest agricultural techniques to the recently ravaged Great Plains. Their interest in the move is both professional and personal: Sally's great-grandfather was one of the first settlers here in 1862. He worked hard on unforgiving lands for decades, only to flee the area for the west coast in the late 1930s in hopes of a fresh start. When Sally's family arrives at the old homestead, they are disappointed to learn it burned down, so they cannot reuse any of the timbers to build their own home. But the beautiful huge oak tree that once shaded the front porch, and which her grandmother Lula planted that first year (according to her diary, which Sally inherited) to commemorate their new venture, is still there. It has recently been accosted by locusts, so Sally's family felled it and made it the main beam in their new home as a way of preserving their family's heritage, if not the tree itself. In an entry dated 10 May 1942, Sally's journal tells us that her father cut the ancestral tree for their new house. Today, archaeologists are concerned about the preservation of Sally's home due to its excellent representation of log cabin architecture from the CCC era. A team of archaeologists is tasked with coring the main beam from the cabin. The core will be analyzed in the laboratory to determine the date of the house and the climactic events that will give more insight into Sally's, and her ancestor's, lives.

Preservation Project 2

Wěi Cheng decided to move his family out to Southern California to find work as a railroad conductor on the Transcontinental Railroad. He felt fated to make this bold move, as his great-grandfather Li had made something of himself in the California Gold Rush during the late 1840s and early 1850s. In fact, despite the odds, and being an immigrant, he did so well as to build a profitable hotel in the northern Grass Valley, which unfortunately burned down in 1855 shortly before his death. His grandfather, Yang, helped build the railroad, making \$35/month under brutal conditions, in the late 1860s. With the success of his Cheng ancestors as inspiration, Wěi and his fellow co-workers started their venture by building a tool shed, also known as a section house, to store necessary equipment. Wei's ledger, preserved at the California State Museum, details that they cut several local pinyon pines for the construction of the section house in 1925. Today, archaeologists are preserving the section house by listing it to the National Register of Historic Places (NHRP) because it symbolizes both working-class America, particularly the contribution of Chinese-Americans, and because it is the only representation of section houses left in Southern California. The LTRR is conducting research on the house by taking a core from one of the beams supporting the section house. The core will allow the determination of the date of construction and climactic events that will give an insight into the past environment.

Preservation Project 3

Luis Cordero is a historical archaeologist specializing in the Spanish Mission era. He is of Native American ancestry—a member of the Chumash Tribe—and currently serves as the Tribal Historic Preservation Officer (THPO) for the Chumash Nation. He is working to nominate an indigenous Chumash plank-house located on the Channel Islands (off the coast of Southern California) to the National Register of Historic Places (NRHP). Very few of these traditional houses are left from the pre-Mission era (1670–1750); this one has been fortuitously preserved by a landslide which dumped almost a meter of mud on it. It has been painstakingly excavated and the site is now protected by the California Office of Archaeology. Cordero (whose great-great grandmother married a Spanish missionary), is studying the effects of Spanish mission life on the Chumash people, as well as what caused over 85% of Chumash to voluntarily move onto Spanish Missions between 1786 and 1804, especially given that they were forced to convert to Christianity, give up their native language, and farm corn and cattle rather than fish as they used to. Recent bioarcheological studies have shown that the bones of many of these converts (now buried in cemeteries on Mission grounds) show signs of acute nutritional stress, making him wonder if environmental changes led to food shortages in acorn and fish, two of the staple food resources on the Channel Islands. He has received a grant from the California Academy of Sciences to analyze a timber from the plank house to investigate climate change and its impact on the Native Chumash populations. The beam has been cross-dated with a beam from one of the Mission structures and another, off-site, pinyon pine (not discussed here), giving them not only a cutting date of 1704 for the plank-house's construction, but also an extensive climate record dating from the early 1800s back to the early 1600s.

Suggestions for Further Exploration and Application

- **"Dendroclimatology: Using Tree Rings to Reconstruct Past Climate"[2] (CCAC 2015)** *(4 minutes)*. The dendrochronologist Rex Adams discusses what tree rings can tell archaeologists about ancient climates.
- **"Tree Rings Do Tell Tales" (Swanberg 2018)** *(4 minutes)*. This overview of tree rings and ancient climate in the American Southwest includes embedded video that shows footage of timber beams in situ in pueblo ruins.
- **"Vikings Unearthed" (PBS 2016)** *(11 minutes)*. This clip episode of *NOVA* includes a history and description of Viking longship, an explanation of dendrochronology and cross dating, and uses trees to reconstruct the climate during Viking times.

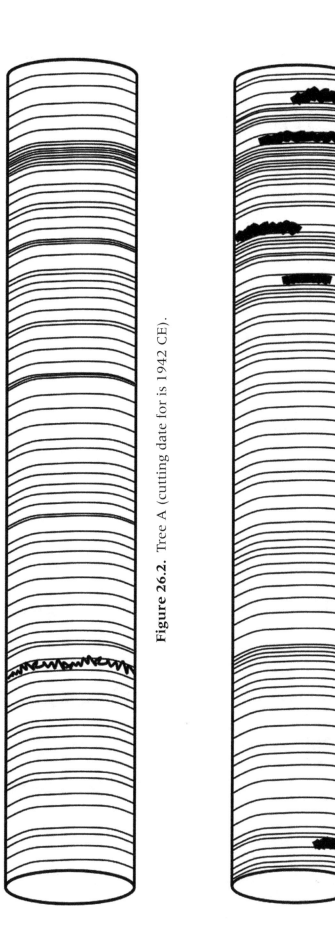

Figure 26.2. Tree A (cutting date for is 1942 CE).

Figure 26.3. Tree B (cutting date is 1925 CE).

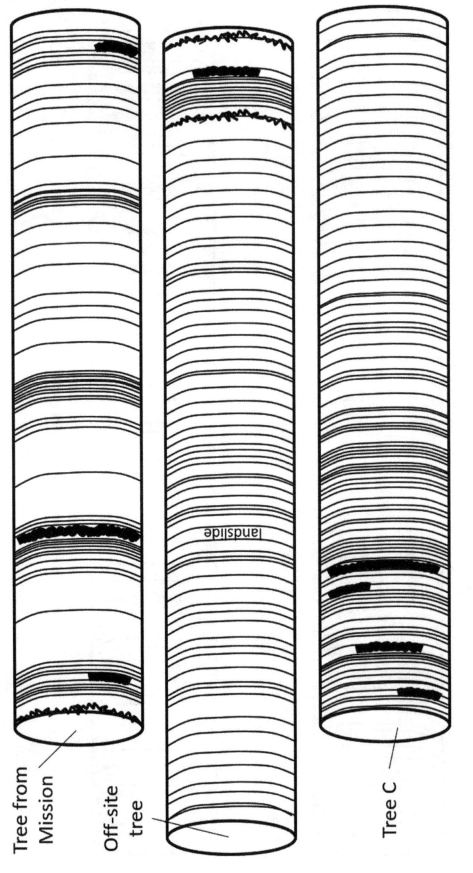

Figure 26.4. Tree C relative to cores from off-site and the Spanish Mission building. Cutting date for Tree C is 1704 CE (Note: You must cross-date these cores to arrive at the construction date.)

Worksheet 26.1

1. **Answer the following questions for Tree A:**

   - What is the date for the first year of growth? _____

   - What climate event(s) can you identify? _____

   _____

   _____

   - Indicate date range(s) of the above event(s): _____

   - What historical/climate event does it most likely represent?_____

   _____

   _____

2. **Answer the following questions for Tree B:**

   - What is the date for the first year of growth? _____

   - What climate event can you identify? _____

   _____

   _____

   - Indicate date range(s) of the above climate event: _____

   - What historical/climate event does it most likely represent?_____

   _____

   _____

3. **Tree C has been cross-dated with other samples to go much further back in time. Answer the following questions for Tree C (but be sure to look at the entire sequence):**

   - What is the date for the first year of growth? _____

   - What year was the landslide that covered the plank house?_____

   - For how many years was the house occupied before the landslide occurred? _____

   - When was this building erected at the Mission? Could the Mission be older than this date?

   _____

   _____

   - What well-known Pacific climate event does this sequence most likely represent?

   _____

   _____

   _____

   _____

   _____

4. Correctly match the tree core to the preservation project:

Project
_____

Project
_____

Project
_____

5. Watch "Tree Rings Do Tell Tales" (Swanberg 2019), which discusses recent research at Chaco Culture National Park, an important historic preservation site in the region. What amazing information has recently come to light and what are the implications of those findings. (The video will tell you *what*, but you have to ponder the cultural significance!)

_____

_____

_____

_____

6. Watch the "Vikings Unearthed" clip (PBS 2016), which discusses recent research at underwater sites in Norway that have preserved amazing intact timbers from these ships. When do the ships date to? And what did cross-dating of the timbers reveal about the manufacture of the ships that was a surprise to everyone?

_____

_____

_____

_____

Worksheet 26.2

For Further Exploration and Application

Your instructor may have you do these questions as part of an in-class discussion or independent reflection.

1. Conduct some online research[3] . . . do you recognize the well-known, cyclical, Pacific Ocean climate events represented in Figure 26.4 (hint: read preservation project 3 carefully for clues)? How might these events have affected the Chumash and the Spanish Missions? In other words, describe the *human ecology* for the time period represented by all three tree cores (i.e., Tree C, Mission tree, and off-site tree). Be as specific as you can, even if you are hypothesizing (but do note if it is a hypothesis!).

_____

_____

_____

_____

_____

_____

_____

_____

_____

_____

_____

_____

_____

_____

_____

_____

_____

_____

Notes

This chapter was contributed by Genevieve Everett and Jessie Hoover, MA candidates in the Applied Archaeology program at Indiana University of Pennsylvania.

1. A video is available at https://www.youtube.com/watch?v=fgwD0OOqs3M.
2. The dendrochronology portion has been edited out and made into an 11-minute clip (the dendrochronology discussion begins at 7:44): "Dendrochronology Used to Date Viking Longships," video, 11:10, uploaded by 2011roads, 28 December 2012, https://www.you tube.com/watch?v=QSOrt8cclMc. Accessed 11 June 2019.
3. Begin by rereading project 3 for clues. If you still have difficulty, your teacher has some resources to help.

References

CCAC (Crow Canyon Archaeological Center). 2015. "Dendroclimatology: Using Tree Rings to Reconstruct Past Climate." Video, 4:42. Uploaded 7 December. https://www.youtube.com/watch?v=GvuLjhdEBoo. Accessed 5 June 2019.

Jackson, Robert H., and Anne Gardzina 1999. "Agriculture, Drought, and Chumash Congregation in the California Missions." *Estudios de Historia Novohispana* 19: 69–90. http://californiamissionsfoundation.org/articles/agriculturedroughtandchumashcongregation. Webpage summary accessed 29 March 2019.

Nash, Stephen E. 2002. "Archaeological Tree-ring Dating at the Millennium." *Journal of Archaeological Research* 10 (3): 243–275.

PBS. 2016. "Vikings Unearthed." *NOVA*, season 43, episode 9. Aired 6 April. https://www.pbs.org/video/nova-vikings-unearthed-pro/. Accessed 5 June 2019.

Rowntree, Lester B. 1985. "Drought During California's Mission Period, 1769–1834." *Journal of California and Great Basin Anthropology* 7 (2): 7–20.

Swanberg, Susan. 2019. "Tree Rings Do Tell Tales: Dendrochronology at Crow Canyon." Western National Parks Association. http://www.wnpa.org/research-item/tree-rings-do-tell-tales. Accessed 29 March 2019.

CHAPTER 27

Kinsman, Can You Spare a Penny?
Economic Anthropology

Reciprocity

Have you ever given a gift to someone, but they failed to reciprocate the gesture? Perhaps you gave a gift to a friend for their birthday, but they failed to give you one on your birthday. Most of us have experienced such disappointment at some point in our lives. Likely, you felt angry or even betrayed. But why do we feel this way? If you really think about it, gifts are not simply the thoughtful gestures we like to think they are. Rather, they represent relationships between people. Giving a gift doesn't just mean you like someone: it also means you have a relationship with that person. This in turn creates a sense of obligation to return the favor with something of equal monetary or sentimental value, not necessarily immediately, but at some point in the future. When our gifts are reciprocated, the bond is strengthened and solidified. But when they are not, the bond is eroded and sometimes lost altogether.

Some nonindustrial (i.e., nonmarket) societies base their entire economic system on gift giving. Anthropologists call this economic system *reciprocity*. Three kinds of reciprocity are recognized. *Generalized reciprocity* (Figure 27.1a) occurs when a gift is given without any expectation of immediate return. The birthday scenario is an example of generalized reciprocity. Similarly, if you are at a dance club with a friend and you buy him a drink, you probably expect him to buy you one in return sometime in the future. But imagine he instead insisted on buying you a drink at the same time you bought him one. Doing so this soon would suggest he does not wish to become involved in a continuing reciprocal exchange with you. In a sense, it is a rejection of your friendship. *Balanced reciprocity* (Figure 27.1b), on the other hand, is one in which the return gift is expected immediately. Such would be the case if you went to a potluck hosted by your boss, who made the main dish; if you fail to reciprocate with a side dish right there and then, you might not be regarded in a good light, and perhaps even seen as a "moocher." Finally, *negative reciprocity* (Figure 27.1c) occurs when there is an attempt to receive a gift of greater value than was given (which may involve coercion or competition, and an imbalance in power). For you *Gilmore Girls* fans, a great example is Rory's relationship with her grandparents, who agree to help pay her private school (and Yale) tuition in return for weekly dinner visits. Obviously, the tuition was worth more than Rory's visits, and Mrs. Gilmore frequently held power over Rory and her mom as a result of the negative imbalance between them.

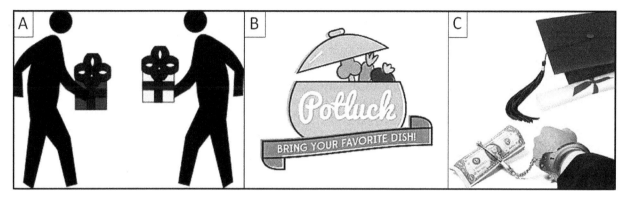

Figure 27.1. Types of reciprocity: generalized (a), balanced (b), and negative (c).

The Kula Ring

Perhaps the most famous example of reciprocity is the Kula Ring, a trade system practiced (pre)historically by the Trobriand Islanders of Papua New Guinea (Figure 27.2). Long, dangerous sea voyages were undertaken to trade, which followed a circular route. A trader traveling in a clockwise direction would give necklaces of red shells (*soulava*) as gifts to his trading partner. A trader traveling in a counterclockwise direction would give armbands of white shells (*mwali*). On the surface, the Kula Ring appears to be simply an exchange of gifts (and feasting with lots of food) designed to solidify bonds between male trading partners. The way in which traders greeted each

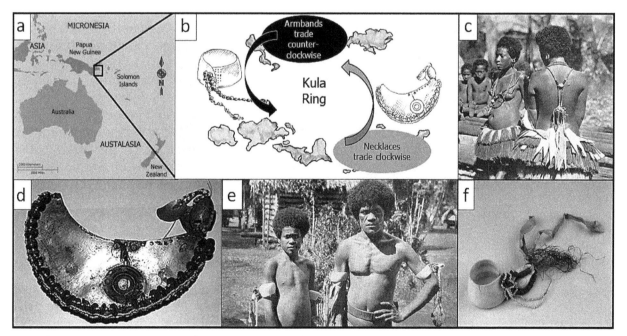

Figure 27.2. Location of Trobriand Islands north of Australia (a), schematic diagram of the Kula Ring (b), historic photographs of women wearing soulava necklaces (c) and men wearing mwali armbands (e), and close-up images of soulava (d) and mwali (f).

other on arriving at an island was rigorously prescribed by tradition: while the senior trading partners formally greeted each other and reinforced their friendship and authority by giving the traditional Kula gifts of armbands and necklaces, the younger men unloaded practical trade items on the beach to be bartered. These mundane items consisted of surplus stock from their home islands. While Kula gifts were exchanged with the assumption of generalized reciprocity (to be repaid in the future), the regular trade goods were bartered for via balanced reciprocity. When asked why they undertook these long distance (and dangerous) trading expeditions, Trobriand Islanders emphasize the social, not just the economic, gain the gifts entailed (Malinowski 2002).

Competitive Gift Giving and Potlatching

One social benefit of gift giving is that it makes us look good in the eyes of others. Givers are viewed as generous and kind, and people like to be around such people. Gift giving can also force others to like them. The anthropologist Lee Cronk (2012) refers to this use of gifts as being able to "flatten people with their generosity." In other words, by giving lavishly or giving rare and priceless gifts that cannot be repaid, at least not immediately, by the receiver. This kind of aggressive gift giving places others in their debt, thereby allowing them a level of control over the debtor and requiring their loyalty. If you have ever heard someone say they don't want to borrow money from a family member, this may be why. It is not just the money that needs to be repaid: it also requires "repayment" in the form of submission to the giver lest the receiver appear unappreciative (especially if the gift can't be reciprocated). This kind of competitive gift giving is the basis of the *potlatch*, a large feast in which the host (called a "Big Man") gives away many gifts to acquire followers. Big Men attempt to out compete one another, each feeling obligated to throw a bigger and better "party" with more elaborate and abundant gifts than the Big Man before him. The acceptance of gifts by attendees affirms the host's generosity and thereby increases their status. The gifts of food and goods essentially places guests in their host's debt until they can at some future time invite them to their own potlatch and give even more than before—essentially balancing the negative reciprocity.[1] Many scholars think this extreme form of competitive gift giving is the basis for the creation and maintenance of social inequality based on wealth and power, a topic that the archaeologist William Rathje (2000) explores in "The Potlatch Plot."

The Activity

This activity is fun—give it a chance! It was originally designed by the anthropologist Cathy Small (1999), who wanted to find a fun and informative way to demonstrate how strategic and nuanced gift giving can be when used as an economic system. As you move around the room making penny exchanges, be conscious of your end goal and the strategy you use to achieve that goal. Fill out Worksheet 27.1 as you make your exchanges. Your instructor will review the rules with you before play begins. Here are a couple reminders that are crucial to the outcome:

- The ultimate goal of this game is to live as comfortable of a life as possible;
- You may not exchange your last penny—you need this to survive on;
- If you make eye contact with a classmate, you *must* exchange;
- You must wear your nametag during the game;
- You may not sit down but must keep moving around the room;
- Exchanges are silent—do not reveal what you are giving prior to the count of three;
- Use Table 27.1 as a guide when recording your exchanges. When exchanging, remember that the number you should record is the difference between exchanges.

Table 27.1. Sample Exchanges.

Gave to (lost pennies)	Evenly exchanged with	Received from (won pennies)
Mary (2)	Quintin (2)	Skylar (1)
Yasmine (2)	Toni-Ann (1)	
Malcom (1)		
Allison (2)		

Gave to (lost pennies)	Evenly exchanged with	Received from (won pennies)
Riley (1)	Quintin (1)	Chris (1)
	Sarah (1)	Yasmine (2)
		Malcom (1)
		Ben (2)

Suggestions for Further Exploration and Application

- **"Eating Christmas in the Kalahari" (Lee 1969).** Richard Lee recounts a lesson learned when he gave the !Kung a prime ox to slaughter for Christmas. Expecting gratitude for his generosity, he was shocked by their ridicule and hurled insults. But the !Kung are well aware that no act is completely generous or free of calculation, and they have a mechanism for dealing with this reality.
- *Ongka's Big Moka* **(Nairn 1974).**[2] This classic documentary follows a Kawelka "Big Man" who is preparing for a large gift-giving exchange called a *moka*. Watch Ongka's stress increase as he negotiates the extremely nuanced feast, which exemplifies the strategy, complexity, competition, and one-upmanship in giving *moka*.
- **"The Potlatch Plot" (Rathje 2000).** Using Microsoft as an example, William Rathje discusses the importance of competitive gift giving by "Big Men" in creating and maintaining power, a process that leads to inequalities in wealth and power.

- **"Reciprocity and the Power of Giving"** (Cronk 2012). Lee Cronk explores the functions of giving using examples from societies around the world. Cronk shows that, in every society, be it !Kung hxaro exchange or US foreign aid, there are "strings attached" to giving that affect how people and groups relate to each other.

Worksheet 27.1

1. Record all your exchanges during the game in the table below.

Gave to (lost pennies)	Even exchanged with	Received from (won pennies)

- How many pennies did you have to start?_____ At the end? _____

- Which characterizes your *economic status* at the end?   Rich   Middle class   Poor

- What characterizes your *strategy*?   Get what I can   Be nice   Avoid contact

- Were you hit (and wiped out financially) by the typhoon?   Yes   No

2. Describe your strategy in Round 1 and why you used it. Had you known about the typhoon at the start, would that have changed your strategy? How did your strategy change in Round 2?

_____

_____

_____

_____

_____

3. Give two examples of reciprocity in our society, one generalized, one negative. Be prepared to share with your class. How does it conform to the principles of this economic system?

_____

_____

_____

_____

_____

4. Why should gift giving be considered strategic and nuanced in its practice?

_____

_____

_____

_____

_____

5. Under what circumstances does reciprocity work *best* as an economic system? Similarly, why would it not work very well in a large state-level society the size of the United States?

_____

_____

_____

_____

_____

Worksheet 27.2

For Further Exploration and Application

Your instructor may have you do these questions as part of an in-class discussion or independent reflection.

1. Read Lee's (1969) "Eating Christmas in the Kalahari." In what way was Lee's "gift" perceived as negative reciprocity? Explain the !Kung's response to what Lee thought was a very generous Christmas gift. Had they simply accepted his gift with profuse thanks, how would that have impacted the relationship between the !Kung and Lee upon his departure?

_____

_____

_____

_____

_____

2. Read "The Power of Giving" (Cronk 2012). How did cultural differences in reciprocity standards lead to deep-rooted misunderstanding that even today is captured in the myth of the "Indian Giver"?

_____

_____

_____

_____

_____

_____

3. Read Rathje's (2000) "The Potlatch Plot." What is the relationship between negative reciprocity, potlatching, and monstrous visual symbols? And what is the byproduct of such competitive gift giving, according to Rathje's hypothesis?

_____

_____

_____

_____

_____

Notes

1. A *potlatch* is a gift-giving feast practiced by Indigenous peoples of the Pacific Northwest Coast of Canada and the United States, including the Haida, Kwakwaka'wakw, and Tlingit cultures.
2. The first half is available at "Kawelka: Ongka's Big Moka," video, 25:24, uploaded by Allan Dawson, 27 August 2016, https://vimeo.com/180445401. Accessed 5 June 2019.

References

Cronk, Lee. 2012. "Reciprocity and the Power of Giving." In *Conformity and Conflict*, ed. James Spradley and David W. McCurdy, 119–124. London: Pearson.

Lee, Richard Borshay. 1969. "Eating Christmas in the Kalahari." *Natural History* 78 (14): 1–6.

Malinowski, Bronislaw. 2002. *Argonauts of the Western Pacific: an Account of Native Enterprise and Adventure in the Archipelagoes of Melanesian New Guinea*. New York: Routledge.

Rathje, William. 2000. "The Potlatch Plot." *Discovering Archaeology* 2 (5): 26–28.

Nairn, Charlie, dir. 1974. *Ongka's Big Moka: The Kawelka of Papua New Guinea*. Disappearing Worlds Series. Granada Television.

Rathje, William. 2000. "The Potlatch Plot." *Discovering Archaeology* 2 (5): 26–28.

Small, Cathy. 1999. "Penny Game: An Exercise in Non-industrial Economics." In *Strategies for Teaching Anthropology*, edited by Patricia Rice and David McCurdy, 71–77. Upper Saddle River, NJ: Prentice Hall.

CHAPTER 28

You Can Dough It?
Linguistic Anthropology

Cuneiform

The earliest form of writing was developed in the Near East by the Sumerians between 3500 and 3200 BCE. It grew out of a symbolic counting and tabulation system using clay tokens representing livestock and commodities. These tokens were stored in clay balls or *bullae* (Figure 28.1a), and notations were made on the outside of the ball indicating what was represented on the inside. Eventually, this system was replaced by a wedge-shaped writing system known as cuneiform (from the Latin word *cuneus*, meaning wedge) (Figure 28.1b). Cuneiform actually refers to the style of writing—creating wedge-shaped symbols with a reed stylus; cuneiform writing was used for many different languages including Sumerian, Akkadian, Elamite, Hittite, and Old Persian. Typically, cuneiform writing was inscribed into clay, but sometimes other materials were used, such as wax, stone, and metal. Clay tablets were often dried in the sun after completion while some may have been fired in a kiln. Sun dried tablets do not preserve very well. Some sun-dried tablets were accidentally burned (often when the buildings in which they were located were burned during an overthrow of power), preserving them until recent times.

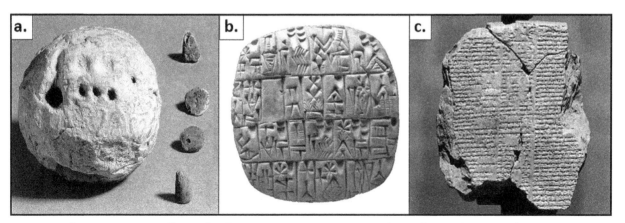

Figure 28.1. Bulla and tokens (a); Sumerian cuneiform from Shuruppak, Iraq, ca. 2500 BCE (b); and Tablet 4 of the *Epic of Gilgamesh* from the Royal Library of Ashurbanipal, 669–627 BCE (c).

While cuneiform served primarily as a means of recording everyday transactions, archaeologists have also gained valuable insight into many more interesting things—from what was known of the cosmos and the planets, to the majestic lives of Assyrian kings and everyday lives of families, to the culinary secrets of making a Babylonian stew and beer, and even the great literature and poetry of the era. Some of this literature has captured the imaginations of readers even today. For example, you are probably familiar with the famous *Epic of Gilgamesh*, but did you know it was originally written in Sumerian cuneiform (Figure 28.1c)? The first version of this poem dates to the 18th century BCE. Humorously, a recent find in Babylonia dating around 1750 BCE, turned out to be what is essentially a customer service complaint. Deciphering the clay tablet revealed the grieving of an irate copper merchant named Nanni, who details at great length his anger at a sour deal, and his dissatisfaction with the quality and service of Ea-nasir (Leafloor 2015). Despite the many advances made in deciphering cuneiform, much remains unknown: at least half a million cuneiform tablets have been excavated in modern times, yet only a fraction have been deciphered or published.

The Activity

This activity allows you to practice deciphering and creating cuneiform texts. First, you will decipher the cuneiform phrase on the worksheet, using one version of a cuneiform "alphabet." Next, using the craft dough and stylus you are provided, you will experiment with writing letters and words in cuneiform. It will take some practice to create the characters with the appropriate depth and shape so that they are recognizable and able to be read by others. Once you feel more confident in your scribal abilities, write a phrase in the "clay" and share it with others. You in turn should try to decipher your classmate's cuneiform phrases.

Suggestions for Further Exploration and Application

- **"Cuneiform" (Khan Academy 2019a).**[1] This is an excellent overview of cuneiform contextualized within Near Eastern archaeology and culture and includes excellent pictures and examples of amazing things the tablets preserve knowledge of, including the *Epic of Gilgamesh*, a map of the Mesopotamian world, observations of the planet Venus, and many more interesting items. There is also a good four-minute video on one graduate student's quest to preserve and transcribe as many of the tablets as possible before it's too late.
- **"The World's Oldest Writing" (Editors 2016).** This is a nice summary article for students or teachers; discusses examples of recipes, laws, medical texts, and more, written in cuneiform.

A Cuneiform "Alphabet"

1. Decipher the phrase below using the cuneiform alphabet provided. Use the lines above each symbol to place the English letter.

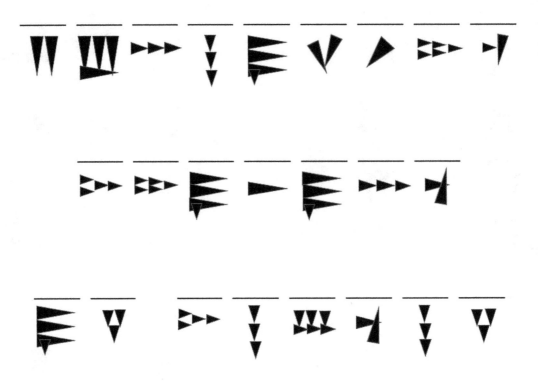

For Further Exploration and Application

Your instructor may have you do these questions as part of an in-class discussion or independent reflection.

2. Create your own inscription using the same alphabet on the dough provided by your instructor.

3. Read "Cuneiform Tablets: Backstory" (Khan Academy 2019b), which highlights large-scale looting of Near Eastern artifacts such as clay tables and cylinder seals. A recent case involved Hobby Lobby, which recently paid the government millions of dollars in fines for illegal (and unprovenienced) import of more than five thousand such artifacts. Archaeologically speaking, why is this a problem (there are several reasons)?

_____

_____

_____

_____

_____

_____

Note

1. While this is generally an excellent site, we do not agree with their discussion of the cradle of civilization, the implication being that without writing and cities, societies are not "civilized."

References

Editors. 2016. "The World's Oldest Writing." *Archaeology* 69 (3): 26–33. https://www.archae ology.org/issues/213-1605/features/4326-cuneiform-the-world-s-oldest-writing. Accessed 5 June 2019.

Khan Academy. 2019a. "Cuneiform." In *The Ancient Near East: An Introduction*. Accessed 2 April. https://www.khanacademy.org/humanities/ancient-art-civilizations/ancient-near-east1/the-ancient-near-east-an-introduction/a/cuneiform. Accessed 12 June 2019.

———. 2019b. "Cuneiform Tablets: Backstory." In *The Ancient Near East: An Introduction*. Accessed 2 April. https://www.khanacademy.org/humanities/ancient-art-civilizations/ancient-near-east1/the-ancient-near-east-an-introduction/a/cuneiform-tablets-backstory. Accessed 2 April 2019.

Leafloor, Liz. 2015. "4,000-Year-Old Ancient Babylonian Tablet Is Oldest Customer Service Complaint Ever Discovered." *Ancient Origins*, 25 April. https://www.ancient-origins .net/artifacts-ancient-writings/4000-year-old-ancient-babylonian-tablet-oldest-complai nt-020313. Accessed 5 June 2019.

MODULE 6

Archaeological Ethics and Stewardship

CHAPTER 29

Draw-an-Archaeologist
Pre- and Posttest

Archaeological Myths and Stereotypes

Many years back, when I was a graduate student, my boss asked me if I would do career day at his son's elementary school. Not an archaeologist himself but knowing his son "wanted to be an archaeologist when he grew up" (we hear that all the time!), he was excited his son would get to meet a "real" archaeologist. I spent lots of time pulling together artifacts to pass around and gathered up the tools of my trade for show and tell: trowel, shovel, shaker sieve, etc. Outside the classroom, I waited for the person ahead of me—an engineer—to finish. As he packed up, I heard the teacher announce that archaeology was next. As I walked into the room, I heard an excited boy whisper loudly to a friend, "Oh good, the dinosaur lady is here!" What a way to start career day—telling 25 excited eight-year-olds that I don't "do dinosaurs." Eyes widened disappointedly, smiles drooped noticeably . . . it felt awful! The good news is that they ended up really liking archaeology—and learning the difference between paleontology and archaeology, something I find that many adults don't know thanks in large part to Hollywood movies that consistently mistake the two. Archaeology students at the Indiana University of Pennsylvania recently sought to remedy this problem during their annual Archaeology Day Open House. They made posters illustrating the difference between archaeology and paleontology and taught the workshops sporting T-shirts reading "Archaeology: Everything but Dinos."

Another common misconception is the Indiana Jones image: trusty whip and fedora, golden treasure, lost arks, narrow escapes from hostile natives, and giant boulders—what's not to love? If I had a dollar for every time someone called me "Indiana Jane," I'd be rich. Don't get me wrong—we love *Raiders of the Lost Ark* as much as the next Harrison Ford fan. But I cringe when I realize that is oftentimes the *only* image the public has of archaeology. Although Indy is a college professor, his ethics leave a lot to be questioned. And as the most famous archaeologist out there (arguably still more popular than Lara Croft), many people have come to associate archaeology with being adventurous, male, white, and dominated by fieldwork. Not to mention the whole looting thing and disrespecting Indigenous cultures. So, while Dr. Jones is hard to beat as a dashing adventurer, by today's standards he would be viewed as no better than an opportunistic relic hunter with little legitimacy, and even less scientific merit.

The Activity

The DART activity will make you more aware of the many myths, misconceptions, and stereotypes that pervade archaeology. (Your teacher will tell you what DART stands for later.) It will also ask you to critically evaluate the origin of these myths, and how we might combat these inaccurate perceptions that really do us more harm than good in the long run. Use Worksheet 29.1 for the pretest and follow your teacher's instructions. Use 29.2 for the posttest. Your teacher may also ask you to complete and turn in Worksheet 29.2 at the beginning of the semester, and the reflection questions in the "For Further Exploration and Application" section at the end of the semester.

Suggestions for Further Exploration and Application

- **"Archaeology Must Open Up and Become More Diverse" (Dave 2016).** Although archaeology classrooms are becoming more representative, there is still a paucity of practitioners with varied backgrounds and perspectives, something that is vitally important to the study of human culture.
- **"Popular Images and Popular Stereotypes: Images of Archaeologists in Popular and Documentary Film" (Baxter 2002).** This article analyzes the source and pervasiveness of common stereotypes emerging from popular film media. Jane Baxter states: "It would be difficult to argue that there is a more popular image of an archaeologist than Indiana Jones . . . [He] has become the stereotypical image of an archaeologist. He is also very white and very male, and his character has become the racial and gendered stereotype of a 'typical' archaeologist" (2002: 16). What about social media? Same problem?

Worksheet 29.1

Pre-DART

Check off the myths and misconceptions represented by the class's DARTs. If there are others not listed here, add them below. Correct these myths in the "Fact" column.

Myth/Misconception	Fact
☐ Archaeology = paleontology	
☐ Archaeology = Indiana Jones	
☐ Archaeology = white male	
☐ Archaeology = fieldwork	
☐ Archaeology is not scientific	
☐ Archaeologists keep/loot artifacts	
☐ Other: _____ Other: _____ Other: _____	

Worksheet 29.2

Post-DART

For Further Exploration and Application

Your instructor may have you do these questions as part of an in-class discussion or independent reflection.

1. How did your first DART (pretest) differ from your second DART (posttest)? Did your changes reflect those of your class in general? Explain why or why not. What did you learn about archaeology that stuck with you the most this semester or unit?

_____

_____

_____

_____

_____

_____

_____

_____

2. Read the recent editorial by the archaeologist Raksha Dave (2016) in _The Guardian_. Why is diversity so important in a discipline like anthropology? Dave argues that our classrooms are more diverse than our discipline. Look around you—does this seem to hold true for your American archaeology classroom, or is it also lacking diversity? If diverse, to what to you attribute this diversity? If not, why do you think that is?

_____

_____

_____

_____

_____

_____

_____

_____

_____

References

Baxter, Jane. 2002. "Popular Images and Popular Stereotypes: Images of Archaeologists in Popular and Documentary Film." *SAA Archaeological Record* 2 (4): 16–17.

Dave, Raksha. 2016. "Archaeology Must Open Up and Become More Diverse." *The Guardian*, 23 May. https://www.theguardian.com/culture-professionals-network/2016/may/23/archaeology-must-open-up-become-more-diverse. Accessed 5 June 2019.

CHAPTER 30

Archaeopolitics
Who Owns the Past?

Archaeological Ethics

Kennewick Man, a male skeleton discovered along a riverbed in Washington State in 1991, serves as the basis for this exploration of archaeological laws and ethics. Kennewick Man's remains immediately became of interest to archaeologists, who initially thought the 9,500-year-old skeleton had "Caucasoid" features, thereby potentially complicating what we thought we knew about the peopling of the Americas. Several Native American tribes, led by the Confederated Tribes of the Umatilla Indian Reservation, argued that their oral traditions teach them they have been here since the beginning of time and that remains so old are clearly Native American, regardless of how long the predate the formation of the Umatilla Tribe. Many archaeologists agreed, noting that archaeologists are anthropologists first and foremost, and as such need to be mindful of cultural sensitivity and interests. Specifically, they point to the *Society of American Archaeology's Principle of Archaeological Ethics no. 2, Accountability*, which states that "Responsible archaeological research . . . requires an acknowledgment of public accountability and a commitment to make every reasonable effort, in good faith, to consult actively with affected group(s), with the goal of establishing a working relationship that can be beneficial to all parties involved" (SAA 2019).

Federal Laws and Regulations Affecting Native Americans

Accountability applies to all descendent communities archaeologists work with, be they African American, Chinese American, or Native American, among many others.[1] While all communities deserve archaeologists' respect and sensitivity, it is especially crucial in our relationships with Native American descendent communities, who are—according to a 1994 federal executive memorandum—*sovereign nations* who may consult and negotiate with the United States on what is called a "government-to-government" basis. In other words, federally recognized Native American tribes, of which there are nearly six hundred, are to be treated as sovereign nations with autonomous governments. Two other federal executive orders (EO) affect the tribes as well: EO 13007, issued in 1996, ensures access to sacred sites on federal land, and EO 13175, issued in 2000, requires government-to-government consultation between tribes and the United States when tribal interests are affected. A final law of importance to this activity is the Native American Graves Protection and Repatriation Act (NAGPRA) of 1990—passed just months before Kennewick Man's discovery. In a nutshell, NAGPRA says all federal agencies (and museums receiving federal funds) inventory Native American human remains and funerary objects, as well as consult with tribes to reach agreements on the *repatriation* (i.e., return of) or other disposition of these remains, which may include reburial at the tribes' discretion. Finally, the law also provides protection for Native American burial sites, careful control over the removal of Native American human remains on federal lands, and consultation with tribes when investigations encounter possible Native human remains.

The Activity

This activity introduces you to key ethical principles and federal laws pertinent to archaeology, specifically as they relate to archaeologists' ethical responsibilities to the descendent communities whose past we study. You'll begin by reading an article (Klinkhammer 2017) and/or watching a short video (PBS 2015) to introduce Kennewick Man, a man who lived in what is now Washington State more than nine thousand years ago. You will then read two pieces of "data": "Claims for the Remains" (PBS 2002), including several of the scientist interviews, and the Umatilla Tribe's 1996 statement on Kennewick Man, whom they call the "Ancient One" (Minthorn 1996). Follow the instructions on Worksheet 30.1.

Suggestions for Further Exploration and Application

- **"African Burial Ground Documentary" (Pham 2008)** (*6 minutes*). Overview of a 17th -century African burial ground found under New York City. While accountability was slow in coming, the area is now a National Historic Landmark, and a granite monument now commemorates the cemetery.
- **"Ancient Technology" (PBS 2002)** (*3 minutes*). Marky Weahkee is a member of the Comanche Nation and an archeologist for the state of New Mexico. From weaving yucca cordage to knowing of medicinal plants, her knowledge highlights what is gained when archaeologists work with, not against, Native Americans.
- **"Comanche Elders Visit Fort Hood and Research Ancestry" (UTSA 2013)** (*7 minutes*). Like all federal agencies, Fort Hood is required to comply with federal laws and regulations such as NAGPRA. They clearly have embraced the spirit, as well as the letter, of these laws.
- **"Developing an Indigenous Archaeology" (Curtis 2010).** Indigenous archaeology is an emerging archaeological perspective that incorporates native culture, arguing that traditional knowledge and scientific knowledge are not mutually exclusive, but rather complement one another in robust ways.
- **"Section 106 Success Story: Discoveries Open Insights into Early History, Strengthen Tribal Relationships" (ACHP 2018).** This summarizes a NAGPRA "success story" in which accountability and compliance exceeded that seen in the Kennewick Man case.
- **"Summer Intensive Course: Public Archaeology" (Stanford Summer 2014)** (*5 minutes*). The archaeologist Barbara Voss describes ongoing archaeological research of the Chinese American descendent community in California and what happens when these groups' histories are erased.

Worksheet 30.1

1. Read Klinkhammer's (2017) article "Kennewick Man's Bones Reburied, Settling a Decade's Long Debate" and/or watching the PBS (2015) video "First Peoples."

2. Get your "data" by navigating to the appropriate websites listed in the references at the end of the chapter. First, read about some of the scientific plaintiffs in the Kennewick Man trials in "Claims for the Remains" (PBS 2002). Then read the Umatilla Tribe's statement (Minthorn 1996) regarding their position on the "Ancient One." As you read both sides of this cold case, place a check in the box of the party (Scientist or Umatilla) you feel is best associated with the value described in the Value column.

Scientists	Umatilla	Value
		Retaining sovereignty over traditional homelands
		Belief that once the body goes into the ground, it is meant to stay there until the end of time so that the spirit remains at rest
		Validity of oral tradition and importance of following religious traditions
		Respect for the living and those who have gone on to be part of the earth
		Responsibility to care for those who are no longer with us
		Honoring treaties and laws and respecting human rights
		Telling the story of Native Americans—who they are, how they lived, and their contribution to the world today
		Need to study human remains since the sample size of well-preserved Paleoindian remains number only a handful
		Discovering how and when people came to the Americas
		Quantitative measurements and exact details
		Understanding ancient migration patterns and lifeways
		Proven, unbroken link to the past

3. Are any of these values shared by both sides? If so, which one(s)? Describe in what way each share this value(s).

_____

_____

_____

_____

_____

_____

4. NAGPRA states that, in order to repatriate human remains, Native Americans must prove lineal descent or "cultural affiliation" with the remains. For scientists, this often means a concrete physical link, but for Native Americans, oral traditions passed down by their elders teach them they have been here since the beginning of time (i.e., they are descended from all ancient remains). What kind of "proof" do you think is appropriate and/or reasonable?

_____

_____

_____

_____

_____

_____

5. Watch the short video "Ancient Technology" (2013) or "Comanche Elders Visit Fort Hood and Research Ancestry (UTSA 2013). How do these videos highlight the principle of accountability? How are scientists and Natives working together to maximize our knowledge of the past while simultaneously respecting both past and present cultures?

_____

_____

_____

_____

_____

_____

Worksheet 30.2

Use the following cards to help organize your main arguments and assertions if your instructor assigns this activity as a Lincoln-Douglas debate.

Evidence Card 1		
Argument/ Assertion	Explanation/Example:	Source Information:
	Explanation/Example:	Source Information:
	Explanation/Example:	Source Information:
Questions for Opposing Team	1. 2.	

Evidence Card 2		
Argument/ Assertion	Explanation/Example:	Source Information:
	Explanation/Example:	Source Information:
	Explanation/Example:	Source Information:
Questions for Opposing Team	1. 2.	

Use the following cards to help organize your main arguments and assertions if your instructor assigns this activity as a Lincoln-Douglas debate.

Evidence Card 3		
Argument/ Assertion	Explanation/Example:	Source Information:
	Explanation/Example:	Source Information:
	Explanation/Example:	Source Information:
Questions for Opposing Team	1. 2.	

Evidence Card 4		
Argument/ Assertion	Explanation/Example:	Source Information:
	Explanation/Example:	Source Information:
	Explanation/Example:	Source Information:
Questions for Opposing Team	1. 2.	

Worksheet 30.3

For Further Exploration and Application

Your instructor may have you do these questions as part of an in-class discussion or independent reflection.

1. Read Wayne Curtis's (2010) "Developing an Indigenous Archaeology." What is "Indigenous archaeology"? How are scientists and Natives working together to maximize our scientific knowledge of the past while simultaneously respecting both past and present cultures?

_____

_____

_____

_____

_____

_____

_____

_____

2. Watch the video on either Chinese American (Stanford Summer 2014) or African American descendent groups (Pham 2008). How are archaeologists accountable to these communities, and why is this accountability important? Really think about this—don't just say everyone is important.

_____

_____

_____

_____

_____

_____

_____

_____

_____

Read the NAGPRA success story (ACHP 2019).

3. Explain why this archaeological project was subject to NAGPRA.

_____

_____

_____

_____

_____

4. How did this NAGPRA cold case prove successful at abiding by the Accountability principle? Don't just say the tribes were more amenable to science—think critically about *why* they were more open to a "white science" approach to their heritage.

_____

_____

_____

_____

_____

_____

_____

_____

_____

_____

_____

_____

_____

_____

_____

_____

_____

Note

1. See "Suggestions for Further Exploration and Application" for video summaries of these descendent communities.

References

ACHP (Advisory Council on Historic Preservation). 2019. "Section 106 Success Story: Discoveries Open Insights into Early History, Strengthen Tribal Relationships." https://www.achp.gov/sites/default/files/2018-07/On%20Your%20Knees%20Cave.pdf. Accessed 29 March 2019.

Curtis, Wayne. 2010. "Developing an Indigenous Archaeology." *American Archaeology* 14 (3): 37–43. http://www.archaeologicalconservancy.org/?wpfb_dl=68. Accessed 5 June 2019.

Klinkhammer, Amy. 2017. "Kennewick Man's Bones Reburied, Settling a Decades Long-Debate." *Discover*, 21 February. http://blogs.discovermagazine.com/d-brief/2017/02/21/kennewick-man-reburied/#.XJ7RWNF7muV. Accessed 5 June 2019.

Minthorn, Armand. 1996. "Human Remains Should Be Reburied." http://www.asd5.org/cms/lib4/WA01001311/Centricity/Domain/629/Human%20Remains%20Should%20Be%20Reburied.pdf. Accessed 29 March 2019.

PBS. 2002. "Claims for the Remains." NOVA Online, last updated December. http://www.pbs.org/wgbh/nova/first/claim.html. Accessed 5 June 2019.

———. 2013. "Ancient Technology." *Time Team America*, season 1 clip. Aired 3 July. https://www.pbs.org/video/time-team-america-ancient-technology. Accessed 5 June 2019.

———. 2015. "First Peoples | Kennewick Man | PBS." Video, 2:30. Uploaded 24 June. https://www.youtube.com/watch?v=Lq1lugMA3hw. Accessed 5 June 2019.

Pham, Jennifer. 2008. "African Burial Ground Documentary." Video, 6:12. Uploaded 3 February. https://www.youtube.com/watch?v=n_h9Xx-a1B0. Accessed 5 June 2019.

SAA (Society for American Archaeology). 2019. "Ethics in Professional Archaeology." https://www.saa.org/career-practice/ethics-in-professional-archaeology. Accessed 30 March 2019.

Stanford Summer. 2014. "Summer Intensive Course: Public Archaeology." Video, 5:00. Uploaded 2 June. https://www.youtube.com/watch?v=Lxb829nMaiE. Accessed 5 June 2019.

UTSA (University of Texas at San Antonio). 2013. "Comanche Elders Visit Food Hood and Research Ancestry." Video, 6:52. Uploaded 2 October. https://www.youtube.com/watch?v=dKPeGAVYGCY. Accessed 5 June 2019.

CHAPTER 31

Common Ground
Glacial Archaeology, Ethics, and Climate Change

Glacial Archaeology

Glacial archaeology is a newer aspect of environmental archaeology that has come about because of the relatively rapid exposure of archaeological remains in mountainous areas across the globe as ice recedes due to rising global temperatures. Sabrina Imbler (2015) describes it well:

> The world's greatest archeologist may not be human, but it is human-made. Global warming, the explorer in question, has melted glaciers that have preserved and hidden many past lives. From a celebrity mummy to graveyards of fish-lizards, ancient remnants have begun to spill out of the disappearing ice—faster, even, than researchers can recover them. And as the artifacts emerge, so has the science. The fledgling field of glacial archaeology seeks to find and recover these relics before the glaciers disappear, a time that may come all too soon.

Given the rich potential for material that is exposed by melting ice across the globe, as well as the complexity in locating, preserving, and studying such findings, there is an opportunity to explore the various perspectives involved when a significant finding is made in one of these locations. But, as the glacial archaeologist James Dixon notes (in Imbler 2015), the aftermath of the melt will mean incalculable losses to scientists' understanding of the past. People mistakenly perceive global warming as beneficial to archaeology: "For every artifact we find, we're losing thousands. And we're never going to be able to replace this data. As long as they're frozen in ice, they're preserved for the future."

The Preservation Ethic

A key concept you will explore in this chapter is the *preservation ethic*. Archaeologists use the preservation ethic as they consider the question of whether they should excavate or instead leave archaeological artifacts buried in the soil. Consider what happens to artifacts that become exposed after being buried for hundreds or thousands of years. Once exposed, artifacts, including their all-important context, are vulnerable to a host of natural and cultural transformations (see chapter 6) such as erosion and looting. Additionally, when we excavate, we often recover thousands of fragile remains that need to be carefully curated to avoid decay and degradation. The space required to keep these materials preserved is expensive, to say the least.

The preservation ethic also asks archaeologists to consider the techniques used in excavation itself—are the methods of excavation damaging to cultural remains, and, if so, should we unearth them? Or should we consider alternate ways to study the archaeological record? There are new high-tech methods emerging that view materials beneath the surface, leaving them in situ and undisturbed. For example, remote-sensing technologies such as ground penetrating radar and Lidar (satellite imagery) may be employed to see what lies beneath the ground well before we excavate. These techniques may also help guide where excavating takes place so that only portions of sites are disturbed while the rest of a site is left for future study.

Before excavating, archaeologists must also ask themselves a very important question: Might we have better technologies in the future that will offer an opportunity to study a site without potentially damaging the archaeological record? Once excavation begins, the work cannot be undone, despite our best efforts to record and preserve the materials we find. We must remember that archaeological resources are essentially nonrenewable resources. Maybe we aren't asking questions future archaeologists or other scientists may have. Maybe we don't have the equipment or theories we will have in the future that can answer key questions about the past. Ultimately, the preservation ethic asks archaeologists to consider the impact of their work on the archaeological record. Sometimes, however, we face a race against the clock where the artifacts and/or site face(s) threats beyond our control. In the emerging field of glacial archaeology, archaeologists may need to ask if we are currently in the best position to excavate and learn what we can before the archaeological record is forever altered or disappears altogether.

The Activity

This activity is a fictitious scenario, but based on the real discovery of Ötzi, the "Iceman," a Copper Age mummy found preserved in a melting alpine glacier on the border of Austria and Italy in the early 1990s. Worksheets 31.1–31.3 contain a series of fictional documents and communications that occurred among the various parties (called *stakeholders*) involved with the archaeological discovery of "Icy." Although all the characters and communications below are fictitious, they represent real-world issues that arose (and some that are still ongoing) during the actual Ötzi discovery. Read the communications carefully, and prepare to defend one person, group, or viewpoint in a class debate to see if the class can reach "common ground" before the 15 September international meeting hosted by the University of Cologne to determine Icy's fate. Your instructor will assign students/groups to each of the following participants in the event. Research the perspective and potential rights of the view they represent to participate in the debate and determine how best to reach common ground, and then answer the questions that follow.

- Couple who discovered the find—Jon and Maeve McWalkabout
- Head archaeologist from Austria (Austrian University)—Dr. Robin I. Fordetail
- Head archaeologist from Italy (Italian Alpine Museum)—Dr. Anthony R. Carbon
- Company that has satellite imagery for this area—Eyes-on-Italy Inc.
- Australian government
- Italian government

Suggestions for Further Exploration and Application

- **"Global Warming Is Thawing Out the Corpses of a Forgotten WWI Battle" (Roet 2014).** This article considers climate change related to a World War I battle site.
- **"Hunting for History through the Eyes of the Ice" (GlacierHub 2018).** In this article Yin (2018) describes the emerging field of glacial archaeology and interviews glacial archaeologists about the effects of thawing glacial ice as it exposes sites to erosion and decay. Includes an embedded 2 minute video.
- **"An Ice-Cold Case" (*Radiolab* 2013a).** This 20-minute *Radiolab* podcast episode attempts to solve the mystery of Ötzi's discovery and death.
- **"The Iceman" (STMA 2019).** The website for the South Tyrol Museum of Archaeology (STMA), which houses Ötzi, includes a "virtual exhibit" of the body (including tattoos), clothing, artifacts, etc.
- **"The Iceman Speaks" (*Radiolab* 2013b).** This podcast is the (13-minute) "sequel to 'An Ice-Cold Case,'" this time a creative take from Ötzi's resurrected perspective.
- **"Melting Mummies Are on Thin Ice, Thanks to Climate Change" (Imbler 2015).** This article discusses how climate change and glacial retreat affects the exposure of mummies in alpine regions.
- **"Argentina: Environmentalists Welcome new Law to Protect Glaciers" (Valente 2010).** This article reviews a controversial new Argentine law to restrict mining and fossil fuel extraction near glacier fields.

Worksheet 31.1

From the Journal of Maeve McWalkabout

"As we hiked along the rugged Watchagonnafind Trail, we decided to take advantage of the unseasonably warm weather and good conditions and ventured off the hiking trail for the afternoon. As we climbed higher in elevation, we enjoyed the cool air, snowcapped views, and wildlife. After about an hour, Jon looked up ahead and noticed the ice patch he was viewing had something protruding from it. We approached and saw what seemed to be a human body wedged in the ice, partially exposed. I must admit to being horrified. Surely, we haven't stumbled on a murdered body way up here?! Shaken up, we ended our afternoon excursion early and hurried to the nearest town to report the body to the local authorities . . ."

Associated Press Release

VIENNA, 22 July 1991—The mummified remains of an ancient body were found by hikers last week a mile south of the rugged Whatchagonnafind Trail, famed for its scenic alpine overlooks. Following the filing of their report by Scottish tourists Jon and Maeve McWalkabout, the couple led the police to the area where they found the body. Austrian police began treating the location as a potential crime scene and worked diligently to expose the body for identification and evidence. As they chipped away at the ice, investigators noted various materials that did not seem typical for hikers who might have been in this area today. Found associated with the highly weathered, but intact body, were a wooden bow, stone-tipped arrows, grass-lined boots and an animal fur coat. The body had tattoos on its back and arms. Italian police deemed the body prehistoric and called in a team of archaeologists from the Austrian University to consult. Archaeologists sent a sample of grass to the Italian Alpine Museum to be evaluated and radiometrically dated. According to Anthony R. Carbon, the sample is more than five thousand years old, confirming suspicions that the body is no modern-day corpse but rather a visitor from the ancient past. The findings raise questions regarding who this individual was, how the body was preserved in such remarkable condition from five thousand years ago until the McWalkabouts' uncanny discovery yesterday. Head archaeologist for the Austrian University's Department of Ancient Civilizations, Robin I. Fordetail, says the McWalkabouts' find may be "the discovery of the century in terms of what we can learn about the life during the Copper Age." The location of this archaeological finding is reported to be on the border between Italy and Austria, raising discussion regarding whose jurisdiction the body belongs; both Italy and Austria have claimed property rights. Archaeologists from both countries caution that the body is of great scientific value and that its condition is rapidly deteriorating now that it has been removed. The McWalkabouts have been approached by the television drama *Ancient Treasures Unearthed* to star in an upcoming episode.

To the Austrian Government: 15 August 1991

While conducting research regarding the age of material discovered at the site discovered by Jon and Maeve McWalkabout on 3 June 1991, it has been revealed that the material dates to 3300 BCE. Thus, the finding is archaeological in nature, and as such, we request that the university here in Austria retain the rights to preserve and study this significant finding. The ancient human discovery is potentially rich with new information about Copper Age alpine cultures of this area. The body appears to be man, a hunter, who is preserved in such remarkable condition that he was initially thought to be a modern death. However, the materials on his person and in his possession are clearly from a time nearly five thousand years prior, as he has unusual tattoos, grass-lined boots, and weapons worthy of study. The potential for paleobotanical study with this finding is also tremendous. As the first archaeologists on-site, it is our sincere hope that you will grant us permission to both house and study the finding we are calling "Icy" for the foreseeable future.

Sincerely,
Dr. Robin I. Fordetail
Austrian University

To the Italian Government: 17 August 1991

It has come to our attention that a significant archaeological finding was made by tourists visiting the area along our country's border last month. This find is currently being studied by a team of archaeologists at the Austrian University led by my colleague Dr. Robin I. Fordetail. Although Dr. Fordetail is a well-respected member of the archaeological community, we strongly believe the mummy resides on Italian soil (see attached map). Thus, my colleagues and I believe the finding should be retained for study at the Italian Alpine Museum under the care of my research team. This is a matter of national pride for our country and its heritage. It is imperative that the Italian government intervenes on behalf of the citizens of Italy to ensure this finding is retained within the borders of its country of origin.

Sincerely,
Dr. Anthony R. Carbon
Italian Alpine Museum

Worksheet 31.2

Dear Dr. Robin I. Fordetail: 19 August 1991

Thank you for your sincere letter seeking permission to continue to house and study the finding known as "Icy" at the laboratories of the Austrian University. We are pleased to grant this request. We ask that you send regular reports regarding progress in your research so that we may be aware of the findings and their significance in the months and years to come.

Sincerely,
The Austrian Government

To the Austrian Government: 20 August 1991

We have been notified of a significant cultural heritage discovery that occurred on 3 June 1991. Upon learning of this finding and its location, we sent a team of geographers to the location to conduct a survey and determine the country of origin for this finding. Upon conclusion of this geographical research (see attached report), it has been determined that the finding Dr. Robin I. Fordetail's team is referring to as "Icy" was discovered approximately 100 meters inside our Italian border.

Given the location of this finding is within Italy, we respectfully request that you return the materials for "Icy" currently housed at the Austrian University to the archaeology department at the Italian Museum. We will be pleased to coordinate the repatriation of these materials to the university's Director of Archaeology, Dr. Anthony R. Carbon. Please contact us with any questions you may have about the logistics of this repatriation effort.

Sincerely,
The Italian Government

To the Italian Government: 15 August 1991

We are the couple who found the ancient man known as "Icy" while hiking on vacation. We understand this finding is tremendously valuable and that, as the individuals who discovered it, we are entitled to a reward or finder's fee. We request this finder's fee be made immediately to us so that we receive what we are due. We also request 5 percent of the proceeds associated with Icy's research, publication, museum tickets for viewings, or sales of books and items about Icy that are generated.

Jon and Maeve Walkabout

To the Austrian Government: 2 September 1991

    It has come to my attention that Italy is requesting the repatriation of the remains and associated materials with the "Icy" find in the Alps last month. I would like to respectfully contest this request. My colleagues in the Department of Geology have also surveyed the area of the finding, and although they concur with the Italian findings that Icy was discovered approximately 100 meters within the Italian border, the mummy appears to have potentially shifted its location over time due to glacial movement and is therefore likely to have originated inside the Austrian border at the time of Icy's death (please see attached report).

    In addition, the complications of repatriating these remains could cause irreparable harm to the archaeological materials themselves. As we find with remains exposed after thousands of years in a well-maintained anaerobic environment, every instance they are exposed to potentially different conditions in our modern climate is a risk to the materials themselves. With every exposure to differing environmental conditions, we lose valuable information due to degradation of the remains from such exposure.

    We currently have Icy in conditions that mimic his preserved state in the ice patch in which he was found. We are including with this letter a proposal for funding to continue our research and preservation. We request that we are allowed to continue to conduct our research without disruption to the materials by returning them to Italy. Please consider an annual grant to our university of $500,000 to continue our research and learn as much from this incredibly significant archaeological finding as possible.

                                                            Sincerely,
                                                    Dr. Robin I. Fordetail
                                                    The Austrian University

---

To the Italian Government and Alpine Museum: 10 September 1991

    We would like to offer our assistance related to the finding of Icy this summer in the Alps. We have worked with several glacial archaeologists of late in Alaska and other alpine areas across the globe, and we believe, based on our studies, Icy will not be an isolated find. We employ a highly qualified team of geologists, geographers, and archaeologists who are well equipped with cutting-edge technologies such as geographic information systems, remote-sensing and satellite imagery, predictive modeling software, aerial photography, and helicopter surveys. The combination of such technologies may be extremely valuable as you consider the potential for other such archaeological findings near the area where Icy was discovered.

    We have included our proposal for $750,000 to use these technologies over the next three years to consider where additional findings may be located within your country's borders. It is imperative that these studies occur soon, or more findings like Icy could be lost as glaciers recede and more ice melts with rising global temperatures. Please let us help.

                                                            Our best,
                                                    Eyes-on-Italy Inc.

Worksheet 31.3

To the Italian Government: 7 September 1991

    As a follow-up to our previous communication and in light of new communications from the archaeological team at the Austrian University, we would like to submit an additional request to house the finding known as "Icy" at the Italian Alpine Museum. This finding was found on Italian soil and thus is ours to research and evaluate.

    We understand the complications associated with preserving and maintaining a safe climate that will not cause further deterioration of Icy's condition. As such, we are submitting a proposal (attached) to expand our laboratory facilities at the museum to appropriately store and research Icy in the years to come. Since we currently do not have these facilities in place, we would be pleased to enable the Austrian University to maintain the find and its associated materials in an appropriate state of preservation until our facility can be upgraded to house Icy. We ask, however, that Dr. Robin I. Fordetail's team suspend any research on Icy until the remains are repatriated to our facility. At that time, we will work with Dr. Fordetail on transferring information and continuing the research by our team. Again, as a piece of Italian heritage, it is important we bring Icy home.

Sincerely,
Dr. Anthony R. Carbon
The Italian Museum

To the Italian Government: 25 September 1991

    We have received your request to repatriate the remains known as Icy for further study at the Italian Alpine Museum by Dr. Anthony R. Carbon and his capable team. The complexity of this repatriation is increasing by the day. Our country currently has the following considerations at stake:

1. We are housing property that may or may not be Italy's;
2. We have a request to continue to house the property in order to retain its integrity in a preserved state;
3. We have a request to continue funding the preservation and research of Icy by the Austrian University team;
4. We understand you are being asked to provide finder's fees to the individuals who discovered the property;
5. We understand there may be additional finds of this nature, and we would like to explore how best to investigate and fund research for these possibilities

    Given these considerations, we would like to meet and discuss the issue further to come to consensus on how best to house, fund, and retain appropriate legal rights to the 3 June finding.

Sincerely,
The Austrian Government

Dear Mr. and Ms. McWalkabout: 25 August 1991

It has come to our attention you were the illustrious hikers fortunate enough to stumble upon Icy, the amazing mummy who is now all the rage among the European public. We have learned from archaeologists that Icy is now believed to have been murdered nearly five thousand years ago. For this reason, we would like to feature your find in an upcoming episode of *Ancient Treasures Unearthed*. If you are not familiar with our popular TV program, it features a different ancient treasure each week. We are the no. 1 rated prime-time show on Saturday nights in both the United Kingdom and France, with more than two million viewers. We have tentatively titled the proposed episode "Iron Age Cold Case." The program includes a recreation of your hike, interviews with locals about similar archaeological finds and their estimated values, and a survey of the Watchagonnafind Trail by both helicopter and foot to find more relicts.

We were impressed with interviews you have given following the find and believe you will be popular with our TV audience. We therefore propose to have you, rather than actors, recreate your fateful hike last month. You will be well compensated, and airfare will be provided to and from the taping location. Please respond favorably by the end of the month.

Sincerely,
The Producers
Ancient Treasures Unearthed

Worksheet 31.4

1. Check your team:

   ☐ Couple who discovered the find—Jon and Maeve McWalkabout

   ☐ Head archaeologist from Austria (Austrian University)—Dr. Robin I. Fordetail

   ☐ Head archaeologist from Italy (Italian Alpine Museum)—Dr. Anthony R. Carbon

   ☐ Company that has satellite imagery for this area—Eyes-on-Italy Inc.

   ☐ Australian government

   ☐ Italian government

2. The debate will proceed in three rounds:

   Round 1: Each team presents a two-minute position statement.

   Round 2: Following a two-minute conference, each team may ask *one* question of *one* other team. Teams have one minute to confer and one minute to answer.

   Round 3: Each team presents a two-minute position statement intended to find common ground.

3. Consider the following issues in developing your opening statement:

   • Who owns Icy and why? Is ownership clear, and how was it determined?

   • Who is the best caretaker of Icy and why? How do you know this?

   • How does the preservation ethic come into play? Why is it important here?

   • Who should finance the preservation/research of Icy (this is not cheap either!)?

   • Why is Icy significant? Does what happen to Icy now set a precedent for later?

   • Will such findings happen again in the future? Why or why not?

   tear here

4. Succinctly describe your team's initial position statement for Round 1:

_____

_____

_____

_____

_____

_____

_____

5. What question(s) was *your* team asked in Round 2? How did you respond?

_____

_____

_____

_____

_____

_____

_____

6. Check the team for whom you have a question. Write your question to the side then tear this section off and deliver your question to the appropriate team after Round 1.

☐ Jon and Maeve McWalkabout

☐ Dr. Robin I. Fordetail

☐ Dr. Anthony R. Carbon

☐ Eyes-on-Italy Inc.

☐ Australian government

☐ Italian government

Worksheet 31.5

1. Did your position change following Round 2? Why or why not?

_____

_____

_____

_____

_____

_____

2. After the debate, was a consensus reached? If so, describe that consensus. What were the key factors in reaching common ground?

_____

_____

_____

_____

_____

_____

_____

_____

3. Which side(s) had the most at stake? Who benefited most from the consensus?

_____

_____

_____

_____

_____

_____

_____

For Further Exploration and Application

Your instructor may have you do these questions as part of an in-class discussion after the debate or as independent reflection.

1. Watch "Hunting for History through the Eyes of the Ice" (Yin 2018) and/or read "Global Warming Is Thawing Out the Corpses of a Forgotten WWI Battle" (Roet 2014). What are some potential additional considerations for the emerging field of glacial archaeology and climate change, both pro and con?

_____

_____

_____

_____

_____

_____

_____

_____

2. What factors do you see playing a role in the "politics of ice?" Consider the recent Argentine law that restricts mining and fossil fuel extraction near glacier fields (for more details, see Valente 2010). Is this something we should consider in the United States? Why or why not?

_____

_____

_____

_____

_____

_____

_____

_____

References

Imbler, Sabrina. 2015. "Melting Mummies Are on Thin Ice, Thanks to Climate Change." *Scientific American*, 28 July. https://www.scientificamerican.com/article/melting-mummies-are-on-thin-ice-thanks-to-climate-change. Accessed 5 June 2019.

Radiolab. 2013a. "An Ice-Cold Case." 19 November. Audio, 21:52. https://www.wnycstudios.org/story/ice-cold-case. Accessed 5 June 2019.

———. 2013b. "The Iceman Speaks." 22 November. Audio, 13:02. https://www.wnycstudios.org/story/iceman-speaks. Accessed 5 June 2019.

Roet, Leander. 2014. "Global Warming Is Thawing Out the Corpses of a Forgotten WWI Battle." Motherboard Blog, 15 January. https://motherboard.vice.com/en_us/article/xywz8d/global-warming-is-thawed-out-the-frozen-corpses-of-a-forgotten-wwi-battle. Accessed 5 June 2019.

STMA (South Tyrol Museum of Archaeology). 2019. "The Iceman." http://www.iceman.it/en/the-iceman. Accessed 30 March 2019.

Valente, Marcela. 2010. "Argentina: Environmentalists Welcome New Law to Protect Glaciers." Inter Press Service, 1 October. http://www.ipsnews.net/2010/10/argentina-environmentalists-welcome-new-law-to-protect-glaciers. Accessed 12 June 2019.

Yin, Sabrina Ho Yen. 2018. "Hunting for History through the Eyes of the Ice." *GlacierHub*, 6 February. http://glacierhub.org/2018/02/06/hunting-history-eyes-ice/. Accessed 5 June 2019.

CHAPTER 32

To List or Not to List?

The National Historic Preservation Act

The National Historic Preservation Act (NHPA), signed into law by US President Lyndon Johnson in 1966 with strong bipartisan support, is legislation intended to preserve historical and archaeological sites. Widely considered to be the most far-reaching preservation legislation ever enacted in the United States, the NHPA requires federal agencies to evaluate the impact all federally funded or permitted projects might have on historic properties (e.g., buildings, archaeological sites, etc.). Specifically, Section 106 of the act mandates that federal agencies "take into account the effect of their undertakings" on historic properties that are included or eligible for inclusion in the National Register of Historic Places (NRHP), the official list of the nation's properties deemed worthy of preservation and maintained by the Department of Interior. Properties on this list that most of us are familiar with include Independence Hall in Philadelphia; the tomb of Martin Luther King Jr., in Atlanta, George; and the Statue of Liberty in New York City.

The NHPA is quite long, but three sections warrant particular mention. In addition to the NRHP, *Section 101* created several important agencies, including a State Historic Preservation Office (SHPO) in every state, a Tribal Historic Preservation Office (THPO) for each federally recognized Native American tribe, and the Advisory Council on Historic Preservation (ACHP). SHPOs and THPOs coordinate statewide inventory of historic properties, nominate properties to the NRHP, maintain a statewide preservation plan, and advise and educate the public. The ACHP, which consists of 23 members appointed by the president, advises the president and Congress on historic preservation issues. *Section 106* stipulates a three-phase process wherein cultural resources must be identified (phase 1), evaluated for NRHP eligibility (phase 2), and mitigated (phase 3) any time federal land, permits, or funds are involved in a project, such as road or pipeline construction. Finally, *Section 110* mandates that federal agencies monitor, manage, and preserve all cultural resources under their purview if they are eligible for the NRHP. These, along with other influential historic preservation laws, led to the development of a subfield of archaeology called "cultural resource management" that today employs nearly three-quarters of all archaeologists in the United States!

Early preservation efforts were driven by patriotism and a desire to protect places integral to the nation's heritage. These early efforts focused primarily on individual structures as opposed to neighborhoods in a city or rural landscapes. The preserved structures were often turned into museums to create a showcase and generate tourism. Toward the end of the 20th century, preservation efforts shifted from patriotism to the aesthetics of structure or areas and ultimately to their relationships with society at large (King 2004). Today, the economic benefits of preservation have emerged as the primary driver of historic preservation; according to Donovan Rypkema (1994), preservation efforts produce the greatest number of jobs in the nation's economy, and these jobs in turn create new businesses and tourism, increase property values, and enhance the quality of life in a community.

The National Register

More than 50 years after the NHPA was passed, more than 90,000 properties are listed on the NRHP (Figure 32.1a). Properties generally fall into one of five broad categories: buildings (e.g., Independence Hall), structures (e.g., Golden Gate Bridge), sites (e.g., Gettysburg Battlefield), districts (e.g., The French Quarter in New Orleans), and objects (e.g., Washington Monument) (see Figure 32.1c). Properties are not protected in any strict sense by NRHP listing (though individual states and local zoning bodies may choose to protect listed historic places), but indirect protection is possible via tax incentives and eligibility for rehabilitation grants. For example, owners of income-producing NRHP properties may be eligible for a 20 percent investment tax credit for the rehabilitation of the historic structure. Many cities and downtown districts take advantage of these incentives to rehabilitate historic buildings, revitalize downtown districts, and bring in investors, businesses, and tourism.

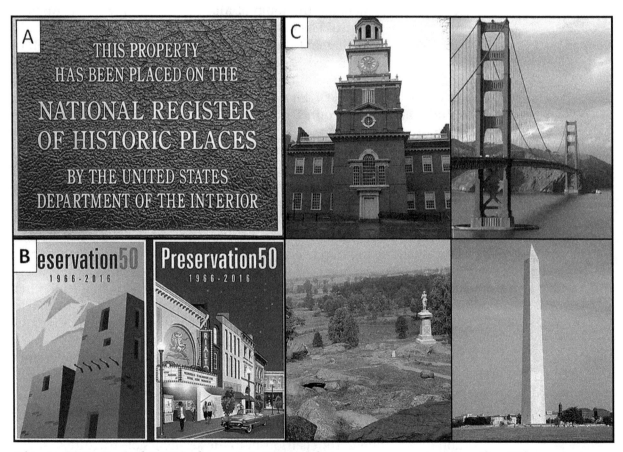

Figure 32.1. Typical NHPA plaque (a), US postal stamps commemorating the 50th anniversary of the NHPA (b), and examples of four types of NHPA properties: clockwise from upper left are a building, a structure, a site and an object (c).

Criteria for National Register Eligibility

At the heart of the NHPA is determining whether an archaeological site or other cultural resource (referred to as an "historic property" in NHPA language) is eligible for inclusion on the NRHP. Eligibility determination is a somewhat equivocal skill for which many students struggle to gain competency. NRHP eligibility hinges on meeting two important criteria. First, a historic property must have "integrity," meaning it must be well preserved, have relatively intact stratigraphy, and be undisturbed by natural and cultural transformation processes (see chapter 9) such as erosion and looting. Second, and more ambiguously, a property must have "significance." Since the definition of significance and meaning can vary substantially from person to person, the NHPA creates four categories; a historic property is significant if it (1) is associated with important events of national, regional, or local history[1] (criteria A); (2) is associated with individuals important to national, regional, or local history (criteria B); (3) represents a distinct architectural style, time period, or the work of a master (criteria C); or (4) has the potential to yield data important to understanding broad historical or prehistoric trends (criteria D). An easy way to remember these four criteria is the pneumonic device "ABCD": A for "association" with important places, B for "big people" in history, C for "cute buildings," and D "data." This is, of course, a simplification, but it is a useful acronym nonetheless. Finally, it is important to note that an historic property need not be a synthetic physical structure. Bulletin 38 by the National Park Service (Parker and King 1990) makes it clear that a historic property can also be a natural landscape, community, neighborhood, or geographic location with significance to the beliefs, customs, and activities of a living community, such as a Native American tribe. These properties are called *traditional cultural properties*, commonly abbreviated as TCPs.

The Activity

In this activity, you will read about two hypothetical (from chapter 26) and three real historic properties.[2] You will first decide if the site has both integrity and significance meeting NRHP eligibility criteria. If so, you will determine which eligibility criteria is most relevant (A, B, C, or D—you may list more than one). Finally, if applicable, provide a justification for accepting the nomination of the site to the NRHP.

Suggestions for Further Exploration and Application

Your instructor may ask you to also complete Worksheet 32.3 (back side) and/or read one of the following articles:

- **"Archaeology Under Attack" (Stewart 2017).** This is a good overview of the state of historic preservation legislation and current threats to historic and archaeological resources.
- **"Heritage Tourism" (Hargrove 2002).** This article describes the relationship between the NRHP and tourism, as well as how to use the NRHP database (NPS 2019).

- **"National Register Criteria for Evaluation" (NPS 2002).** This publication details the official criteria for NRHP eligibility.
- *National Register of Historic Places* **(NPS 2019).** This database provides resources for how to list a property, as well as sample NRHP nomination forms (NPS 2016), answers frequently asked questions about NRHP eligibility, and provides access to the national database (organized by state) of NRHP properties.

Worksheet 32.1

NRHP Nomination 1

In 1942, Sally Müllenberger and her family moved across the country to southeastern Colorado to take advantage of new opportunities in the developing West after the great Dust Bowl catastrophe of the 1930s. Her father, a soil scientist, was hired by the Civilian Conservation Corp (CCC) to bring the latest agricultural techniques to the ravaged Great Plains. Their interest in the move was both professional and personal: Sally's great-grandfather was one of the first settlers here in 1862. He worked hard on unforgiving lands for decades, only to flee the area for the West Coast in the late 1930s in hopes of a fresh start, leaving the Müllenberger homestead behind on the prairie. When Sally's family arrived at the old homestead, they were disappointed to discover it was too damaged in a fire to reuse as their own home as they had originally planned. But the beautiful huge oak tree that once shaded the front porch, and that her grandmother Lula planted that first year (according to her diary, which Sally inherited) to commemorate their new venture, was still there, so Sally's family felled it and used it as the main beam in their new home as a way of preserving their family's heritage, if not the tree itself. In an entry dated 10 May 1942, Sally's journal tells us her father cut the ancestral tree for their new house. Today, archaeologists are concerned about the preservation of Sally's family homestead because of its excellent representation of log cabin architecture from the CCC era. A team of archaeologists was recently tasked with coring the main beam to get a precise date for construction. Despite some damage by locusts, the main beam is in good enough condition to date the house using dendrochronology, as well as to examine climactic events that will give more insight into Sally's, and her ancestors', lives both before and during the Dust Bowl. Does the Müllenberger homestead belong on the NRHP?

Integrity (Y/N)	Significance (Y/N)	Significance Criteria (A, B, C, or D)	Eligible (Y/N)	Justification for listing or not listing:

The Trice site in western Kentucky was originally documented as a typical mid- to late 19th-century homestead consisting of a main house, an out-building, and a cistern—one of hundreds documented in the region. Historically, the site was located along the bank of the Cumberland River, near Canton, a thriving town before the dissolution of the railroad after the Civil War. During its heyday, Canton was a popular destination and boosted a well-known hotel at which several famous people stayed, including President James Polk in 1851, General Marquis de Lafayette, and the famous opera singer Jenny Lind. After the Tennessee Valley Authority damned the river in the 1940s to create Lake Barkley, Canton became something of a "ghost town," and the Trice homestead slowly began to erode into the lake at an average rate of about a foot per year. By 2010, an estimated 30–40 percent of the site was gone. As a result, the site was deemed ineligible for the NRHP, but shortly afterward, wooden coffins were reported eroding out of the lake bank, resurrecting the question of eligibility. Archaeological survey and historic research determined additional coffins were unlikely and that the small family plot that once existed had long ago eroded in the lake. However, the new archaeology survey identified an additional homestead (also eroding into the lake) not originally discovered, as well as an unknown prehistoric component, dating to the Archaic period. Based on the presence of lithic debris, shell, fire-cracked rock, and campfires, the site probably functioned as a temporary fishing camp for prehistoric bands of hunter-gatherers. During the Section 106 review of the site, the Office of State Archaeology suggested the site be reconsidered eligible for the NRHP based on the features and the possible preservation of organic food remains, something not common in Kentucky. They also worried about local residents' concern over the eroding historic period coffins. What is your determination?

Integrity (Y/N)	Significance (Y/N)	Significance Criteria (A, B, C, or D)	Eligible (Y/N)	Justification for listing or not listing:

Worksheet 32.2

NRHP Nomination 3

Luis Cordero is an archaeologist specializing in the Spanish Mission era. He is of Native American ancestry—a member of the Chumash Nation—and currently serves as the tribal historic preservation officer for the Chumash Nation. He is working to nominate an Indigenous Chumash plank house located on the Channel Islands (off Southern California) to the NRHP. Very few of these traditional houses are left from the pre-Mission era (1670–1750); this one has been fortuitously preserved intact by a landslide that dumped almost a meter of mud on it. It has been painstakingly excavated, and the site is now protected by the California Office of Archaeology. Cordero (whose great-great-grandmother married a Spanish missionary) is studying the effects of Spanish mission life on the Chumash people, as well as what caused more than 85 percent of Chumash to voluntarily move onto Spanish Missions between 1786 and 1804 (Jackson and Gardzina 2019), especially given that they were forced to convert to Christianity, give up their native language, and farm corn and cattle rather than fish as they used to. Recent bioarchaeological studies have shown that the bones of many of these converts (now buried in cemeteries on Mission grounds) show signs of acute nutritional stress, making him wonder if environmental changes led to food shortages in acorn and fish, two of the staple food resources on the Channel Islands. He has received a grant from the California Academy of Sciences to analyze a timber from the plank house to investigate climate change and its impact on the Native Chumash populations. The beam has been cross-dated with a beam from one of the Mission structures and another, off-site, pinyon pine (not discussed here), giving them not only a cutting date of 1704 for the plank house's construction but also an extensive climate record dating from the early 1800s back to the early 1600s. Does the Chumash plank house meet the criteria for listing in the NRHP?

Integrity (Y/N)	Significance (Y/N)	Significance Criteria (A, B, C, or D)	Eligible (Y/N)	Justification for listing or not listing:

The Squirrel Hill Site, in western Pennsylvania, is a Late Prehistoric (ca. 1300–1600 CE) Monongahela village located near the north-south running Catawba Trail, a major prehistoric road running north into what is now New York, and south into what is now North Carolina. The site is a typical Monongahela-period village, of which there are nearly four hundred recorded in Pennsylvania, Ohio, and West Virginia (the Monongahela "homeland"). The site contains several dozen round house structures with attached storage pits, a central plaza, and a stockade wall surrounding the village. It is one of the largest known Monongahela sites in the tristate region. Several burials were reportedly identified during the original excavations in the 1950s, although today it is uncertain how many there are or in what condition they may be in. The site has been heavily collected since the 1950s, mostly by locals collecting arrowheads and pottery from the field after the plows have been through. Some of these collections have recently been donated to the state museum by family members, and contain arrowheads, bone tools such as fishhooks, large pieces of decorated pottery, faceted and polished hematite beads, and bone and shell beads and pendants. Because of the collection by non-archaeologists, the Archaeological Conservancy purchased the farmland to protect it from further collection and/or looting of the sensitive burials thought to be present. Recent work in the 2000s used high-tech ground penetrating radar to map the site. These recent excavations showed the stratigraphy to be intact below the plow zone. This work also found—to everyone's surprise—a long, rectangular structure (nearly 60 feet long) with internal divisions, very different from the round houses typical of Monongahela villages. It has been proposed that the structure may be an Iroquois longhouse; if so, it would be the first recorded instance of an Iroquoian presence at a Monongahela site anywhere. Initial excavations, albeit on a small scale, confirmed the structure is prehistoric and domestic in nature—most of the artifacts consist of pottery, lithics flakes, and fire-cracked rock (used in both cooking and sweat bathing). Is the Squirrel Hill site NRHP eligible?

Integrity *(Y/N)*	Significance *(Y/N)*	Significance Criteria *(A, B, C, or D)*	Eligible *(Y/N)*	Justification for listing or not listing:

Worksheet 32.3

NRHP Nomination 5

To the Washoe Tribe of Nevada and California, Lake Tahoe is the center of the Washoe world, both geographically and spiritually.[3] According to oral tradition, Lake Tahoe, which today is a popular tourist attraction and resort, has been sacred since the beginning of time. Specifically, De'ek Wadapush (translated as Standing Gray Rock), a prominent physical feature on the eastern shore of Lake Tahoe, has been a sacred place of extreme spiritual power. It is to be respected and avoided by all but a few traditional Washoe doctors or traditional practitioners. Moreover, the Tribe gathers at De'ek Wadapush during sacred events throughout the year; they also collect medicinal plants and reeds for ceremonial baskets from a nearby section of the shoreline during the spring of each year. Thus, Cave Rock, as it is commonly known by local (non-tribal) residents, is the most important historic property in existence to the Washoe people. In 1993, the Washoe Tribe alerted land management and regulatory agencies at the US Forest Service of the sacredness and significance of Cave Rock and its surrounding environs when they learned that the Nevada Division of State Parks had submitted a permit application to the Tahoe Regional Planning Agency to extend and renovate the boat ramp at Cave Rock Lake Tahoe State Park. The tribe also shared its concerns regarding threats to Cave Rock's traditional religious and cultural significance by rock climbing and that the tribe considered such activity to be desecration of, and damaging to, a most sacred site. The tribe argued the site should be listed on the NRHP, which would require Section 106 review to evaluate any adverse effects resulting from any federal undertakings, including proposed renovation of the boat ramp but also several other activities allowed by the US Forest Service in sensitive areas of the lake, including rock climbing and hiking during sacred times of the year, which the Washoe feel are incompatible with the sacred nature of this area during these times. Is De'ek Wadapush eligible for the NRHP?

Integrity (Y/N)	Significance (Y/N)	Significance Criteria (A, B, C, or D)	Eligible (Y/N)	Justification for listing or not listing:

For Further Exploration and Application

Your instructor may have you do these questions as part of an in-class discussion or independent reflection.

1. Use the NRHP database (NPS 2019) to find a listed property in your hometown or country by searching by state and country.[4] Pick one and complete the following:

Name of property: _____

Resource type: SITE   STRUCTURE   OBJECT   BUILDING   DISTRICT

Applicable criteria *(may circle more than one)*:   A   B   C   D

Traditional cultural property?   Yes   No

Describe property and significance:

_____

_____

_____

_____

_____

2. Read "Archaeology Under Attack" (Stewart 2017). What are some recent threats to historic preservation efforts and archaeological resources?

_____

_____

_____

_____

_____

_____

_____

_____

Notes

1. Either US history, or the history of a relevant descendent community, such as Native Americans, Chinese Americans, or African Americans.
2. Some facts and details have been changed to fit the needs of this exercise and/or to protect the sites being described.
3. Adapted and modified from a real De'ek Wadapush case study; some facts have been changed to fit the needs of this exercise. For more information, see ACHP (2018).
4. The Department of the Interior is in the process of scanning and uploading listings for each state. Depending on where you live, you may have access to pictures and the full NRHP nomination form as a PDF, or you may only be able to see a summary of the listing.

References

ACHP (Advisory Council on Historic Preservation). 2019. "Section 106 Success Story: Discoveries Open Insights into Early History, Strengthen Tribal Relationships." https://www.achp.gov/sites/default/files/2018-07/On%20Your%20Knees%20Cave.pdf. Accessed 29 March 2019.

Hargrove, Cheryl M. 2002. "Heritage Tourism." *CRM* 25 (1): 10–11.

Jackson, Robert H., and Anne Gardzina 1999. "Agriculture, Drought, and Chumash Congregation in the California Missions." *Estudios de Historia Novohispana* 19: 69–90. http://californiamissionsfoundation.org/articles/agriculturedroughtandchumashcongregation. Webpage summary accessed 29 March 2019.

King, Thomas F. 2004. *Cultural Resource: Law and Practice.* 2nd ed. New York: Altamira Press.

NPS (National Park Service). 2002. "National Register Criteria for Evaluation." In *National Register Bulletin 15: How to Apply the National Register Criteria for Evaluation*, 2. Washington, DC: NPS. https://www.nps.gov/nr/publications/bulletins/nrb15/nrb15_2.htm. Accessed 5 June 2019.

———. 2016. "National Register of Historic Places Program: Sample Nomintions." Last updated 21 September. https://www.nps.gov/nr/sample_nominations.htm. Accessed 5 June 2019.

———. 2019. *National Register of Historic Places.* https://npgallery.nps.gov/nrhp. Accessed 30 March 2019.

Parker, Patricia, and Thomas King. 1990. *National Register Bulletin 38: Guidelines for the Evaluation and Documentation of Traditional Cultural Properties.* Washington, DC: National Park Service.

Rypkema, Donovan D. 1994. *The Economics of Historic Preservation: A Community Leader's Guide.* Washington, DC: National Trust for Historic Preservation.

Stewart, Tamara Jager. 2017. "Archaeology under Attack: Archaeologists are Responding to a Series of Threats." *Archaeology* 21 (1). https://www.archaeologicalconservancy.org/archaeology-under-attack. Accessed 5 June 2019.

CHAPTER 33

The Ethical Archaeologist

Archaeological Ethics

Archaeology has a way of conjuring up images of adventure and exotic artifacts. When we tune into the History Channel or National Geographic, it is easy to be swept away to the ancient world, which is often romanticized and its artifacts glorified. Often, the mysterious past is so compelling that we want to be a part of it, to have a keepsake of it, making it tempting to pick up artifacts when we find them. Most of us are quick to criticize *looters*, those who dig at sites with the sole purpose of selling artifacts to make a quick buck, but fail to realize that recreational collecting can be just as destructive as looting. While collecting may initially seem benign, it masks a poorly understood fact: every place has a past (often of great antiquity), and every past is important—particularly to the descendants of those that lived in the past. As discussed in chapter 7, the context of artifacts is crucial to reconstructing that past; artifacts by themselves tell us very little. Collecting recreationally also has the unintended side effect of depleting what is essentially a nonrenewable resource. Once an artifact is gone (along with its context), we can never get that scientific knowledge back. For these reasons, among others, professional archaeologists abide by the nine Principles of Archaeological Ethics established by the Society for American Archaeology in 1996 and recently revised in 2017. Ethics help guide our decisions as professionals, thereby helping to preserve the archaeological record which allows us to understand past human cultures. Without a code of ethics, we would be no better than the treasure hunters who loot and damage sites. These principles (Table 33.1) can be grouped into three broad categories: (1) stewardship and accountability, (2) commercialization and site documentation, and (3) public education and professional responsibilities.[1]

Stewardship (Principle no. 1) and Accountability (Principle no. 2)

The Stewardship principle says the archaeological record (including in situ archaeological sites, artifact collections, and digital records) is irreplaceable. It is therefore the responsibility of archaeologists to work toward the long-term conservation and protection of archaeological resources, which we recognize to be nonrenewable. Stewards are both caretakers of, and advocates for, the archaeological record for the benefit of *all* people. They should therefore use their knowledge to promote public understanding and support for its long-term preservation. The Accountability principle says responsible archaeological research requires an acknowledgment of public accountability and a commitment to make every reasonable effort, in good faith, to consult actively with affected group(s) and descendent communities, with the goal of establishing a working relationship that can be beneficial to all parties

Table 33.1. Summary of the Archaeological Principles of Ethics.

Principle no.	Principle	Purpose
1	Stewardship	Archaeological stewards are caretakers of, and advocates for, the archaeological record for the benefit of *all* people; they will use their knowledge to promote public understanding and support for its long-term preservation.
2	Accountability	Responsible archaeological research requires an acknowledgment of public accountability and a commitment to make a reasonable and good faith effort to sensitively consult with affected descendent communities and interested parties.
3	Commercialization	Archaeologists will discourage, and themselves avoid, activities that enhance the commercial value of archaeological objects.
4	Public Education and Outreach	Archaeologists should (1) enlist public support for the stewardship of the archaeological record, (2) explain and promote the use of archaeological techniques in understanding past cultures, and (3) communicate knowledge to the public.
5	Intellectual Property	The knowledge and documents created through the study of archaeological resources should be treated in accord with the principles of stewardship rather than as personal possession; these materials and documents should be made available to others.
6	Public Reporting and Publication	Within a reasonable time, archaeological research/knowledge must be presented in accessible form (through publication or other means) to as wide a range of interested publics as possible.
7	Records and Preservation	Archeologists will responsibly use and preserve the portion of the archaeological record that has been removed, including collections, records, and reports.
8	Training and Resources	Archaeologists must have adequate training, experience, and facilities to conduct research in a manner consistent with the standards of professional practice.
9	Safe Educational and Workplace Environments	Archaeologists will foster a supportive and safe environment for trainees, including knowing the laws/policies of their home nation and institutional workplace that pertain to discrimination and harassment based upon sex, gender identity, sexual orientation, ethnicity, disability, national origin, religion, or marital status.

involved. Archaeologists do not own the past but rather should view themselves as *stewards* of the past.

Commercialization (Principle 3) and Site Documentation (Principle 7)

Archaeological collections often represent the only surviving evidence of the past (particularly prehistory) and can provide new information about where, when, and how people lived in the past. Their scientific value, therefore, cannot be quantified in, or replaced by, dollars. Even if you are not an archaeologist yourself, you can preserve this information by keeping good records and recording any sites or artifacts that you come across. Most state historic preservation offices (SHPO) have a means of recording sites you may encounter and can provide advice about how best to preserve them. They will encourage you to record the site; recording sites is an important for the preservation of them, especially to prevent possible destruction caused by state and/or federal projects. In Pennsylvania, for example, archaeologists record sites on the Pennsylvania Archaeological Site Survey (PASS) form (PHMC 2018). Every site receives a unique site number that encodes important information, including the state, the county, and the numerical sequence within the county. For example, the Squirrel Hill Sites number is 36Wm0035: the 36 represents the state of Pennsylvania (i.e., the 36th state alphabetically), Wm stands for Westmoreland County, and 0035 means it was the 35th site identified in Westmoreland County. These unique site numbers help identify each site, which in turn allows for the preservation of the archaeological record. While the Squirrel Hill Site is currently owned and protected by the Archaeological Conservancy, if something were to destroy it, we at least still have a PASS record of the site's location and types of artifacts found there.

Public Outreach and Professional responsibilities

The rest of the principles deal mostly with issues of public education and professional responsibilities—to each other as well as the public at large. Principle no. 4 mandates archaeologists to reach out to the public and share our knowledge for the sake of stewardship. Principle nos. 5, 6, and 7 mandate archaeologists to report their findings in a timely manner though public education and academic publication and that they take physical care of the records resulting from excavation. Finally, Principle nos. 8 and 9 directs archaeologists to conscientiously train the next generation of archaeologists in a robust and ethical manner and to foster safe and respectful educational and workplace environments free of discrimination or sexual harassment.

The Activity

In this activity, you will "create your own adventure" to determine what type of archaeologist you would be (ethical or unethical). Each scenario will prompt you to choose between two alternatives. Based on your choices, you will discover if you would be an ethical or unethical archaeologist. Use

Worksheets 32.1–32.3 to record your choices by checking the box next to the option you choose, then move onto the next question based on your choice.

Suggestions for Further Exploration and Application

- **"Respect and Protect" (Tread Lightly! 2019).** This national conservation group partners with state agencies in Utah to help preserve cultural resources on public and to facilitate balancing recreation with stewardship and preservation efforts. The homepage hosts six very nicely filmed short videos (two to four minutes each) featuring their campaign slogans "respect and protect" and "look, don't loot." Your instructor may show one or two of these; if not, we recommend the "Rock Art" and/or the "Campaign Overview" videos.

Worksheet 33.1

Scenario 1: Finding an Artifact

Box 1

You're walking through a field on your way to meet up with some friends to go fishing. The outdoors is like a second home to you, and since you plan to be an archaeologist, you spend most of your time looking at the ground and examining the world around you. As you walk, you kick some stray rocks that are in your path. As you look down, you see something that catches your eye. You stop and bend down to take a closer look. When you brush the dirt and dried grass away, you notice that what you've found is stone and looks like an arrowhead . . .

☐ **Option 1:** You pick it up and pocket it as you continue on your way (go to box 2).

☐ **Option 2:** You admire it but then return it to its original location (go to box 3).

Box 2

You pick up the arrowhead and put it in your pocket. You continue on your way. You meet up with your friends and show them the cool arrowhead you found on your way to see them. Your friends are really interested in the arrowhead you found and suggest it's worth quite a bit of money. In fact, one of your friends says he saw something similar go for more than $100 on eBay just last week . . . .

☐ **Option 1:** You go ahead and list the arrowhead and get $110 for it (go to box 4).

☐ **Option 2:** You decide to not sell the arrowhead and keep it for yourself (go to box 5).

Box 3

You take a picture of the arrowhead before you leave, wondering how old it is and who made it. As you keep walking, you notice several sherds of historic whiteware and a few brick fragments nearby, so you begin to look a bit more. Realizing you'll be late, you continue to meet your friends. Later that evening, you google arrowheads to learn more about your find. While doing so, you stumble onto the SHPO's website, which is featuring a similar arrowhead in its "Artifact of the Month" section . . .

☐ **Option 1:** You contact the SHPO and record the site on a PASS form (go to box 6).

☐ **Option 2:** You don't see anything else, so you decide it is an isolated find and therefore fine to keep for yourself (go to box 7).

Box 4

You take the $100 and buy a Nintendo Wii with the money. The End. You are an unethical archaeologist ☹

Box 5

You start to get curious about the arrowhead and contact a professor at the local university to tell them about the find so that they can help you figure out what the next steps are. She explains it is a Late Prehistoric Madison point used by the Monongahela cultural tradition. She refers you to the SHPO. After calling . . .

☐ **Option 1:** You contact the SHPO, record the site on a PASS form, and donate the point (whose exact location you forget) to the SHPO educational collection (go to box 6).

☐ **Option 2:** You decide it is too much trouble and just keep the artifact for yourself as a keepsake, displayed in a nice shadow box (go to box 7).

Box 6

You took the responsible road to securing the posterity of the potential site. The End. You are an ethical archaeologist ☺

Box 7

Collecting objects and keeping them for yourself destroys the artifact's archaeological context, depletes a nonrenewable resource, and disrespects the community whose ancestors made it. The End. You are not an ethical archaeologist ☹

1. In this scenario, what box did you end in? #_____ Were you an ethical or unethical archaeologist *(circle one)*? If you were "unethical," which choices led your astray and why? Regardless of whether you were "ethical" or "unethical," would you feel confident about how to approach this scenario in real life, with the outcome of being an ethical archaeologist?

_____

_____

_____

_____

_____

_____

Worksheet 33.2

Scenario 2: National Register Eligibility

Box 1

You are a professional archaeologist on a "phase 1" survey at a site near the coast. The sun is brutally hot, and the smell of saltwater and fish permeates your senses. You are tired of schlepping through heavy sand in your heavy workbooks lugging equipment. On a wave-cut bank about 30 feet above the shore you find shell, ceramic, and bone, so there is potentially a prehistoric site in this area, which could prompt a "phase 2" excavation. But it would need to happen fast, because the site will surely be washed away if a few more storms hit . . .

☐ **Option 1:** You tell your supervisor you found cultural material that is indicative of a site but note that the site integrity is very poor (go to box 2).

☐ **Option 2:** You tell your supervisor there was no material found because it's obviously going to wash into the ocean soon (go to box 3).

Box 2

Your supervisor requests a survey, which shows the area of artifacts to be large, and several diagnostic ceramics help date the site to the Late Archaic, a period for which little is known in this region of the country. You and your supervisor must decide what to do . . .

☐ **Option 1:** You both decide that despite the quantity of artifacts the area has experienced too much erosion to be of any use to archaeologists (go to box 5).

☐ **Option 2:** You realize the site is significant and therefore eligible for the National Register of Historic Places (go to box 4).

Box 3

Fudging data is unethical and you are not qualified to determine when, or even if, the site will erode—that's for a consulting geologist to say. Go back to and rethink your decision. ☹

Box 4

But you are still concerned about the integrity of the site due to all the erosion, so you . . .

☐ **Option 1:** Finish your survey and discover a large portion of the site is still intact, but recommend the site ineligible due to erosion (go to box 5)

☐ **Option 2:** Recommend a consulting geologist be hired to evaluate how severe the erosion is and how stable/unstable the site might be (go to box 6).

Box 5

The SHPO and Advisory Council on Historic Preservation are concerned with your recommendation and will not concur with your findings, calling your stewardship and ethical practices into question. ☹

Box 6

The consulting geologist notes that the rainy season has ended, and erosion will be negligible for the next year, allowing time for phase 2 excavation of the site before it washes. More importantly, she notes the bank could be stabilized by adding riprap to protect it from the storm surge. That, coupled with the significance of the Late Archaic site and the potential for burials, prompts her to encourage you to rethink your eligibility recommendation.

    ☐ **Option 1:** You remain stubborn and disregard the geologist's advice, arguing that you are the archaeologist after all (go to box 7).

    ☐ **Option 2:** Based on the geologist's findings you recommend the site eligible, and further recommend expediting phase 2 excavation in case unexpected erosion occurs, as well as consultation with interested Native American Tribes (go to box 8).

Box 7

Archaeological interpretation requires the expertise of many professionals, including geologists. Plus, the possibility of burials warrants consultation with Native American tribes who may have concern with them possibly eroding out to the bank. Sorry, but you are an unethical archaeologist. ☹

Box 8

Your actions balanced both the stewardship and accountability principles of ethics. You are an ethical archaeologist. ☺

2. In this scenario, what box did you end in? #_____ Were you an ethical or unethical archaeologist *(circle one)*? If you were "unethical," which choices led your astray and why? Regardless of whether you were "ethical" or "unethical," would you feel confident about how to approach this scenario in real life, with the outcome of being an ethical archaeologist?

_____

_____

_____

_____

Scenario 3: Finding Human Remains

Box 1

You are a professional archaeologist working at a Mississippian mound site (ca. 1250 CE) in western Kentucky. The site was found while recording and documenting burials at an African American diaspora site (ca. 1870) just to the east, which includes a small cemetery plot. Both sites are located on a strip of land slated for a strip mall and Starbucks. Test excavations in the prehistoric plot reveal a tooth that appears human and some funerary artifacts . . .

☐ **Option 1:** You continue excavating the Mississippian site, carefully documenting and mapping any human remains you encounter to preserve their context (go to box 2).

☐ **Option 2:** You stop excavating, record both sites with the Kentucky SHPO, and recommend both sites to be eligible for the NRHP (go to box 3).

Box 2

The Chickasaw Nation learns of the excavation and becomes very upset. They contact the SHPO to register a complaint and demand that excavations stop until a tribal representative can be on site, which is the following week . . .

☐ **Option 1:** You are pressured by the client building the mall to "work around" the burials because he is losing money every day they wait (go to box 4).

☐ **Option 2:** You immediately stop excavating and wait for the Tribal representative to arrive, preparing a report of your findings for the representative to evaluate (go to box 5).

Box 3

After receiving your site documentation, the SHPO concurs that excavation should stop while representatives of the appropriate descendent communities are contacted for consultation on the project. Your supervisor asks you to initiate contact . . .

☐ **Option 1:** You reach out to the Chickasaw Nation to discuss repatriation and/or reburial since such consultation is required under NAGPRA (go to box 6).

☐ **Option 2:** You reach out to the both the Chickasaw Nation and the local African American descendants still living near the diaspora site (go to box 5).

Box 4

Your supervisor learns you failed to consult with the Chickasaw Nation and comply with NAGPRA. The End. You are an unethical archaeologist and have been fired. ☹

Box 5

The Chickasaw Nation representative arrives on site, as does a representative from the African American community you reached out to while waiting. After two days of consultation, a consensus is reached among all parties: the human remains will be reburied during a ceremony, and a historical marker will be placed to highlight the African American accomplishments at the diaspora site and commemorate those who died there. With both consultation and excavation complete three months later . . .

☐ **Option 1:** You immediately begin work at another diaspora site, realizing there is a rich history of such sites in the region and hoping this will eventually become a master's thesis, though that is probably years away (go to box 7).

☐ **Option 2:** You carefully write up a report and accept an invitation to speak at the local amateur archaeology society about the two sites and the consultation process (go to box 8).

Box 6

Your supervisor learns you failed to consult with the African American descendent community. You have failed to abide by the Accountability principle and have been fired. ☹

Box 7

By not responsibly publishing and presenting your results in a timely manner, or sharing your knowledge with the public and consulting parties, you have failed to abide by the Public Outreach and Education principle. You are an unethical archaeologist. ☹

Box 8

By reaching out to both descendent communities, you have complied with NAGPRA and the Accountability principle to be accountable to, and consult with, all interested parties. By presenting your findings at the local archaeology chapter, you have abided by the Public Outreach and Education principle. You are an ethical archaeologist. ☺

3. In this scenario, what box did you end in? #_____ Were you an ethical or unethical archaeologist *(circle one)*? If you were "unethical," which choices led your astray and why? Regardless of whether you were "ethical" or "unethical," would you feel confident about how to approach this scenario in real life, with the outcome of being an ethical archaeologist?

_____

_____

_____

_____

_____

Notes

This chapter was contributed by Eleanor Schultz (master's degree student in Museum Studies at Johns Hopkins University and Harley Burgis (master's degree student in Anthropology at Florida State University) while undergraduates in Indiana University of Pennsylvania's anthropology program.

1. For more information and details on each principle, see SAA (2019).

References

PHMC (Pennsylvania Historical and Museum Commission). 2019. "Recording Sites." Accessed 2 April. http://www.phmc.state.pa.us/portal/communities/archaeology/resources/recording-sites.html.

SAA (Society for American Archaeology). 2019. "Ethics in Professional Archaeology." https://www.saa.org/career-practice/ethics-in-professional-archaeology. Accessed 30 March 2019.

Tread Lightly! 2019. "Respect and Protect." https://www.treadlightly.org/programs/respect-and-protect. Accessed 30 March 2019.

IMAGE AND TEXT CREDITS

Figure 4.1. Created by the author.

Worksheet 4.3. Created by the author.

Figure 5.1. Created by the author.

Worksheet 5.2. Reprinted by permission. Extract from Janet D. Spector. 1993. *What This Awl Means: Feminist Archaeology at a Wahpeton Dakota Village.* St. Paul, MN: St. Paul Minnesota Historical Society Press.

Worksheet 6.2. Penny. Wikimedia Commons, Public Domain;
Charred Corn Kernel. Wikimedia Commons, Public Domain;
Cave Paintings. Wikimedia Commons, Public Domain.

Figure 7.1. Created by the author.

Figure 7.2. Three hypothetical scenarios illustrating archaeological association.
(a) Adapted from Microsoft Word clip art, public domain;
(b) Adapted from Microsoft Word clip art, public domain;
(c) Reproduced by permission. "12 burial illustrations from Appendix 1" Courtesy Jeffrey Quilter from original drawings by Bernardino Ojeda, *Life and Death at Paloma: Society and Mortuary Practices in a Preceramic Peruvian Village* (Iowa City: University of Iowa Press, 1989), 87-162.

Figure 7.3. Created by the author.

Figure 8.1. Created by the chapter author (Angela Lockard Reed).

Figure 8.2. Created by the chapter author (Angela Lockard Reed).

Figure 10.1. Created by the author.

Figure 10.2. Created by the author.

Worksheet 10.2. Created by the author.

Figure 11.1. Reproduced by permission courtesy Sarah C. Sherwood. Example of stratigraphy from the archaeological site of Dust Cave, Alabama. "Figure 8.9 (Prile N63, W67 to W64), p. 204," in "The Geoarchaeology of Dust Cave," Sherwood 2001, Figure 8.9.

Worksheet 11.1. Reproduced by permission. "Figure from 'Lab 1: Seriation and Stratigraphy,'" Courtesy James Denbow, University of Texas at Austin.

Worksheet 11.2. Reproduced by permission. Images from "Stratigraphy: Establishing a Sequence from Excavated Archaeological Evidence" and "Seriation: Ordering Archaeological Evidence by Stylistic Differences" from James Patterson. *The Theory and Practice of Archaeology: A Workbook* (Prentice Hall PTR, 1993) © 1994 Taylor & Francis Group LLC Books.

Figure 13.1. Created by the author.

Figure 13.2. Reproduced by permission. Deetz's seriation for the Stoneham cemetery in eastern Massachusetts. "Figure 1. Stylistic Sequence from a Cemetery in Stoneham, Massachusetts" from James Deetz and Edwin Dethlefsen, "The Plymouth Colony Archive Project" From *Natural History*, March 1967, copyright © Natural History Magazine, Inc., 1967.

Figure 14.1.   Evolution of the BMW 5 Series over time. Image created in Microsoft Word's online picture gallery, Creative Commons CC-BY-SA.

Figure 14.2.   Stylistic elements for use in seriation. Image created in Microsoft Word's online picture gallery, Creative Commons CC-BY-SA.

Figures 14.3.–14.5. Reproduced by permission. Stirrup Bottles A-D; Stirrup bottles E-H; Stirrup bottles I-L. Images from "Stratigraphy: Establishing a Sequence from Excavated Archaeological Evidence" and "Seriation: Ordering Archaeological Evidence by Stylistic Differences" from James Patterson. *The Theory and Practice of Archaeology: A Workbook* (Prentice Hall PTR, 1993) © 1994 Taylor & Francis Group LLC Books.

Worksheet 14.1.   Reproduced by permission. Images from "Stratigraphy: Establishing a Sequence from Excavated Archaeological Evidence" and "Seriation: Ordering Archaeological Evidence by Stylistic Differences" from James Patterson. *The Theory and Practice of Archaeology: A Workbook* (Prentice Hall PTR, 1993) © 1994 Taylor & Francis Group LLC Books.

Figure 15.1.   Adapted from "Dendrochronology," Courtesy Crow Canyon Archaeological Center, https://crowcanyon.org/index.php/dendrochronology.

Figure 15.2.   (a) Created by the chapter author (Tracy Michaud);
(b) Example of a bristlecone pine, the oldest tree species on earth. Images created in Microsoft Word's Online Pictures, Creative Commons CC-BY-SA;
(c) Created by the author.

Figure 15.3.   Reproduced by permission. Images courtesy Marc Bermann.

Figure 16.1.   Created by the author.

Worksheet 16.1a.   Created by the author.

Worksheet 16.1b.   Created by the author.

Worksheet 16.1c.   Created by the author.

Worksheet 16.2.   Reproduced by permission. Example of carbon-dating myth. Illustration created by Joseph Bomberger.

Figure 17.1.   Created by the author.

Figure 17.2.   Created by the author.

Figure 17.3.   Created by the author.

Figure 17.4.   Created by the author.

Worksheet 17.1.   Created by the author.

Figure 18.1.   Created by the author.

Figure 18.2.   Created by the author.

Figure 18.3.   Created by the author.

Figure 18.4.   Created by the author.

Figure 19.1.   Created by the chapter author (Pascale Meehan).

Figure 19.2.   Created by the chapter author (Pascale Meehan).

Figure 19.3.   Created by the chapter author (Pascale Meehan).

Figure 19.4.   Created by the chapter author (Pascale Meehan).

Figure 19.5.   Created by the chapter author (Pascale Meehan).

Figure 19.6.   Created by the chapter author (Pascale Meehan).

Figure 19.7.	Created by the chapter author (Pascale Meehan).
Figure 20.1.	Created by the author.
Figure 20.2.	Created by the author.
Figure 20.3.	Created by the author.
Figure 20.4.	Created by the author.
Figure 20.5.	Created by the author.
Figure 20.6.	Created by the author.
Figure 21.1.–21.4.	Reproduced by permission. Burial descriptions for burials # 10, 54, 87, 110, 115, 138, 142, 152, 202, 224, 84, 119, 65, 15, and 220. "12 burial illustrations from Appendix 1," Courtesy Jeffrey Quilter from original drawings by Bernardino Ojeda, *Life and Death at Paloma: Society and Mortuary Practices in a Preceramic Peruvian Village* (Iowa City: University of Iowa Press, 1989), 87–162.
Worksheet 21.1.	Created by the author.
Worksheet 21.2.	Created by the author.
Figure 22.1.	Created by the author.
Figure 23.1.	(a) Reproduced by permission. Example of western gender stereotypes in the *Flintstones*. "Flintstones Cartoon" Courtesy Everett Collection; (b) Reconstructions of our hominin ancestors. Wikimedia Commons, Creative Commons CC-BY-SA.
Worksheet 23.1. and Worksheet 23.2.	Arrowhead. Microsoft online pictures, CC-BY-SA; Hoe. "GUID 20C2B15D-839A-FB59-EB4F-FEFB5998B667," Missouri History Museum, http://images.mohistory.org/?guid=20C2B15D-839A-FB59-EB4F-FEFB5998B667, public domain; "Mississippian Notched Hoe Blade Collected by J.J.R. Patrick in St. Clair County, Illinois, With Modern Haft." Image Source, Missouri History Museum, https://mohistory.org/collections/item/resource:462308, Wikimedia Commons, public domain, https://commons.wikimedia.org/w/index.php?curid=61722825; Ceramic Vessel. Microsoft online pictures, CC-BY-SA; Earspools. Microsoft online pictures, CC-BY-SA; Bone fishhook. Microsoft online pictures, CC-BY-SA; Grinding stone. Microsoft online pictures, CC-BY-SA; Bone needle. Image by José-Manuel Benito, Wikimedia Commons, public domain, https://commons.wikimedia.org/w/index.php?curid=550562; Wolf-tooth pendant. Adapted from "Canis lupus Canine perceé MHNT PRE 2010.0.12.2 Henri Filhol.jpg" by Didier Descouens, Wikimedia Commons, public domain, https://commons.wikimedia.org/w/index.php?curid=37075970, CC BY-SA, https://creativecommons.org/licenses/by-sa/4.0/deed.en; Cave art. Microsoft online pictures, CC-BY-SA; Scraper. Microsoft online pictures, CC-BY-SA.
Figure 24.1.	All adapted from public domain images: (a) https://commons.wikimedia.org/wiki/File:Pech_Merle_cave,_painting.JPG. (b) Microsoft Online images, CC-BY-SA. (c) https://commons.wikimedia.org/wiki/File:Lascaux,_replica_05.JPG.

Figure 24.2.   Created by the author.

Worksheet 25.1.   a) Created by the Joseph Bomberger.

Figure 26.1.   Created by the author.

Figure 26.2.   Created by the author.

Figure 26.3.   Created by the author.

Figure 26.4.   Created by the author.

Worksheet 26.1.   Created by the author.

Figure 27.1.   Created by the author.

Figure 27.2.   (a) Location of Trobriand Islands north of Australia. Image created in Microsoft Word's online picture gallery, Creative Commons CC-BY-SA;
(b) Created by the author;
(c) Women wearing soulava necklaces. Wikimedia Commons, public domain;
(d) Close-up images of soulava. Modified from Microsoft online images, CC-BY-SA;
(e) Historic photographs of men wearing white shell armbands. Wikimedia Commons, public domain;
(f) Mwali. Modified from Microsoft online images, CC-BY-SA.

Figure 28.1.   Created by the chapter author (Angela Lockard Reed). These images are all public domain from Microsoft online pictures, unknown author, Creative Commons license CC-BY-SA.

Worksheet 28.1a. Reproduced by permission. Extract from "Life in Ancient Mesopotamia p. 47," Courtesy of the Oriental Institute of the University of Chicago.

Worksheet 28.1b. Created by the chapter author (Angela Lockard Reed).

Figure 32.1.   (a) NHPA plaque. Wikimedia Commons, public domain, https://commons.wikimedia.org/wiki/File:HistoricPlacesNationalRegisterPlaque.JPG;
(b) NHPA posters, public domain;
(c) Independence Hall: Wikimedia Commons, CC BY-SA 3.0, https://commons.wikimedia.org/w/index.php?curid=46500, https://creativecommons.org/licenses/by-sa/3.0/deed.en;
(c) Golden Gate. Wikimedia Commons, CC BY-SA 1.0, https://commons.wikimedia.org/w/index.php?curid=10087;
(c) Gettysburg National Military Park. Wikimedia Commons, CC-BY-SA 3.0, https://upload.wikimedia.org/wikipedia/commons/6/62/Gettysburg_National_Military_Park_31.JPG, https://creativecommons.org/licenses/by-sa/3.0/deed.en;
(c) Washington Monument. Wikimedia Commons, CC BY-SA 2.5 https://commons.wikimedia.org/w/index.php?curid=1430046.

INDEX